THE INTEGRATED PERSONALITY TREATMENT FRAMEWORK

A Clinical Treatment Manual and Client Workbook for Personality Disorder Recovery

A Stage-Based Guide for Clinicians and the Individuals They Treat

Jayden Josh James
MSc, PGDip CBT, PGDip DBT, MBT, EMDR
Advanced Psychotherapist
Talking Therapies UK

Companion Volume to
The Definitive British Textbook of Personality Disorders: Science, System, and Synthesis

THE INTEGRATED PERSONALITY TREATMENT FRAMEWORK A Clinical Treatment Manual and Client Workbook for Personality Disorder Recovery

Published by Talking Therapies UK

www.talkingtherapies.co.uk

The information contained in this treatment manual is intended for qualified mental health professionals who have undertaken appropriate training in the therapeutic modalities upon which the Integrated Personality Treatment Framework draws, including Dialectical Behaviour Therapy, Cognitive Behavioural Therapy for Personality Disorder, Schema-Focused Therapy, and Mentalisation-Based Treatment. The client workbook sections are intended for individuals receiving treatment under the supervision of such professionals. This manual is not intended as a substitute for professional clinical supervision, and the author and publisher accept no liability for any outcomes arising from the application of the material presented herein.

The Integrated Personality Treatment Framework (IPTF) is an original clinical model developed by the author. Clinicians wishing to implement the IPTF within National Health Service or independent practice settings are encouraged to undertake appropriate training and to ensure that their use of the framework is supported by regular clinical supervision.

All clinical examples and case vignettes presented in this manual are fictionalised composites. Any resemblance to actual individuals, whether living or deceased, is

For every person who has been told they are untreatable, and for every clinician who refused to believe it.

Contents

Part VI: The Client Workbook

Part VII: Implementation, Training, and Quality Assurance

Appendices

Preface: From Textbook to Treatment Room

This manual exists because a textbook, however comprehensive, is not the same thing as a treatment guide. In 2026, I published The Definitive British Textbook of Personality Disorders: Science, System, and Synthesis, a work that traced the history, theory, politics, law, and treatment of personality disorder within the British National Health Service context, and that proposed the Integrated Personality Treatment Framework as a new model for organising and delivering personality disorder care. That textbook was written for scholars, trainees, policymakers, and clinicians who wished to understand the intellectual and scientific foundations upon which the IPTF rests. It was, by design, a discursive, academic, and comprehensive work, spanning twenty-five chapters and over one hundred and thirty thousand words.

What that textbook could not provide, without distorting its academic purpose, was the session-by-session, handout-by-handout, worksheet-by-worksheet operational detail that a clinician needs in order to actually implement the IPTF in their clinical practice. The textbook tells the reader why the IPTF exists and what it does. This manual tells the reader how to do it.

The distinction is not a trivial one. It is the same distinction that exists between Marsha Linehan's Cognitive-Behavioral Treatment of Borderline Personality Disorder, published in 1993, which provided the theoretical architecture of Dialectical Behaviour Therapy, and the DBT Skills Training Manual, which provided the practical tools for delivering it. Nobody would accuse Linehan of duplicating herself in producing both publications, because the relationship between a theoretical textbook and a treatment manual is one of complementary dependency, not redundancy. The textbook provides the rationale; the manual provides the recipe. Both are necessary. Neither is sufficient alone.

This manual is structured in seven parts. Part I provides the clinician with the foundational knowledge needed to understand and implement the IPTF, including a concise theoretical summary, a detailed assessment and formulation guide, and the fully developed IPTF Formulation Worksheet. Parts II, III, and IV correspond to the three stages of the IPTF, providing detailed clinician guidance for Stage 1 (Stabilisation and Safety), Stage 2 (Cognitive Mapping and Schema Work), and Stage 3 (Functional Recovery and Identity Consolidation), including session-by-session protocols, therapist scripts, and reproducible clinical tools. Part V addresses specialist adaptations for forensic settings, neurodivergent populations, primary care, and adolescents. Part VI contains the Client Workbook: a complete set of plain-language psychoeducation materials, skills handouts, and worksheets designed to be used by individuals receiving IPTF treatment. Part VII addresses implementation, training, fidelity, and the research agenda.

A note on terminology. Throughout this manual, I use the term 'patient' rather than 'client', 'service user', or 'person with lived experience', not because I am unaware of the political sensitivities surrounding diagnostic terminology, which I examine at length in the parent textbook, but because this manual is intended primarily for use within the National Health Service, where 'patient' remains the standard clinical term, and because clarity of communication requires consistency of language. I use the term 'personality disorder' in accordance with the International Classification of Diseases, Eleventh Revision (ICD-11), whilst acknowledging the ongoing debate about terminology that the textbook explores in Chapters 9 and 11. Where the term 'Complex Emotional Needs' is preferred by a particular service or patient, clinicians should adapt their language accordingly.

This manual should be read alongside the parent textbook, but it can also be used as a standalone clinical resource by clinicians who are already familiar with the evidence-based therapies upon which the IPTF draws. Where a topic is covered in greater depth in the textbook, I provide a cross-reference. Where a topic is new to this manual, I provide the full treatment here.

The IPTF is not a finished product. It is a clinical framework that will evolve as evidence accumulates, as clinicians provide feedback from their implementation experience, and as the individuals who receive IPTF treatment contribute their perspectives to its ongoing development. I invite clinicians, researchers, and experts by experience to engage with the framework, to test it, to critique it, and to help me improve it. The ultimate measure of any treatment manual is not the elegance of its theory but the quality of the lives it helps to build.

Jayden Josh James
Liverpool, 2026

PART I

Foundations for the Clinician

Chapter 1

Introduction to the IPTF: Purpose, Scope, and How to Use This Manual

> *The gap between knowing what works and actually doing what works is the gap between a textbook and a treatment manual. This manual exists to close that gap.*
>
> — Jayden Josh James, 2026

The Purpose of This Manual

The Integrated Personality Treatment Framework, as described in Part VII of The Definitive British Textbook of Personality Disorders (James, 2026), represents an original contribution to the field of personality disorder treatment: a staged, modular, formulation-driven framework that synthesises the evidence-based mechanisms of change identified across Dialectical Behaviour Therapy (DBT; Linehan, 1993a, 1993b), Schema-Focused Therapy (SFT; Young, Klosko, and Weishaar, 2003), Cognitive Behavioural Therapy for Personality Disorder (CBT-PD; Davidson, 2007), and Mentalisation-Based Treatment (MBT; Bateman and Fonagy, 2004) into a coherent programme of care deliverable within the structural, financial, and workforce realities of the National Health Service. The textbook provides the scientific rationale for this framework, drawing upon attachment theory, developmental neuroscience, epigenetics, the ICD-11 dimensional diagnostic model, and a critical analysis of the political and ethical landscape within which personality disorder care operates in the United Kingdom.

This treatment manual serves a fundamentally different purpose. It translates the conceptual architecture of the IPTF into practical, implementable clinical guidance. Where the textbook explains why emotional dysregulation should be addressed before schema-level cognition, this manual provides the session plans, the therapist scripts, the group facilitation guides, and the client worksheets that enable a clinician to actually deliver that sequenced intervention. Where the textbook describes the five active ingredients that effective personality disorder treatments share, this manual operationalises those ingredients into specific clinical behaviours, assessment tools, and fidelity measures. Where the textbook presents three illustrative case studies, this manual provides the detailed protocols, worked examples, and reproducible materials that would enable a trained clinician to generate similar outcomes with their own patients.

The relationship between the textbook and this manual is therefore one of complementary dependency. The textbook provides the evidence and the argument; the manual provides the tools and the technique. Clinicians who wish to understand the full theoretical foundations of the IPTF are directed to the parent textbook. Clinicians who are already familiar with the evidence base for DBT, SFT, CBT-PD, and MBT, and who wish to begin implementing the IPTF in their clinical practice, will find in this manual everything they need to do so.

Who This Manual Is For

This manual is intended for qualified mental health professionals who possess existing competence in at least one of the evidence-based therapeutic modalities upon which the IPTF draws. The primary intended readership includes clinical psychologists, counselling psychologists, psychological therapists, cognitive behavioural therapists, mental health nurses with advanced therapy training, and psychiatrists with psychotherapy training who work within NHS personality disorder services, community mental health teams, forensic mental health services, or independent practice settings where personality disorder is a significant component of the clinical caseload. The manual is also intended as a training resource for therapists undertaking postgraduate clinical training in personality disorder treatment.

It is important to state clearly who this manual is not for. The IPTF is a complex, integrative clinical framework that requires the clinician to move flexibly between therapeutic modalities in response to the patient's evolving presentation. This requires a level of clinical sophistication that cannot be acquired from a manual alone. Clinicians who have not received formal training in at least one of the constituent modalities, specifically DBT, CBT-PD, SFT, or MBT, should not attempt to deliver the IPTF without first undertaking such training and securing appropriate clinical supervision. The manual is a map, not a substitute for the skills of navigation. A map in the hands of an untrained navigator is not merely useless; it can be dangerous, because it creates the illusion of competence where competence does not yet exist.

The client workbook sections of this manual, contained in Part VI, are written at an accessible reading level and are designed to be used by individuals receiving IPTF treatment under the supervision of a qualified clinician. These sections are not intended for unsupervised self-help use, because the psychological material they address, including trauma, attachment disruption, and schema-level cognition, requires professional guidance to process safely.

The Dual-Audience Format

One of the distinctive features of this manual is its dual-audience design. Each stage of the IPTF is presented in two complementary formats: a clinician's guide, which provides detailed therapeutic rationale, session protocols, and clinical decision-making guidance; and a client workbook, which provides accessible psychoeducation, skills handouts, and personal worksheets. This dual format reflects the IPTF's philosophical commitment to the collaborative therapeutic relationship as a mechanism of change, a commitment grounded in the common factors research reviewed in Chapter 20 of the parent textbook and operationalised throughout the IPTF's clinical practice.

The practical implication of this design is that the manual can be used in multiple ways. A clinician preparing to deliver a Stage 1 skills group session would consult Part II of this manual for the session plan, the facilitator's script, and the troubleshooting guidance, and would then photocopy the corresponding client handout from Part VI to distribute to the group. A patient who wished to review the skills taught in the session, or to complete a between-session practice assignment, would use the client workbook section. A clinician and patient working together on the IPTF Formulation Worksheet would use both the clinician's completion guide in Chapter 4 and the client-facing version of the worksheet in Part VI, sitting side by side as the IPTF's relational stance requires.

How This Manual Is Organised

The manual is organised into seven parts, each serving a distinct function within the overall clinical implementation of the IPTF.

Part I: Foundations for the Clinician (Chapters 1 to 4) provides the preparatory knowledge that a clinician needs before beginning to deliver the IPTF. Chapter 1 (this chapter) orients the reader to the manual's purpose and structure. Chapter 2 provides a concise clinical summary of the theoretical model, distilling the parent textbook's twenty-five chapters into a practical reference. Chapter 3 provides a detailed assessment and ICD-11 dimensional formulation protocol, including structured clinical interview schedules, psychometric guidance, and differential diagnostic considerations. Chapter 4 presents the fully developed IPTF Formulation Worksheet with detailed completion guidance and worked examples.

Part II: Stage 1 — Stabilisation and Safety (Chapters 5 to 9) provides the complete clinician's guide to Stage 1 of the IPTF. This includes a stage overview, the full session-by-session skills group facilitator's guide across all four skills modules and thirty-two sessions, the individual therapy component, crisis management and safety planning protocols, and the Stage 1 to Stage 2 transition assessment.

Part III: Stage 2 — Cognitive Mapping and Schema Work (Chapters 10 to 14) provides the complete clinician's guide to Stage 2. This includes the mentalising therapeutic stance, the four-phase sequential clinical guide (developmental history and schema identification, schema mapping and mode identification, experiential processing and cognitive restructuring, and consolidation), with detailed protocols for imagery rescripting, chair work, cognitive restructuring, and behavioural experiments, and the Stage 2 to Stage 3 transition assessment.

Part IV: Stage 3 — Functional Recovery and Identity Consolidation (Chapters 15 to 18) provides the complete clinician's guide to Stage 3. This includes vocational recovery, social recovery, identity consolidation, values clarification, relapse prevention, and the planned therapeutic ending.

Part V: Specialist Adaptations (Chapters 19 to 22) addresses the delivery of the IPTF in four specialist contexts: forensic settings and the Offender Personality Disorder Pathway, neurodivergent populations (autism spectrum conditions and attention deficit hyperactivity disorder), primary care and stepped care for personality difficulty, and adolescents and young adults.

Part VI: The Client Workbook (Chapters 23 to 30) provides the complete set of client-facing materials, written at an accessible reading level and designed for photocopying. This includes psychoeducation about personality disorder, skills handouts and worksheets for all four Stage 1 modules, a guide to schema work, the recovery workbook for Stage 3, the safety plan, the client-facing formulation, and the relapse prevention plan.

Part VII: Implementation, Training, and Quality Assurance (Chapters 31 to 34) provides the organisational and systemic guidance needed to set up and sustain an IPTF service, including implementation planning, training and supervision structures, fidelity measurement, outcome monitoring, and the research agenda.

Navigating Between the Textbook and the Manual

Throughout this manual, cross-references to the parent textbook are provided in the format [Textbook, Chapter X]. These references indicate points at which the reader may wish to consult the textbook for a fuller treatment of the theoretical, historical, or scientific material that underpins the clinical guidance provided here. The manual is designed to be usable without the textbook, but clinicians who have access to both publications will benefit from the richer understanding that the textbook provides.

Conversely, the parent textbook references this manual at several points, directing the reader to the manual for the operational detail that the textbook's academic format does not provide. The two publications are designed to function as a complementary pair: the textbook provides the depth of understanding, and the manual provides the breadth of application.

Symbols and Conventions Used in This Manual

The following conventions are used throughout the manual to assist the reader in navigating the material efficiently. Sections marked with the symbol ◆ denote Clinical Pearls: brief, practical tips distilled from clinical experience that address common pitfalls or highlight particularly important points. Sections marked with the symbol ▶ denote Patient Perspectives: composite quotations from individuals who have received treatment for personality disorder, included to ground the clinical material in the lived experience of those the IPTF serves. Sections marked with the heading 'NHS Delivery Context' address the practical realities of delivering the described intervention within the resource constraints, workforce configurations, and organisational structures of the National Health Service. Sections marked with the heading 'Reproducible Worksheet' or 'Reproducible

Handout' indicate materials that may be photocopied for clinical use under the terms described in the copyright notice.

> **◆ CLINICAL PEARL**
> Before you begin reading this manual in detail, take thirty minutes to read the one-page IPTF summary provided in the parent textbook and to familiarise yourself with the IPTF Formulation Worksheet in Chapter 4 of this manual. These two documents provide the conceptual scaffold upon which everything else in this manual hangs. If you understand the three-stage model and the formulation worksheet, you have the map. The rest of this manual fills in the terrain.

The IPTF at a Glance: A Summary for Quick Reference

The IPTF is organised into three sequential stages, each addressing a different level of personality dysfunction and each drawing primarily upon a different evidence-based therapeutic tradition. The model is underpinned by five active ingredients, identified through a common factors analysis of effective personality disorder treatments, that operate across all three stages. The framework is formulation-driven, meaning that the specific clinical content of each stage is individualised to the patient's presentation rather than delivered in a one-size-fits-all protocol. The framework is modular, meaning that its three stages can be delivered in different configurations depending on the resources available: a specialist personality disorder service may deliver all three stages in sequence, whilst a community mental health team may deliver Stage 1 as a standalone skills programme and refer to a specialist service for Stage 2.

The Five Active Ingredients

The IPTF identifies five mechanisms of change that are common to all effective personality disorder treatments and that operate across all three stages of the framework. These five active ingredients, described in full in Chapter 20 of the parent textbook, provide the theoretical glue that holds the integrative framework together. They are: first, structure and consistency, the provision of a predictable, reliable therapeutic environment that functions as a secure base; second, validation and empathy, the communication to the patient that their distress is understood, that their difficulties make sense in context, and that they are not to blame for their condition; third, the therapeutic alliance, the deliberate cultivation and utilisation of the therapeutic relationship as a vehicle for change, including the recognition that alliance ruptures are opportunities for therapeutic work rather than signs of treatment failure; fourth, affect regulation and distress tolerance, the development of the patient's capacity to identify, understand, modulate, and tolerate their emotional experiences without resorting to destructive coping strategies; and fifth, agency and self-efficacy, the fostering of the patient's sense of personal competence, autonomy, and capacity to influence their own life.

The Three Stages

Stage 1: Stabilisation and Safety draws primarily upon Dialectical Behaviour Therapy and addresses the neurobiological level of personality dysfunction: the emotional dysregulation, the impulsive behaviour, and the crisis-driven self-harm that constitute the most immediate and most dangerous manifestations of personality disorder. The primary aim of Stage 1 is to establish behavioural safety and emotional stabilisation, providing the patient with a functional repertoire of emotion regulation and distress tolerance skills. The treatment targets of Stage 1, adapted from Linehan's target hierarchy, are organised in order of priority: life-threatening behaviours, therapy-interfering behaviours, and quality-of-life-interfering behaviours. Stage 1 does not attempt to explore the origins of the patient's difficulties; it focuses on providing the skills and strategies needed to manage distress, maintain safety, and engage consistently with treatment. Typical duration: six to twelve months.

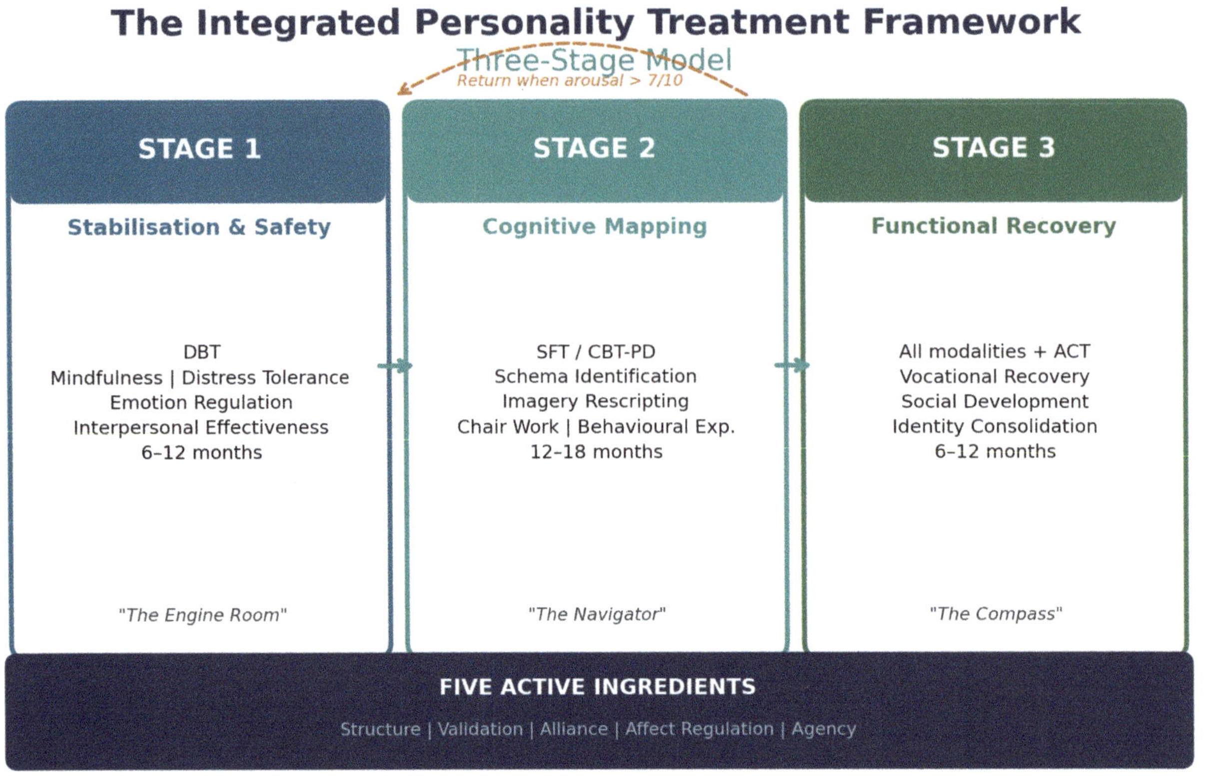

Figure 1. The IPTF Three-Stage Model with Five Active Ingredients.

Stage 2: Cognitive Mapping and Schema Work draws primarily upon Schema-Focused Therapy and CBT-PD, delivered within a mentalising therapeutic stance, and addresses the cognitive and relational level of personality dysfunction: the maladaptive core beliefs, the dysfunctional coping modes, and the distorted internal working models that maintain the personality disorder. The primary aim of Stage 2 is to help the patient understand and modify the deep-seated patterns that generate the crises addressed in Stage 1. The clinical content includes developmental history exploration, schema identification and mapping, mode identification, imagery rescripting, chair work, cognitive restructuring, and behavioural experiments. Typical duration: twelve to eighteen months.

Stage 3: Functional Recovery and Identity Consolidation draws upon all three therapeutic traditions and upon additional approaches from occupational therapy, social prescribing, and vocational rehabilitation, and addresses the social and developmental level of personality dysfunction: the vocational difficulties, the social isolation, the identity confusion, and the absence of a meaningful, purposeful life. The primary aim of Stage 3 is to support the patient in translating the psychological changes achieved in Stages 1 and 2 into sustained improvements in everyday life. Typical duration: six to twelve months.

The 7/10 Arousal Rule

A critical clinical principle governs the transitions between stages, both at the macro level of the overall treatment trajectory and at the micro level of individual sessions. The 7/10 Arousal Rule states that the clinician should never attempt to move from stabilisation work to exploratory cognitive or schema work if the patient's current emotional arousal exceeds approximately 7 on a subjective 0 to 10 scale. When emotional arousal is at this level, the prefrontal regulatory capacity required for reflective engagement is neurobiologically compromised, and attempting to conduct schema exploration or cognitive restructuring is not merely ineffective but potentially harmful. At the start of every session, the clinician asks the patient to rate their current arousal. If the rating is 7 or above, the session begins with Stage 1 skills work regardless of where the patient is in the overall treatment trajectory. This non-linear movement between stages is a core feature of the IPTF's design, not a treatment failure.

A Note on Evidence and Intellectual Honesty

It is important to be candid about the current evidence base for the IPTF. The IPTF is a new framework that has not yet been subjected to a randomised controlled trial. Its evidence base is, at this stage, theoretical and derivative: that said it is an evidence based intervention, it draws upon the established evidence bases of DBT, SFT, CBT-PD, and MBT, and upon the common factors research that identifies the mechanisms of change shared across these modalities. The IPTF's claim is not that it is a new therapy with a novel evidence base, but rather that it provides a more effective way of organising and sequencing established, evidence-based techniques within the real-world constraints of NHS delivery. The distinction is important. The individual components of the IPTF, the DBT skills, the schema-focused techniques, the cognitive restructuring, the mentalising stance, all have robust evidence bases in their own right. What has not yet been empirically tested is the specific staged, modular configuration in which the IPTF organises them.

This manual is therefore offered in the spirit of clinical innovation rather than clinical certainty, that said, it is underpinned by robust research evidence which supports the efficacy of the individual components of the IPTF (DBT,MBT,SFT,CBT-PD). Part VII includes a detailed research agenda that sets out the empirical programme needed to evaluate the IPTF, including feasibility studies, pilot trials, and pragmatic randomised controlled trials. Clinicians who implement the IPTF are encouraged to contribute to this evidence base by collecting routine outcome data and sharing their implementation experience. The framework will evolve in response to evidence, and this manual will be updated accordingly in future editions.

What the IPTF does offer, even in advance of trial evidence, is a principled, theoretically coherent, and practically implementable framework for doing what NHS clinicians are already doing in an ad hoc and unsupported way: integrating techniques from multiple evidence-based modalities in response to the complex, evolving presentations of their personality disorder patients. The alternative to the IPTF is not the delivery of a single, pure, manualised modality; the alternative is the unprincipled, unsupervised, atheoretical eclecticism that currently characterises much personality disorder treatment in community mental health teams. The IPTF aims to bring structure, coherence, and accountability to this integration, and this manual provides the tools to do so.

Chapter 2

The Theoretical Model in Brief: A Clinician's Summary

> *The clinician who understands why a treatment works is better equipped to adapt it when the manual does not quite fit the patient in front of them. Theory is not an academic luxury; it is a clinical necessity.*
>
> — Jayden Josh James, 2026

Purpose of This Chapter

This chapter provides a concise summary of the theoretical foundations of the IPTF, drawn from the extensive treatment provided across the twenty-five chapters of the parent textbook. Its purpose is not to replicate the textbook's scholarly depth but to provide the working clinician with the conceptual framework they need to understand why the IPTF is structured as it is, why the stages are sequenced as they are, and why the integration of specific therapeutic modalities at specific stages is not arbitrary but grounded in a coherent model of personality disorder aetiology and maintenance. Clinicians who wish to explore any of the topics summarised here in greater depth are directed to the relevant textbook chapters, which are cross-referenced throughout.

What Is Personality Disorder? A Dimensional Understanding

The IPTF is built upon the dimensional model of personality disorder introduced by the International Classification of Diseases, Eleventh Revision (ICD-11; World Health Organisation, 2019), which has replaced the categorical system of the ICD-10 and which represents the most significant reconceptualisation of personality disorder diagnosis in the history of psychiatric classification [Textbook, Chapters 7 and 8]. Under the dimensional model, personality disorder is understood not as a collection of discrete diagnostic categories, such as Borderline, Narcissistic, or Antisocial Personality Disorder, but as a single diagnostic entity that varies along two dimensions: severity and trait expression.

Severity is classified into three levels, Mild, Moderate, and Severe, with an additional sub-threshold category of Personality Difficulty for individuals who display personality-related impairments that do not meet the threshold for a formal diagnosis. The severity classification is determined by the degree of impairment in two core domains of personality functioning: the functioning of the self, encompassing identity, self-worth, self-direction, and the capacity for accurate self-appraisal; and interpersonal functioning, encompassing the capacity for empathy, intimacy, and the management of conflict within relationships. This dimensional approach to severity has profound implications for treatment planning within the IPTF, because the intensity, duration, and modality mix of the treatment should be calibrated to the severity of the patient's personality dysfunction rather than determined by a categorical label.

Trait expression is described across five trait domains: Negative Affectivity, the tendency towards intense, unstable, and negatively valenced emotional experiences; Detachment, the tendency towards emotional and interpersonal withdrawal; Dissociality, the tendency towards disregard for the rights and feelings of others, encompassing callousness, deceitfulness, manipulativeness, and hostility; Disinhibition, the tendency towards impulsive, reckless, and irresponsible behaviour; and Anankastia, the tendency towards rigidity, perfectionism, and emotional and behavioural constriction. In addition, the ICD-11 retains a single Borderline Pattern Specifier for individuals whose presentation is characterised by the specific features associated with the former Borderline Personality Disorder construct: emotional instability, impulsivity, identity disturbance, and a pervasive pattern of unstable and conflicted interpersonal relationships.

For the IPTF clinician, the dimensional model means that every patient receives an individualised diagnostic formulation that specifies their severity level, their trait domain profile, and whether the Borderline Pattern Specifier applies, rather than being assigned to a categorical box. This formulation directly informs the treatment plan: the severity level determines the overall intensity and duration of treatment; the trait profile informs the selection and emphasis of specific therapeutic techniques within each stage; and the Borderline Pattern Specifier, when present, indicates that the full three-stage IPTF pathway is likely to be needed.

Why Do Personality Disorders Develop? The Aetiological Model

The IPTF rests upon a bio-psycho-social-developmental model of personality disorder aetiology. This model holds that personality disorder does not arise from a single cause but from the dynamic interaction of three broad classes of causal factor: biological vulnerability, adverse relational experience, and the wider social and environmental context. Understanding this model is clinically indispensable, because it shapes everything about how the IPTF conceptualises the patient's difficulties, how it approaches formulation, and why it is structured in the particular sequence it adopts. The sections that follow set out this aetiological model in full, drawing upon the convergent evidence from attachment theory, developmental neuroscience, and epigenetics that together constitute its scientific foundation.

The Attachment Foundation

No single theoretical contribution has done more to explain why personality disorders develop than attachment theory, and no working clinician in the field of personality disorder can afford to be without a thorough grasp of its core propositions. Developed by the British psychiatrist and psychoanalyst John Bowlby across four decades of clinical observation and theoretical synthesis, attachment theory proposes that the quality of the infant's earliest relationships with primary caregivers creates a set of internalised relational templates — known as internal working models — that shape the individual's expectations, emotional responses, and interpersonal behaviour in all subsequent relationships across the entire lifespan (Bowlby, 1969, 1973, 1980). The central insight of attachment theory is at once simple and profound: what happened to us in our earliest relationships does not stay in the past. It becomes the lens through which we perceive and navigate every relationship that follows.

Bowlby proposed that attachment is an evolved behavioural system, biologically primed to promote the survival of the vulnerable infant by maintaining proximity to a protective caregiver. The set goal of this system is the maintenance of what Bowlby called a "felt sense of security": the experience of the caregiver as both a safe haven to retreat to when threatened and a secure base from which to explore the world when safe. When the caregiver is perceived as reliably available and responsive, the attachment system is quiescent and the infant is free to explore, to play, and to develop. When the infant perceives a threat — whether through separation, the caregiver's emotional unavailability, or environmental danger — the attachment system is activated and a cascade of proximity-seeking behaviours is mobilised: crying, clinging, searching, and protesting. These are not symptoms of pathology; they are the outputs of a finely calibrated biological system designed to keep the infant close to its source of protection.

The empirical revolution in attachment research was initiated by the Canadian-American developmental psychologist Mary Ainsworth, whose Strange Situation Procedure provided the first systematic method for observing and classifying individual differences in the quality of infant-caregiver attachment (Ainsworth, Blehar, Waters, and Wall, 1978). Ainsworth's research identified three principal attachment patterns: Secure, Insecure-Avoidant, and Insecure-Ambivalent. The securely attached infant, whose caregiver has been consistently sensitive and responsive, develops an internal working model of the self as worthy of care and of others as available and reliable, providing the relational foundation for confident exploration, flexible emotional regulation, and the capacity for trusting relationships in adult life. The insecure-avoidant infant, whose caregiver has consistently rejected attachment behaviour, develops an internal working model of the self as unworthy of emotional support and of others as rejecting and unavailable, a model that generates the compulsive self-reliance, emotional constriction, and dismissal of attachment needs that characterise the Detachment trait domain in the ICD-11. The insecure-ambivalent infant, whose caregiver has been inconsistently responsive, develops an internal working model of the self as uncertain and ineffective and of others as unreliable, generating the hypervigilance to relational threat and the intense, unstable emotional responses that characterise the Negative Affectivity domain.

The attachment pattern most consistently associated with moderate to severe personality disorder is the fourth pattern identified by Mary Main and Judith Solomon in the 1980s: Disorganised or Disoriented attachment (Main and Solomon, 1986). This pattern arises in a specific and deeply damaging relational context: when the primary caregiver is simultaneously the source of comfort and the source of fear. The infant of an abusive, severely neglectful, or chronically frightened caregiver faces what Main described as "fright without solution": the biological imperative to approach the caregiver for safety and the equally powerful impulse to flee from a figure who is experienced as dangerous cannot be simultaneously satisfied. Because neither approach nor avoidance resolves the dilemma, the attachment system breaks down into the contradictory, confused, and often dissociative behaviours that characterise the disorganised classification — freezing, simultaneous approach and avoidance, trance-like states, and stereotyped repetitive movements.

The longitudinal research of Karlen Lyons-Ruth and colleagues at Harvard Medical School has demonstrated that disorganised attachment in infancy is the single most powerful relational predictor of later personality disorder, particularly of presentations characterised by emotional dysregulation, identity disturbance, and the chaotic, unstable interpersonal relationships associated with what was formerly termed Borderline Personality Disorder (Lyons-Ruth, 2008; Levy, 2005; Agrawal, Gunderson, Holmes, and Lyons-Ruth, 2004). The infant with disorganised attachment has no stable relational mirror in which to develop a coherent sense of self, because the figure who should provide that mirror has been simultaneously terrifying and unreachable. The consequence, traceable from infancy through adolescence and into adult life, is the hallmark features of moderate to severe personality disorder: identity fragmentation, an unstable and often deeply negative self-concept, and relationships characterised by the same irresolvable paradox — desperately needed and desperately feared — that characterised the original attachment relationship.

A critical feature of internal working models, and the feature that makes them so clinically significant, is their self-perpetuating character. Once established in early childhood, internal working models operate largely outside conscious awareness, selectively directing attention towards relationship information that confirms existing expectations and away from information that might challenge them. The individual with an avoidant model does not merely expect rejection; they behave in ways that elicit rejection, by withdrawing from intimacy and suppressing emotional expression in a manner that drives potential attachment figures away. The individual with a disorganised model does not merely expect danger in relationships; they may recreate dangerous relational dynamics, not through choice but through the activation of relational schemas formed before explicit memory was possible. This self-perpetuating quality gives personality disorder its characteristic stability and explains why it does not simply resolve with time, good intentions, or standard supportive care. The internal working models that drive it are not beliefs to be reasoned away; they are deep relational structures that require sustained, relationally-based therapeutic experience to revise. This insight is foundational to the entire architecture of the IPTF.

The concept of mentalisation, developed by Peter Fonagy and colleagues building upon Bowlby's foundations, adds a further critical dimension to this understanding (Fonagy, Gergely, Jurist, and Target, 2002). Mentalisation refers to the capacity to understand one's own and others' behaviour in terms of underlying mental states — thoughts, feelings, wishes, beliefs, and intentions. A secure attachment relationship promotes mentalisation by providing an environment in which the infant's mental states are consistently recognised, named, and responded to by a caregiver who is "thinking about the infant thinking." The infant of a frightening or dissociated caregiver has no such environment. Instead, they may actively suppress mentalisation of the caregiver's mental states — because understanding what the abusive parent is thinking is too frightening — producing the generalised failures of mentalisation that are central to personality disorder pathology: the inability to reflect upon one's own emotional states, the misreading of others' intentions, and the collapse of reflective function under interpersonal stress. The restoration of mentalisation capacity is one of the core mechanisms of change in the IPTF, pursued across all three stages through the consistent application of a mentalising therapeutic stance.

The clinical implication of attachment theory for IPTF practice is fundamental and pervasive. Personality disorder is, at its core, a disorder of relational adaptation. The patient's difficulties are not defects of character, failures of moral will, or deliberate strategies of manipulation. They are adaptations to adverse relational environments: strategies developed to survive intolerable relational circumstances that persist into adult life because the internal working models that generated them continue to organise the individual's perception of, and response to, their relational world. Every presentation of personality disorder carries within it the logic of a survival strategy. The IPTF clinician's task is to understand that logic, to communicate it compassionately to the patient, and to provide, through the therapeutic relationship itself, a new relational experience sufficiently consistent, safe, and containing to begin to revise the internal working models that the original relational environment produced.

The Neurobiological Foundation

The relational experiences described in the preceding section do not merely shape the individual's psychology in the abstract; they produce measurable, documented alterations in the structure and function of the developing brain. The neuroscience of personality disorder provides the biological substrate that makes sense of what clinicians observe every day in their clinical work: the explosive emotional reactions that appear disproportionate to their triggers, the impulsivity that the patient genuinely cannot control in the moment, the paralysis of cognitive function under interpersonal stress, and the capacity for ordinary reflective thinking to vanish entirely when the individual feels threatened. These are not behavioural choices. They are the observable outputs of a nervous system that has been shaped by early adversity to operate in a particular way.

The two neural systems most consistently implicated in personality disorder are the amygdala-centred threat detection system and the prefrontal cortex-based regulatory system, and understanding the relationship between them is essential to understanding both the phenomenology of personality disorder and the rationale for the IPTF's staged structure. The amygdala, a small almond-shaped structure located deep within the temporal lobe, functions as the brain's primary threat detection and emotional processing centre. It receives sensory input through both slow, cortically mediated pathways that permit conscious appraisal and fast, subcortical pathways that bypass conscious awareness entirely, enabling the rapid mobilisation of a defensive response before the individual has had time to consciously evaluate whether a threat is actually present (LeDoux, 1996). This design is evolutionarily adaptive in environments of genuine physical threat, where a fraction of a second may determine survival. It becomes maladaptive when the threat detection system has been calibrated by early experience to fire in response to social and relational cues that represent echoes of past danger rather than present reality.

Neuroimaging research has consistently demonstrated that individuals with Borderline Personality Disorder show heightened amygdala reactivity to emotionally salient stimuli, particularly to stimuli associated with social threat, rejection, and interpersonal abandonment (Donegan et al., 2003; Herpertz et al., 2001). Critically, this heightened reactivity extends to ambiguous social stimuli — neutral facial expressions, for example — which the amygdala of the individual with personality disorder evaluates as threatening in the absence of any objective threat signal. The individual with personality disorder does not simply overreact to obvious threats; their threat detection system has been calibrated by early relational adversity to read danger into the social environment with a frequency, sensitivity, and intensity that far exceeds that of individuals with secure attachment histories. The Psychiatrist Bessel van der Kolk's formulation that the amygdala acts as the brain's "smoke detector" is apt: in personality disorder, the smoke detector has been set to a hair-trigger sensitivity that generates full alarm responses to stimuli that are ambiguous at best and benign at worst (van der Kolk, 2014).

The counterpart to the amygdala's accelerator function is the prefrontal cortex's brake. The prefrontal cortex, particularly the medial prefrontal cortex, the dorsolateral prefrontal cortex, and the orbitofrontal cortex, performs the executive functions of evaluation, reflection, planning, impulse control, and the top-down regulation of limbic emotional responses. It is the prefrontal cortex that enables the individual to pause between stimulus and response, to evaluate whether an apparent threat is genuinely dangerous, to consider the consequences of a proposed action, and to generate alternative responses to the one that the emotional brain is demanding. Neuroimaging research has demonstrated that individuals with personality disorder show reduced prefrontal regulatory capacity, particularly in the dorsolateral and ventromedial prefrontal regions associated with impulse control, emotion regulation, and decision-making (Silbersweig et al., 2007; New et al., 2007). The prefrontal cortex exerts top-down regulation of the amygdala through a dense network of inhibitory connections; when this regulatory capacity is reduced, the amygdala's outputs are less effectively modulated, generating the emotional intensity and impulsive reactivity that characterise personality disorder presentations.

The third neural system of central importance in personality disorder is the hypothalamic-pituitary-adrenal (HPA) axis, the brain and body's primary neuroendocrine stress response system. The HPA axis governs the release of cortisol in response to stress and plays a fundamental role in regulating arousal, energy mobilisation, and the return to baseline calm following a stressor. Research has demonstrated that individuals who have experienced significant childhood adversity show characteristic HPA axis dysregulation, including elevated baseline cortisol, blunted cortisol responses to acute stress, and impaired negative feedback regulation, all of which contribute to the chronic stress sensitivity and the difficulty returning to a regulated baseline that characterise personality disorder presentations (Rinne et al., 2002; Zimmerman and Choi-Kain, 2009). The HPA axis is not a fixed, predetermined system; it is calibrated during sensitive periods of early development by the quality of the caregiving environment, precisely mirroring the attachment processes described in the preceding section. A caregiving environment characterised by unpredictability, threat, or chronic emotional unavailability programmes the HPA axis towards hyperreactivity in a manner that serves short-term survival in dangerous environments but generates long-term emotional vulnerability.

This neurobiological evidence provides the scientific rationale for the IPTF's staged structure, and specifically for the sequencing of Stage 1 before Stage 2. Stage 1 addresses the amygdala-level dysregulation: the emotional intensity, the impulsive reactivity, and the crisis-driven behaviour that occur when the threat detection system is hyperactivated and the prefrontal regulatory system is overwhelmed and unable to modulate the response. The skills taught in Stage 1, drawn primarily from Dialectical Behaviour Therapy, directly target these neurobiological mechanisms: the TIP skills work by rapidly altering physiological arousal through temperature, intense exercise, and paced breathing; the distress tolerance skills provide alternative behavioural pathways through acute crises; and the emotion regulation skills build the prefrontal regulatory capacity that has been impaired by early adversity. Stage 2, which requires the patient to engage in reflective, mentalising, cognitively flexible thinking of the kind mediated by the prefrontal cortex, simply cannot be effectively delivered until Stage 1 has established a sufficient degree of amygdala-level stabilisation for the prefrontal regulatory system to come back online. This is the neurobiological basis of the 7/10 Arousal Rule: when emotional arousal exceeds the threshold at which prefrontal regulation is overwhelmed, the cognitive and relational work of Stage 2 is not merely difficult but neurobiologically impossible. The clinician who attempts schema restructuring with a patient whose amygdala is in a state of hyperactivation is not merely inefficient; they are working against the brain's own architecture.

The third element of the aetiological model is the wider social and environmental context within which personality disorder develops and is maintained [Textbook, Chapter 6]. Epigenetic research has demonstrated that adverse experiences, including childhood maltreatment, neglect, and poverty, can alter gene expression through mechanisms such as DNA methylation and histone modification, without altering the underlying DNA sequence (McGowan et al., 2009; Perroud et al., 2011). These epigenetic modifications can affect the functioning of the hypothalamic-pituitary-adrenal (HPA) axis, the body's primary stress response system, producing lasting alterations in cortisol regulation that contribute to the emotional volatility and stress sensitivity characteristic of personality disorder. The critical implication of the epigenetic evidence is that the boundary between biology and environment is far more permeable than was previously understood: adverse experience literally gets under the skin, modifying the biological systems that regulate emotion and behaviour.

For the IPTF clinician, the practical significance of this neurobiological evidence is threefold. First, it provides a compassionate, non-blaming framework for understanding the patient's difficulties: the patient's emotional dysregulation is not a choice, a manipulation, or a character defect, but a neurobiologically mediated consequence of adverse experience that has altered the structure and function of their brain and their stress response system. This understanding is therapeutically essential, because it enables the clinician to respond to emotional intensity and impulsive behaviour with curiosity and compassion rather than with the frustration or therapeutic pessimism that can arise when these phenomena are misunderstood as volitional. Second, it provides a basis for hope: if adverse experience can modify these neural systems in a maladaptive direction, then therapeutic experience can, in principle, modify them in an adaptive direction. The concept of neuroplasticity underpins the IPTF's fundamental therapeutic optimism. Third, it underscores the importance of addressing the patient's wider social environment alongside the psychological work of therapy, because the social determinants of health that contributed to the development of personality disorder will continue to maintain dysregulation if they are not addressed. This is why Stage 3 of the IPTF incorporates vocational rehabilitation, social prescribing, and community engagement as integral therapeutic components.

The Epigenetic and Environmental Context

The third element of the IPTF's aetiological model concerns the molecular mechanisms through which the environmental experiences described in the preceding sections become literally embedded in the biology of the developing individual. The science of epigenetics — the study of heritable changes in gene expression that occur without alteration of the underlying DNA sequence — provides the missing bridge between the relational world of early attachment and the neurobiological alterations that shape personality disorder. Its central insight may be summarised as follows: genes are not fixed, deterministic blueprints that dictate developmental outcomes regardless of environmental conditions. They are better understood as a repertoire of possible expressions, a set of potentials that are activated, silenced, amplified, or dampened by signals from the environment. The most extensively studied epigenetic mechanism is DNA methylation, a biochemical process in which a methyl group is attached to a cytosine nucleotide in the DNA sequence, typically silencing the transcription of the affected gene. The significance of this for personality disorder lies in the fact that methylation patterns are dynamically responsive to environmental signals, particularly during the sensitive periods of prenatal and early postnatal development when the epigenome is being established. Two children with identical DNA sequences can develop substantially different emotional and regulatory profiles if raised in sufficiently different environments, because their environments will produce different patterns of gene expression.

The landmark research of Michael Meaney and colleagues at McGill University established the direct link between early caregiving quality and epigenetic modification of the stress response system (Meaney, 2001). Meaney's programme demonstrated that rat pups raised by mothers providing high levels of attentive caregiving developed into adults that were less anxious, more exploratory, and more efficient in their cortisol stress response than pups raised by low-care mothers. These differences were mediated by a specific epigenetic mechanism: high maternal care produced demethylation of the promoter region of the glucocorticoid receptor gene in the hippocampus, increasing glucocorticoid receptor expression and enhancing the efficiency of HPA axis negative feedback regulation. Low maternal care produced the opposite pattern. Crucially, cross-fostering experiments demonstrated that it was the quality of caregiving — not genetic relatedness — that determined the epigenetic outcome. The translation of these findings to human populations was accomplished by Patrick McGowan and colleagues, who demonstrated that individuals who had experienced childhood abuse showed increased methylation of the same glucocorticoid receptor gene promoter in post-mortem hippocampal tissue, directly mirroring the pattern observed in Meaney's low-care pups (McGowan et al., 2009). This was the first direct evidence that the quality of human caregiving produces measurable epigenetic modifications in the human brain.

The Adverse Childhood Experiences (ACE) study, involving over seventeen thousand adults, provided the epidemiological framework through which the health consequences of childhood adversity have been most extensively documented (Felitti et al., 1998). The study demonstrated a powerful, graded dose-response relationship between the number of categories of childhood adversity — encompassing physical, emotional, and sexual abuse; physical and emotional neglect; and household dysfunction including parental mental illness, substance misuse, domestic violence, and parental imprisonment — and the risk for adverse health and psychological outcomes in adulthood. For personality disorder specifically, the ACE framework illuminates the severity gradient of the ICD-11 dimensional model: individuals with low ACE scores are more likely to develop sub-threshold personality difficulty, whilst those with high ACE scores reflecting cumulative adversity across multiple domains are substantially more likely to develop moderate or severe personality disorder. The epigenetic evidence has two further implications of profound clinical significance. First, epigenetic modifications are not permanent in the way that DNA sequence changes are; they are, in principle, reversible. Emerging evidence that sustained positive relational experience can modify the methylation patterns that adversity has established provides the molecular basis for the IPTF's therapeutic optimism (Perroud et al., 2011). Second, the epigenetic evidence demonstrates that social determinants of health — poverty, housing insecurity, community violence, and social exclusion — are not merely background factors in personality disorder; they are the environmental conditions that, through epigenetic pathways, alter gene expression and produce the neurobiological vulnerabilities that treatment is subsequently required to address.

Taken together, the attachment, neurobiological, and epigenetic evidence converges on a single, clinically vital conclusion: personality disorder is a condition of adaptation, not defect. It arises from the transaction between a biological temperament and an adverse relational environment that, through processes operating simultaneously at the level of internal working models, neural circuitry, and gene expression, produces enduring patterns of self-dysfunction and interpersonal dysfunction that serve a survival function in the original context but generate suffering in every context that follows. This understanding shapes every clinical interaction within the IPTF: the compassionate stance towards behaviours that might otherwise provoke frustration, the formulation-based approach to risk, the sequencing of stages in correspondence with neurobiological readiness, the inclusion of the social environment within the scope of treatment, and the fundamental conviction that people who have been changed by adverse experience can be changed again by therapeutic experience.

The Common Factors Rationale: Why Integration?

The IPTF's integrative approach is grounded not in therapeutic eclecticism, the unprincipled mixing of techniques from different traditions, but in the common factors research that has, over eight decades, consistently demonstrated that the specific techniques of any given therapeutic modality account for a relatively small proportion of the variance in therapeutic outcomes, whilst factors common to all effective treatments account for a substantially larger proportion [Textbook, Chapter 20]. This finding, first articulated by Rosenzweig (1936) and confirmed by successive generations of meta-analytic research (Wampold, 2001, 2015; Norcross and Lambert, 2019), does not imply that technique does not matter; it implies that technique matters less than the therapeutic context within which it is delivered.

The five active ingredients identified in the parent textbook, structure and consistency, validation and empathy, the therapeutic alliance, affect regulation and distress tolerance, and agency and self-efficacy, represent the IPTF's operationalisation of the common factors that effective personality disorder treatments share. These ingredients are not the property of any single modality; they are present in DBT, in MBT, in SFT, and in CBT-PD, though each modality operationalises them differently. What the IPTF does is to identify these ingredients explicitly, to monitor their delivery across all three stages, and to ensure that the specific techniques drawn from each modality are deployed in the service of these common mechanisms rather than in the service of adherence to a single therapeutic brand.

The practical consequence for the clinician is a form of principled flexibility. Within the IPTF, the clinician is not required to adhere rigidly to the protocols of any single modality; they are required to ensure that the five active ingredients are consistently present in every session, every stage, and every therapeutic interaction, and to select the specific techniques, from whichever modality is most appropriate, that best serve the therapeutic goals of the current stage for the current patient. This is not eclecticism; it is integration guided by a coherent model of change.

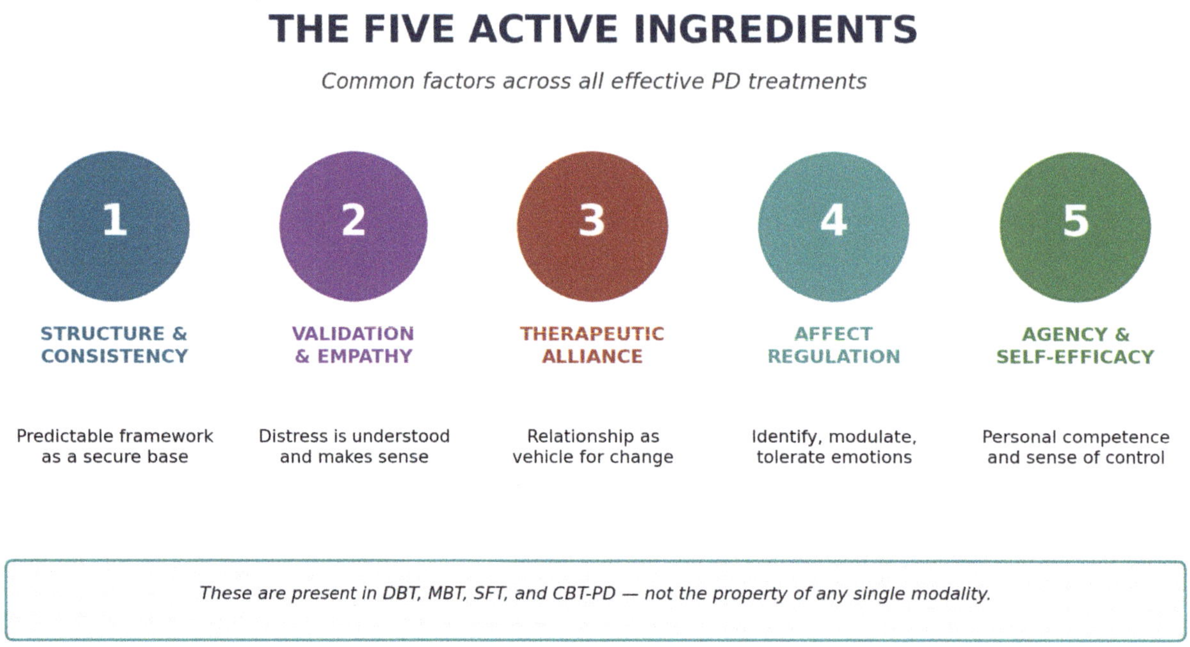

Figure 5. The Five Active Ingredients across effective PD treatments.

The Staged Logic: Why This Sequence?

The three-stage structure of the IPTF is not arbitrary. It reflects a specific model of how therapeutic change occurs in personality disorder, a model that can be summarised in the following proposition: the patient must be safe before they can think, and they must understand before they can build. Each stage addresses a successively deeper level of personality dysfunction, and each stage creates the conditions that make the next stage possible.

Stage 1, by establishing behavioural safety and emotional stabilisation, creates the conditions under which the reflective, mentalising, cognitively flexible engagement required by Stage 2 becomes possible. A patient who is in acute crisis, who is cutting themselves every evening, who is presenting to the accident and emergency department every week, who is unable to sit through a session without dissociating, is not in a position to explore the developmental origins of their core beliefs or to engage in imagery rescripting of childhood trauma. The amygdala must be calmed before the prefrontal cortex can be recruited. The fire must be contained before the building can be inspected.

Stage 2, by mapping and modifying the cognitive and relational patterns that maintain the personality dysfunction, creates the conditions under which the life-building work of Stage 3 becomes possible. A patient who has learned to regulate their emotions but who continues to operate from the conviction that they are fundamentally defective, that others will inevitably abandon them, and that the world is a dangerous place, will find that their Stage 1 skills are insufficient to sustain the demands of returning to employment, building new relationships, and constructing a coherent identity. The schemas must be understood and modified before the life can be rebuilt.

Stage 3, by supporting the patient in translating psychological change into practical, social, and vocational achievement, consolidates the gains of Stages 1 and 2 into a sustainable recovery. Without Stage 3, there is a risk that the patient achieves symptomatic improvement in the consulting room but remains functionally impaired in the real world, a phenomenon that is familiar to any clinician who has discharged a personality disorder patient who was 'doing well in therapy' only to find them re-referred six months later because they could not sustain the gains outside the therapeutic relationship.

The Non-Linear Reality: Moving Between Stages

Whilst the three stages are presented as a sequential framework, the clinical reality of personality disorder treatment is that patients do not progress through the stages in a smooth, linear trajectory. The IPTF explicitly anticipates and accommodates this non-linearity. A patient who has progressed to Stage 2 may experience a crisis, a bereavement, a housing loss, a relationship breakdown, that reactivates their emotional dysregulation and necessitates a return to Stage 1 skills within the current session or across a series of sessions. A patient who is engaged in Stage 3 life-building may encounter a vocational setback that activates a Defectiveness schema and requires a brief return to Stage 2 exploration. The 7/10 Arousal Rule operationalises this non-linearity at the session level: if the patient's arousal rises above the threshold for reflective engagement, the clinician shifts to the stage that addresses the current level of functioning, regardless of where the patient is in the overall treatment trajectory. This approach is similar to that used in MBT when emotional arousal increases in a therapy session, the demand for Mentalising is reduced in session to a lower intensity, returning to validation.

This non-linear design is one of the IPTF's most important features, because it reflects the clinical reality that recovery from personality disorder is not a straight line but a spiral: the patient returns, again and again, to earlier challenges, but each time from a position of greater skill, greater understanding, and greater resilience. The clinician who treats the return to Stage 1 as a failure, rather than as a normal and expected feature of the recovery process, risks communicating to the patient that their difficulties are evidence of their inadequacy, which is precisely the schema-confirming message that the treatment is designed to disrupt.

Chapter Summary

This chapter has provided a concise clinical summary of the theoretical foundations of the IPTF: the ICD-11 dimensional model that shapes the assessment and formulation; the bio-psycho-social-developmental aetiological model that explains why personality disorder develops; the common factors rationale that justifies the integrative approach; and the staged logic that determines the sequencing of therapeutic interventions. The chapters that follow translate these theoretical foundations into practical clinical tools, beginning with the assessment and formulation protocol in Chapter 3.

Chapter 3

Assessment and ICD-11 Dimensional Formulation

> *Assessment is not something you do to the patient before the therapy begins. Assessment is the first act of therapy. The way you listen, the questions you ask, the curiosity you bring, and the respect you show in those opening sessions will determine whether the patient trusts you enough to do the work that follows.*
>
> — Jayden Josh James, 2026

Purpose of This Chapter

This chapter provides the IPTF clinician with a comprehensive assessment protocol for personality disorder, from the initial referral screening through to the production of a complete ICD-11 dimensional formulation. The assessment process described here serves three simultaneous functions: diagnostic, in that it establishes whether a personality disorder diagnosis is warranted and, if so, determines its severity and trait profile; formulative, in that it generates the initial data needed to begin populating the IPTF Formulation Worksheet described in Chapter 4; and therapeutic, in that it establishes the therapeutic relationship, communicates the clinician's competence and trustworthiness, and begins the process of validation that is the first of the five active ingredients.

The assessment protocol is designed to be completed across three to four assessment sessions, each lasting approximately sixty to ninety minutes, supplemented by the administration of standardised psychometric measures. At the conclusion of the assessment, the clinician should have sufficient information to complete Section One ('The Now') of the IPTF Formulation Worksheet, to make a preliminary ICD-11 dimensional diagnosis, and to agree a treatment plan with the patient that specifies which stage of the IPTF is the appropriate starting point and what the initial treatment targets will be.

Referral Screening and Pre-Assessment Preparation

Before the first face-to-face assessment session, the clinician should review the referral information and any available clinical records to establish a preliminary understanding of the patient's presenting difficulties, risk history, previous treatment history, and current service involvement. This pre-assessment review is not a substitute for the clinical interview, but it enables the clinician to use the interview time more efficiently and to identify areas that will require particular attention.

The Standardised Assessment of Personality, Abbreviated Scale (SAPAS; Moran et al., 2003) may be used as a screening tool at the point of referral, either administered by the referring clinician or by the personality disorder service as part of the triage process. The SAPAS is an eight-item, self-report screen that takes approximately five minutes to administer and that has demonstrated good sensitivity and specificity for the detection of personality disorder in clinical populations. A score of three or above on the SAPAS indicates a high probability of personality disorder and warrants a full diagnostic assessment. However, the SAPAS should not be used as a diagnostic instrument; it is a screening tool only, and a full clinical assessment is required to establish the presence, severity, and trait profile of personality disorder.

◆ **CLINICAL PEARL**

When reviewing clinical records before the first assessment session, pay particular attention to the language used by previous clinicians. Terms such as 'manipulative', 'attention-seeking', 'difficult', 'non-compliant', and 'untreatable' in the patient's records are red flags not for the patient's pathology but for the system's response to it. These labels often indicate that the patient has experienced invalidation and rejection from services, and they should alert you to the need for a particularly careful, validating, and curious approach in the assessment. The patient who has been described as 'manipulative' in their records will be expecting you to treat them accordingly. Your job is to provide a different experience.

Assessment Session One: Engagement, Presenting Difficulties, and Current Functioning

The Opening Minutes: Setting the Tone

The first minutes of the first assessment session are among the most therapeutically consequential moments in the entire IPTF treatment pathway. The patient who presents for a personality disorder assessment has typically experienced multiple previous contacts with mental health services, many of which have been characterised by invalidation, dismissal, or the withdrawal of care. They arrive at the assessment carrying not only their presenting difficulties but a history of being assessed, labelled, and found wanting. The clinician's task in the opening minutes is to communicate, through their behaviour rather than through their words, that this assessment will be different: that the clinician is interested in the patient's experience, that the clinician takes their difficulties seriously, and that the clinician is not looking for reasons to exclude them from treatment.

The clinician begins by introducing themselves, explaining their role, and describing the purpose and structure of the assessment process. The following script provides a suggested framework for this introduction, which should be adapted to the clinician's own style and the specific service context:

> **Therapist Script:** '*Thank you for coming today. My name is [name], and I am a [role] working in the [service name]. I want to start by explaining what this assessment is about, because I think it is really important that you know what to expect. Over the next few sessions, I would like to spend some time getting to understand your difficulties from your perspective. I am not here to test you or to catch you out. I am here to listen carefully to your experience and to work with you to develop an understanding of what has been going on for you and what might help. Some of the things we talk about may be difficult, and I want you to know that you are in control of what you share and when. If anything feels too much, we can slow down or take a break. There is no rush. Does that sound alright?*'

This introduction accomplishes several therapeutic objectives simultaneously. It communicates transparency about the assessment process, reducing the anxiety associated with the unknown. It positions the clinician as a listener rather than an examiner, enacting the collaborative stance that the IPTF requires. It explicitly addresses the power dynamic by assuring the patient that they are in control of what they share. And it validates the potential difficulty of the process, communicating that the clinician understands that talking about these experiences may be painful.

Presenting Difficulties and Current Functioning

Following the introduction, the clinician invites the patient to describe their current difficulties in their own words. The question should be open-ended and non-directive: 'I would like to hear from you about what has been going on. What are the main difficulties that have brought you here today?' The clinician listens carefully, tracking both the content of the patient's account and the process of the telling: the emotional tone, the coherence of the narrative, the areas of avoidance or disconnection, and the language the patient uses to describe themselves and their experiences.

As the patient describes their difficulties, the clinician begins to map the information onto the domains of the IPTF Formulation Worksheet Section One ('The Now'). The domains that should be covered, either through the patient's spontaneous account or through the clinician's follow-up questions, include the following. Current emotional difficulties: the frequency, intensity, duration, and triggers of emotional distress; the patient's capacity to identify and name their emotions; the strategies, both adaptive and maladaptive, that they use to manage emotional distress. Current interpersonal difficulties: the quality and stability of the patient's significant relationships; patterns of conflict, withdrawal, idealisation, or devaluation; the patient's capacity for trust, intimacy, and the management of interpersonal boundaries. Current risk: self-harm behaviours, including method, frequency, intent, and function; suicidal ideation, planning, and previous attempts; substance misuse; and any other behaviours that place the patient at risk of harm. Current functional impairment: the impact of the patient's difficulties on their daily life, including employment or education, housing, finances, self-care, and social participation. Current service involvement: the patient's current and recent contact with mental health services, including any ongoing treatment, medication, or care coordination.

◆ CLINICAL PEARL

In the first assessment session, resist the temptation to take a full developmental history. The patient has not yet established enough trust in you to share their most painful experiences, and pushing too early for trauma details risks replicating the experience of previous assessments in which the patient was asked to recount their history to a stranger who then did nothing with the information. The developmental history is the focus of Assessment Session Two. In Session One, stay in the present: the patient's current difficulties, their current life, and what they want from treatment. This is 'The Now'.

Psychometric Assessment: Administration Guidance

At the conclusion of Assessment Session One, the clinician provides the patient with the self-report psychometric measures that will be completed before the next session. The recommended assessment battery for the IPTF initial assessment includes the following instruments.

Instrument	What It Measures	Administration Time
Personality Inventory for ICD-11 (PiCD; Oltmanns and Widiger, 2018)	ICD-11 trait domain scores (Negative Affectivity, Detachment, Dissociality, Disinhibition, Anankastia)	15–20 minutes
Level of Personality Functioning Scale — Brief Form 2.0 (LPFS-BF; Weekers et al., 2019)	Severity of impairment in self and interpersonal functioning	5–10 minutes
Young Schema Questionnaire — Short Form 3 (YSQ-S3; Young and Brown, 2005)	Early Maladaptive Schemas across five domains	20–30 minutes
Clinical Outcomes in Routine Evaluation (CORE-OM; Evans et al., 2002)	Global psychological distress, risk, and functioning	5–10 minutes
Patient Health Questionnaire-9 (PHQ-9; Kroenke, Spitzer, and Williams, 2001)	Depression symptom severity	3–5 minutes
Generalised Anxiety Disorder-7 (GAD-7; Spitzer, Kroenke, Williams, and Löwe, 2006)	Anxiety symptom severity	3–5 minutes
Borderline Symptom List-23 (BSL-23; Bohus et al., 2009)	Borderline-specific symptomatology	5–10 minutes

The clinician should explain the purpose of the questionnaires to the patient, emphasising that they are not tests that can be passed or failed, that there are no right or wrong answers, and that the results will be used collaboratively to build a shared understanding of the patient's difficulties. Patients should be advised to complete the questionnaires in a quiet environment where they will not be interrupted, and to answer based on their experience over the past two weeks for the PHQ-9 and GAD-7, or as otherwise specified in the instrument's instructions.

Assessment Session Two: Developmental History and Attachment Exploration

The second assessment session is devoted to the exploration of the patient's developmental history, with particular attention to the attachment relationships, adverse experiences, and environmental factors that have shaped their personality development. This session provides the raw material that will later populate Section Two ('The Why') of the IPTF Formulation Worksheet, although the formal completion of Section Two does not occur until the transition from Stage 1 to Stage 2, when the patient has established sufficient stability and therapeutic trust to engage in this reflective work.

The developmental history interview follows a chronological structure, moving from early childhood through adolescence and into adulthood, and attending to the following domains at each developmental stage. Family composition and primary caregivers: who was in the household, who provided the primary caregiving, and how stable the family structure was over time. Quality of attachment relationships: the patient's experience of their primary caregivers' emotional availability, responsiveness, consistency, and capacity for warmth and affection. Adverse experiences: any experiences of abuse (physical, sexual, emotional), neglect (physical, emotional), household dysfunction (parental mental illness, substance misuse, domestic violence, incarceration), and other adversity (bullying, bereavement, institutional care, forced migration). Emotional expression in the family: how emotions were expressed, tolerated, and responded to within the family, including whether the patient's emotional needs were acknowledged, validated, dismissed, or punished. Peer relationships: the quality of the patient's friendships and social relationships, including experiences of social isolation, bullying, or relational victimisation. Educational and occupational history: the patient's educational trajectory, including any disruptions, exclusions, or significant achievements, and their employment history. Significant adult relationships: the quality, stability, and pattern of the patient's adult intimate relationships, friendships, and relationships with authority figures. Previous mental health treatment: a detailed account of all previous contacts with mental health services, including what was offered, what was helpful, what was unhelpful, and why treatment ended.

◆ CLINICAL PEARL

When exploring the developmental history, attend as much to what is not said as to what is said. The patient who describes their childhood as 'fine' or 'normal' but whose adult presentation includes severe emotional dysregulation, self-harm, and chaotic relationships is telling you something important in the gap between their narrative and their symptoms. Do not challenge this narrative in the assessment; note it. In Stage 2, the collaborative exploration of this gap, between the story the patient tells themselves about their childhood and the impact that childhood has had on their adult life, becomes some of the most therapeutically productive work in the entire IPTF.

Assessment Session Three: Risk Assessment and Formulation Feedback

Structured Risk Assessment

The third assessment session begins with a structured risk assessment that builds upon the risk information gathered in Sessions One and Two. The IPTF approach to risk assessment follows the structured professional judgement model described in Chapter 15 of the parent textbook, which holds that risk assessment in personality disorder should be formulation-based rather than checklist-based: it should seek to understand the function that risk behaviours serve for the patient and the conditions under which risk is elevated, rather than simply cataloguing the presence or absence of risk factors.

The risk assessment domains include the following. Self-harm: a detailed functional analysis of the patient's self-harm behaviours, including method, frequency, intensity, triggers, function (emotional regulation, self-punishment, communication of distress, dissociation management), and the patient's own understanding of why they self-harm. Suicidality: a careful exploration of current suicidal ideation, including frequency, intensity, duration, content (passive ideation, active ideation, planning, intent), access to means, and protective factors. The clinician should be direct and compassionate in asking about suicidality: 'I want to ask you about something that is really important, and I hope you will be honest with me. Have you had thoughts of ending your life? If so, how often, and how strong are those thoughts?' Substance misuse: an assessment of the type, frequency, quantity, and function of any substance use, including whether substance use is used as a coping strategy for emotional distress or as a means of managing interpersonal difficulties. Risk to others: an assessment of any history of aggression, violence, or offending behaviour, including the context, triggers, and function of such behaviour. Vulnerability: an assessment of the patient's vulnerability to exploitation, abuse, or harm from others, including their current living situation, relationships, and social support.

Formulation Feedback Session

The latter part of Assessment Session Three, and, where needed, a fourth session, is devoted to feeding back the assessment findings to the patient in a collaborative, non-pathologising manner and to agreeing the treatment plan. This is one of the most therapeutically significant moments in the assessment process, because it is the point at which the patient learns how the clinician understands their difficulties, and the manner in which this understanding is communicated can either validate or invalidate the patient's experience.

The formulation feedback should be delivered using the language and structure of the IPTF Formulation Worksheet. The clinician begins by summarising 'The Now': the patient's current difficulties, their current risk, and their current coping strategies, using the patient's own words wherever possible and checking at each point that the summary resonates with the patient's experience. The clinician then provides the ICD-11 dimensional diagnosis, explaining the severity level and the trait profile in accessible, non-technical language. A suggested framework for this explanation is as follows:

> **Therapist Script:** '*Based on everything we have talked about over the past few sessions, and the questionnaires you have completed, I think that the best way to understand your difficulties is as a personality disorder of moderate severity. I know that the term "personality disorder" can feel really loaded, and I want to be clear about what I mean by it. I do not mean that there is something wrong with who you are as a person. What I mean is that the experiences you went through growing up, the things that happened to you that should not have happened, have shaped the way you experience your emotions, the way you see yourself, and the way you relate to other people, in ways that are causing you a great deal of pain and making it really hard for you to build the kind of life you want. The good news is that these patterns, because they were learned through experience, can be changed*

> *through new experience, and that is what our treatment is designed to do.'*

The clinician then outlines the treatment plan, explaining the three stages of the IPTF in accessible language, identifying which stage is the recommended starting point, and describing the practical arrangements including session frequency, duration, group and individual components, and the expected treatment timeline. The treatment plan is agreed collaboratively with the patient, and the patient's informed consent is obtained and documented.

The ICD-11 Dimensional Diagnostic Process: A Step-by-Step Guide

The following section provides a step-by-step guide to producing an ICD-11 dimensional personality disorder diagnosis from the assessment data gathered in the sessions described above.

Step One: Determine Whether a Personality Disorder Diagnosis Is Warranted

The first step is to determine whether the patient's difficulties meet the general diagnostic requirements for personality disorder under ICD-11. These requirements specify that the disturbance must be manifest in patterns of cognition, emotional experience, emotional expression, and behaviour that are pervasive across a range of personal and social situations, not limited to specific relationships or social roles; that the disturbance must be of long duration, typically evident from late childhood or adolescence, though it may not come to clinical attention until adulthood; that the disturbance must cause significant distress or significant impairment in personal, family, social, educational, occupational, or other important areas of functioning; and that the disturbance must not be better explained by another mental disorder, the direct physiological effects of a substance, or a general medical condition.

If the patient's difficulties are personality-related but do not meet the threshold for a full diagnosis, the sub-threshold category of Personality Difficulty may be applied. Personality Difficulty, under ICD-11, describes individuals who display some features of personality dysfunction that may cause problems in daily living but that are not of sufficient severity or pervasiveness to warrant a personality disorder diagnosis.

Step Two: Determine the Severity Level

The severity of the personality disorder is determined by assessing the degree of impairment across two core domains: self-functioning and interpersonal functioning. Self-functioning encompasses the individual's capacity for a stable, coherent sense of identity; the capacity for accurate self-appraisal; the capacity for self-direction, including the ability to set and pursue meaningful goals; and the capacity for self-worth that is not wholly dependent on external validation. Interpersonal functioning encompasses the capacity for empathy, the ability to understand and respond to the perspectives and emotions of others; the capacity for intimacy, the ability to form and maintain close, mutually satisfying relationships; and the capacity for cooperation, the ability to manage conflict, negotiate competing needs, and maintain social reciprocity.

Severity Level	Self-Functioning	Interpersonal Functioning	Typical IPTF Pathway
Personality Difficulty (Sub-threshold)	Some difficulties with identity, self-worth, or self-direction that are context-dependent and do not significantly impair daily functioning.	Some difficulties in empathy, intimacy, or cooperation that are context-dependent and do not significantly impair relationships.	Scaled-down IPTF: may benefit from Stage 1 skills group alone or a brief Stage 2 intervention. See Chapter 21 (Primary Care Adaptation).
Mild	Difficulties in some but not all areas of self-functioning. Identity may be somewhat unstable, or self-appraisal may be distorted in specific areas, but the individual can generally maintain a sense of self and pursue meaningful goals.	Difficulties in some but not all aspects of interpersonal functioning. Relationships may show some recurrent patterns of difficulty but are not pervasively impaired.	Full IPTF pathway, typically at reduced intensity. Stage 1 may be briefer (3–6 months); Stage 2 may focus on one or two core schemas; Stage 3 may be brief.
Moderate	Significant difficulties across multiple areas of self-functioning. Identity may be markedly unstable; self-appraisal may be significantly distorted; the capacity for self-	Significant difficulties across multiple areas of interpersonal functioning. Relationships are characterised by recurrent patterns of conflict, instability, withdrawal, or	Full IPTF pathway at standard intensity. All three stages are typically required. Treatment duration: 24–42 months.

	direction may be substantially impaired.	dysfunction.	
Severe	Pervasive and profound impairment across all areas of self-functioning. Identity may be fragmented or absent; self-appraisal may be profoundly distorted; the capacity for self-direction may be minimal.	Pervasive and profound impairment across all areas of interpersonal functioning. Relationships are severely impaired, chaotic, or largely absent. The individual may pose significant risk to themselves or others.	Full IPTF pathway at maximum intensity. Stage 1 will be extended (9–12+ months). Stage 2 may be protracted. Stage 3 will require intensive multi-agency support. Treatment duration: 36–60 months.

Step Three: Determine the Trait Domain Profile

Clinical interview prompts for Negative Affectivity: 'How would you describe your emotional life? Do your emotions tend to be intense, or do they tend to be fairly steady?' 'When you get upset, how quickly does that happen, and how long does it take to settle down?' 'Do you worry a lot, and do you sometimes find yourself expecting the worst in situations?' 'Do you often feel ashamed or like you have done something wrong, even when you are not sure what?' 'How do you feel about yourself on a typical day?' 'Are you very sensitive to how people respond to you — for example, to whether they seem pleased with you or displeased?' 'Do you get very anxious when you think someone important to you might leave or pull away?'

Clinical interview prompts for Detachment: 'Do you find that you tend to keep people at a distance?' 'Do you prefer to be on your own rather than with other people?' 'Would you say that you find it hard to feel close to people, or that you do not really want closeness?' 'Do you find it hard to know what you are feeling, or to put your feelings into words?' 'Is there much in your life that you genuinely enjoy?' 'Do you often feel numb or cut off from your emotions?' 'When people try to get close to you, what happens — do you tend to pull back?' 'Has anyone ever said to you that you seem cold or difficult to reach?'

Clinical interview prompts for Dissociality: 'Would you say that you are someone who generally cares a great deal about how other people feel, or does that not concern you very much?' 'Have you ever used dishonesty or manipulation to get what you wanted? How did that feel?' 'Do you feel that you are someone who deserves more than most people get?' 'Do you tend to feel that rules apply to everyone else but not necessarily to you?' 'When someone wrongs you, what do you tend to want to do?' 'Have other people described you as hard, cold, or ruthless?' 'Is it important to you to win, even at others' expense?'

Clinical interview prompts for Disinhibition: 'Do you tend to act on impulse, without thinking things through?' 'Have you done things that you regretted immediately afterwards, without understanding quite why you did them?' 'Do you find it hard to stick at things — to follow through on plans or commitments?' 'Do you get bored easily, and do you find yourself looking for excitement or stimulation?' 'Have you done risky things — things that most people would consider dangerous — without really thinking about what might happen?' 'Do you find it hard to think about the long term — do you tend to focus on what you want right now rather than what might be better for you in the future?' 'Have you had consistent difficulties with money, work, or relationships because of acting too quickly?'

Clinical interview prompts for Anankastia: 'Would you describe yourself as a perfectionist? Do you find it hard to feel that things are ever quite good enough?' 'Do you find it hard to cope when things do not go according to plan?' 'Is it important to you that things are done in the right way — your way?' 'Do you find it difficult to be spontaneous, or to be comfortable with things being uncertain or open-ended?' 'Do you tend to make very detailed plans and feel anxious or irritated when they have to change?' 'Would people close to you describe you as stubborn or inflexible?' 'Do you find yourself very focused on rules, order, or doing things correctly, even when a more flexible approach might be more effective?' 'Do you find it hard to delegate, because you worry others will not do things to your standard?'

Having assessed the prominence of each trait domain, the clinician records the trait domain profile in the clinical notes and on the IPTF Formulation Worksheet, noting which domains are prominent, which are present but not prominent, and which are not significantly elevated. The profile is used to inform the emphasis of the treatment: a patient with prominent Negative Affectivity and the Borderline Pattern Specifier will require all three stages of the full IPTF pathway with an intensive Stage 1 skills curriculum; a patient with prominent Detachment will require particular attention to the therapeutic relationship and to the systematic, gentle challenging of avoidance in Stage 2; a patient with prominent Disinhibition will require particular emphasis on impulse management skills in Stage 1 and on behavioural experiments targeting impulsive patterns in Stage 2; and a patient with prominent Anankastia will require particular work on cognitive flexibility, schema rigidity, and the cost of perfectionism in Stage 2, with attention to the interpersonal consequences of their rigid standards. The clinician references the IPTF Assessment Template in Appendix A when recording and synthesising the trait domain profile as part of the full diagnostic formulation.

Step Four: Apply the Borderline Pattern Specifier

The ICD-11 retains a single Borderline Pattern Specifier for individuals whose presentation is characterised by the specific features associated with the former Borderline Personality Disorder construct. The specifier is applied when the patient demonstrates a pervasive pattern of instability of interpersonal relationships, self-image, and affects, and marked impulsivity, as indicated by several of the following: frantic efforts to avoid real or imagined abandonment; a pattern of unstable and intense interpersonal relationships characterised by alternating between extremes of idealisation and devaluation; identity disturbance, manifested in markedly and persistently unstable self-image or sense of self; a pattern of impulsive behaviour in at least two areas that are potentially self-damaging; recurrent episodes of self-harm; affective instability due to marked reactivity of mood; chronic feelings of emptiness; and inappropriate, intense anger or difficulty controlling anger. When the Borderline Pattern Specifier is applied, the full three-stage IPTF pathway is typically indicated, with Stage 1's DBT-informed skills training being particularly critical.

Differential Diagnostic Considerations

The Neurodiversity Overlap

> *Interview prompts — Developmental Trajectory: 'Can you tell me about yourself as a young child, even before you started school? Were there things that were particularly difficult for you, or that people noticed about you?' 'Were you ever described as different from other children in some way, even when nothing bad was happening at home?' 'Did you have any difficulties with learning, concentration, or sitting still from a very early*

age?' 'Were there certain things — sounds, textures, lights, or tastes — that bothered you a great deal as a child, more than they seemed to bother other children?' 'Did you find it easier or harder than other children to understand unwritten social rules — the things that everyone else seemed to know without being told?' 'When do you think your difficulties really began? Can you link them to something that happened, or were they just always there?'

Interview prompts — Emotional Dysregulation: 'When you have a very intense emotional reaction — what we might call a meltdown or crisis — what tends to set it off?' 'Is it usually something that happens between you and another person, or are there other kinds of triggers?' 'Are you affected by sensory things — noise, crowds, bright lights, certain textures or smells — in a way that can overwhelm you?' 'Does a sudden change to your plans or routine throw you badly?' 'When you are very upset, does being reassured by someone help, or do you need to be alone and have quiet instead?' 'How long does a big emotional reaction tend to last? Does it come and go quickly, or does it linger for hours or days?' 'Is there a particular point — a kind of limit — after which you feel overwhelmed and unable to cope, and what tends to bring you to that point?'

Interview prompts — Interpersonal Functioning: 'Do you find social situations confusing — like other people are following rules that you were never told?' 'Do you find it hard to read people — to work out what they mean, what their facial expressions convey, or what they want from you?' 'Do you find social interaction exhausting? Do you need a lot of time alone to recover from being around people?' 'When you have a conflict with someone, is it usually because you misread what they meant, or because you were very sensitive to something in the way they treated you?' 'Do you struggle more with understanding what people mean, or with managing your feelings about what they do?' 'Have you ever learnt social rules consciously — by watching others and working out what you were supposed to do, rather than by instinct?' 'Do people sometimes say that you seem not to realise the effect you have had on them?'

Interview prompts — Identity: 'Do you have a clear sense of who you are, what you value, and what kind of person you are?' 'Do you feel like a different person in different situations, or with different people?' 'Do you ever feel like you are performing — putting on a social mask — rather than being yourself?' 'If you are masking, do you know who you are underneath?' 'Do you sometimes feel like you do not know who you really are, or what you actually want?' 'Has your sense of yourself changed dramatically depending on who you were with, or which relationship you were in?' 'Do you feel as though you absorb the personality or preferences of people around you?'

Interview prompts — Executive Function: 'Do you find it hard to concentrate, or does your mind wander a great deal?' 'Do you lose track of what you were doing, forget what people have said to you, or lose things regularly?' 'Is it very hard to start tasks, even ones you want to do?' 'Do you find it difficult to organise your time, or to judge how long things will take?' 'Do you tend to leave things to the last minute, or not finish things you have started?' 'Were you ever described as a daydreamer at school, or as not reaching your potential despite being intelligent?' 'Do you hyperfocus — becoming so absorbed in something that interests you that everything else disappears?'

Where neurodevelopmental features are identified through clinical interview, the ASRS-v1.1, and behavioural observation, referral for specialist neurodevelopmental assessment is strongly recommended. The IPTF treatment can proceed alongside this referral process, but the neurodiversity adaptations described in Chapter 20 of this manual should be applied from the outset. These adaptations include modifications to the communication style used in sessions, the structure and predictability of the therapeutic frame, the delivery of psychoeducation, and the selection of skills practice activities that take account of the individual's neurodevelopmental profile. The IPTF Assessment Template in Appendix A provides a dedicated section for recording neurodevelopmental screening findings.

Complex Post-Traumatic Stress Disorder

Interview prompts — PTSD Core Symptoms: 'Do you ever find that memories of things that happened to you in the past suddenly come back to you when you are not expecting them — memories that feel very vivid, as though they are happening again right now?' 'Do you ever have the experience of suddenly feeling as though you are back in the past, re-living something that happened to you?' 'Do you have nightmares about things that happened to you?' 'Are there places, people, or situations that you actively avoid because they remind you of things that happened in the past?' 'Do you feel constantly on edge, as though something bad is about to happen? Are you easily startled by sudden noises or movements?' 'Do you ever feel as though you are not quite real, or as though the world around you is not quite real? Do you ever find that time has passed and you cannot account for where you were or what you were doing?'

Interview prompts — Temporal Relationship: 'Can you tell me about the most difficult things that have happened to you in your life? Do you think there are particular experiences that have had the biggest impact on how you are now?' 'When did your difficulties really begin? Can you connect them to something specific that happened?' 'When you have an emotional crisis or feel very bad about yourself, is that usually triggered by something that reminds you of the past, or does it seem to come from something happening right now?' 'Are there particular topics, images, smells, sounds, or situations that can suddenly take you back to your worst experiences?' 'Do you feel that the things that happened to you have fundamentally changed who you are, or how you feel about yourself?' 'How much of your everyday distress do you think is connected to specific things that happened, versus being part of a more general pattern of how you are?'

Interview prompts — Self-Concept: 'How do you see yourself as a person? How would you describe yourself?' 'Do you feel that the experiences you went through have permanently damaged or changed you in some way?' 'Do you carry feelings of shame or guilt about things that happened to you — as though what was done to you was somehow your fault, or as though it has left a mark on you that you cannot get rid of?' 'Do you ever feel dirty or damaged in a way that goes very deep?' 'Does your sense of yourself tend to stay fairly consistent, or does it change dramatically depending on how a day has gone, or how someone has treated you?' 'Do you ever have periods where you do not feel like yourself at all, or feel completely empty?'

Where CPTSD is identified, either alone or in conjunction with personality disorder, the treatment plan should be adjusted accordingly. The IPTF's Stage 1 stabilisation work is well suited to the initial management of both conditions, since the emotion regulation, distress tolerance, and safety planning components are directly relevant to the management of trauma-driven emotional dysregulation and crisis behaviour. However, where CPTSD is present, the Stage 2 schema work will need to be supplemented with specific trauma-processing interventions, including EMDR (Eye Movement Desensitisation and Reprocessing) or trauma-focused CBT, delivered in accordance with the NICE guidelines for PTSD (NICE, 2018). It is essential that trauma processing is not commenced before Stage 1 has established sufficient emotional regulation capacity: commencing trauma-focused work with a patient who has not yet developed robust distress tolerance skills risks destabilising the patient, activating trauma material without providing the regulatory scaffolding to contain it, and replicating the experience of being overwhelmed by their own history without adequate support. The IPTF's sequenced structure is, in this context, not merely an organisational preference but a clinical safety requirement. The IPTF Risk Assessment Template in Appendix B and the IPTF Assessment Template in Appendix A both include dedicated sections for the recording of CPTSD-related clinical information.

Chapter Summary

This chapter has provided a comprehensive assessment protocol for the IPTF, covering the referral screening process, the three to four assessment sessions including engagement, developmental history, risk assessment, and formulation feedback, the recommended psychometric battery, the step-by-step ICD-11 dimensional diagnostic process, and the key differential diagnostic considerations including the neurodiversity overlap and the relationship between personality disorder and CPTSD. The assessment culminates in the production of an ICD-11 dimensional diagnosis and the collaborative agreement of a treatment plan. The IPTF Comprehensive Assessment Template in Appendix A provides a structured, reproducible clinical tool for recording and synthesising all assessment data across the full assessment sequence, and should be used alongside this chapter's guidance. The IPTF Risk Assessment Template in Appendix B provides the structured professional judgement framework for formulation-based risk assessment and safety planning, and should be completed as part of Assessment Session Three and reviewed at each stage transition. The chapter that follows presents the IPTF Formulation Worksheet in full detail, providing the tool through which the assessment data is organised into a clinically usable, collaboratively owned document.

Chapter 4

The IPTF Formulation Worksheet: A Detailed Clinician's Guide

> *The formulation is not a document that the clinician writes about the patient. It is a document that the clinician and the patient write together, looking at the same page, building the same understanding. The act of co-producing a formulation is itself a therapeutic intervention.*
>
> — Jayden Josh James, 2026

Purpose of This Chapter

This chapter presents the IPTF Formulation Worksheet in its fully developed form, with detailed completion guidance for each of its three sections. The worksheet was described in narrative form in Chapter 21 of the parent textbook; this chapter provides the operational detail that will enable clinicians to use the worksheet in their clinical practice, including worked examples showing completed worksheets for different patient presentations, guidance on the collaborative completion process, and the therapeutic rationale for each section.

The IPTF Formulation Worksheet is the single most important clinical tool in this manual. It serves as the organising framework for the entire treatment, providing a visual, tangible, collaboratively owned document that connects the patient's current difficulties to their developmental history and to their recovery goals. It is not an administrative form to be filed in the patient's notes; it is a living document that is updated at each stage transition and that is used actively in sessions as a reference point for the therapeutic work.

The Relational Stance: Sitting Alongside the Patient

Before the content of the worksheet is discussed, the manner in which it is used must be addressed, because the relational stance adopted by the clinician during the formulation process is itself a therapeutic intervention that embodies the IPTF's core philosophical commitments. The IPTF specifies that the clinician should, wherever practicable, sit next to the patient rather than opposite them when completing the Formulation Worksheet. This physical arrangement is a deliberate and symbolically significant departure from the traditional clinical consultation in which the clinician sits behind a desk, facing the patient, in a configuration that implicitly establishes the clinician as the expert who examines and the patient as the subject who is examined.

By sitting next to the patient, looking at the worksheet together, the clinician communicates a fundamentally different relational message: that the formulation is a shared project, that clinician and patient are collaborative investigators examining the patient's experience together, and that the expertise in the room is distributed rather than concentrated. The clinician contributes clinical knowledge; the patient contributes experiential knowledge. This side-by-side stance physically enacts the collaborative empiricism that the IPTF inherits from the CBT tradition and the limited reparenting that it inherits from Schema-Focused Therapy.

For patients with personality disorder, whose formative relational experience has typically been characterised by power imbalance, control, and the subordination of their perspective to the authority of others, the experience of sitting alongside a professional who treats them as an equal partner in the construction of their own story can be profoundly corrective. It directly challenges the Subjugation and Defectiveness schemas that many patients carry: the belief that their perspective is worthless, that they have nothing to contribute, and that the professional knows better than they do about their own experience.

◆ CLINICAL PEARL

If your consulting room has a fixed desk-and-chairs arrangement that places you opposite the patient, rearrange the furniture for IPTF sessions. Place two chairs side by side with a small table or clipboard between them. If room constraints prevent this, use a clipboard held between you at an angle that both can see. The physical act of rearranging the room signals to the patient that something different is happening here, that this is not the usual clinical encounter, and that their active participation is not just welcome but required. Give the patient a copy of the worksheet to take home after each session. This simple act communicates that the formulation belongs to both of you.

Section One: 'The Now' — Stage 1: Stabilisation and Safety

Section One of the IPTF Formulation Worksheet captures the patient's current presentation and identifies the immediate treatment targets for Stage 1. It is completed collaboratively across the first three assessment sessions and updated throughout Stage 1 as the patient's presentation changes. Section One includes the following domains.

ICD-11 Severity Rating

This domain records the patient's ICD-11 dimensional diagnosis, including the severity level (Personality Difficulty, Mild, Moderate, or Severe), the trait domain profile (which domains are prominent and which are present but not prominent), and whether the Borderline Pattern Specifier applies. The clinician should include a brief narrative justification for the severity rating, expressed in accessible language that the patient can understand. For example: 'Moderate severity, because the difficulties affect several important areas of your life including your relationships, your ability to work, and the way you feel about yourself, but you are still able to manage some aspects of your daily life and you have some important strengths that we can build on.'

Current Risk Profile

This domain records the patient's current risk profile, organised according to the IPTF treatment hierarchy adapted from Linehan's target hierarchy. Life-threatening behaviours are recorded first, including the type, frequency, intensity, method, and function of any self-harm or suicidal behaviour, the most recent episode, and the patient's current level of suicidal ideation. Therapy-interfering behaviours are recorded next, including patterns of non-attendance, non-engagement, boundary violations, or other behaviours that have compromised previous therapeutic relationships. Quality-of-life-interfering behaviours are recorded last, including substance misuse, housing instability, unemployment, social isolation, and any other factors that significantly impair the patient's daily functioning.

Current Coping Strategies

This domain records the patient's existing strategies for managing distress, divided into adaptive strategies that the treatment can build upon and maladaptive strategies that the treatment will seek to replace. Adaptive strategies might include exercise, creative expression, contact with a trusted friend, or religious or spiritual practice. Maladaptive strategies might include self-harm, substance use, dissociation, interpersonal conflict, or withdrawal. The inclusion of both adaptive and maladaptive strategies is important because it communicates to the patient that the clinician recognises their existing strengths and resources, not just their difficulties, and because the adaptive strategies provide the foundation upon which Stage 1 skills are built.

Collaborative Safety Plan

This domain contains the patient's collaboratively developed safety plan, organised as a hierarchical sequence of strategies to be deployed in response to escalating distress. The safety plan follows a stepped format: personal warning signs that indicate that distress is increasing; internal coping strategies that the patient can use independently, including the specific DBT skills taught in Stage 1; social coping strategies, including named individuals whom the patient can contact for support; professional contacts, including the crisis team telephone number and the patient's care coordinator; and the emergency plan, including the nearest accident and emergency department. The safety plan is developed collaboratively with the patient, using their own language and reflecting their own preferences.

Stage 1 Skills Targets

This domain records the specific DBT skills modules that are prioritised for this patient based on their current presentation. For most patients, all four modules (Mindfulness, Distress Tolerance, Emotion Regulation, and Interpersonal Effectiveness) will be delivered through the Stage 1 skills group curriculum. However, the clinician may identify specific modules that require additional emphasis in the individual therapy component. For example, a patient whose predominant presentation is acute crisis-driven self-harm may require intensive Distress Tolerance skills work in the early weeks of Stage 1, whilst a patient whose predominant presentation is chronic interpersonal conflict may benefit from early emphasis on Interpersonal Effectiveness.

Section Two: 'The Why' — Stage 2: Cognitive Mapping and Schema Work

Section Two is completed once the patient has achieved sufficient stabilisation to engage in reflective therapeutic work, typically at the transition from Stage 1 to Stage 2. It captures the developmental, cognitive, and relational information that will guide the Stage 2 therapeutic process. The completion of Section Two is itself a significant therapeutic event, because it is the point at which the patient begins to make explicit connections between their early experiences and their current difficulties, connections that have often been felt but never articulated, understood intuitively but never mapped.

Developmental Timeline

This domain records a structured chronological timeline of the patient's significant life events, attachment relationships, and adverse experiences from birth to the present. The timeline is constructed collaboratively, with the clinician drawing a horizontal timeline on the worksheet and inviting the patient to identify the events that they consider most significant at each developmental stage. The clinician attends not only to the content of the events but to the developmental stage at which they occurred, because the timing of adversity has a significant impact on its psychological consequences: adversity in infancy affects the formation of attachment patterns; adversity in early childhood affects the formation of core schemas; adversity in adolescence affects identity development and peer relationships.

Attachment Pattern

This domain records the patient's predominant attachment pattern as assessed through the clinical interview and, where available, formal assessment. The clinician uses the information gathered in Assessment Session Two, including the patient's descriptions of their early caregiving relationships, their adult relationship patterns, and their response to separation and loss, to make a clinical judgement about whether the patient's attachment style is best characterised as secure, anxious-preoccupied, dismissing-avoidant, or disorganised-fearful. The attachment pattern is recorded in accessible language, with a brief explanation of what it means and how it connects to the patient's current relational difficulties.

Early Maladaptive Schemas and Core Beliefs

This domain records the patient's identified Early Maladaptive Schemas, drawing upon the Young Schema Questionnaire results and the clinical interview data from the assessment. The schemas are organised by domain: Disconnection and Rejection (including Abandonment, Mistrust/Abuse, Emotional Deprivation, Defectiveness/Shame, and Social Isolation), Impaired Autonomy and Performance (including Dependence, Vulnerability to Harm, Enmeshment, and Failure), Impaired Limits (including Entitlement and Insufficient Self-Control),

Other-Directedness (including Subjugation, Self-Sacrifice, and Approval-Seeking), and Overvigilance and Inhibition (including Negativity/Pessimism, Emotional Inhibition, Unrelenting Standards, and Punitiveness). For each identified schema, the clinician records the core belief in the patient's own words, the developmental experience that is hypothesised to have given rise to it, and the current situations that most commonly trigger it.

Schema Modes

This domain records the patient's predominant schema modes and the triggers and contexts associated with each. The five core schema modes relevant to personality disorder are the Vulnerable Child, the emotional state in which the patient experiences the raw, unprocessed pain of their unmet childhood needs; the Angry Child, the state in which the patient protests the injustice of their treatment with rage and hostility; the Detached Protector, the state in which the patient cuts off from emotional experience and withdraws from interpersonal contact to avoid the pain of schema activation; the Punitive Parent, the state in which the patient attacks themselves with the internalised critical voice of their caregivers; and the Healthy Adult, the state in which the patient responds with compassion, rationality, and flexibility. The relative strength and frequency of each mode is recorded, along with the typical triggers that activate each mode.

The Schema Map

The Schema Map is the centrepiece of Section Two and of the Stage 2 therapeutic process. It is a visual diagram, constructed collaboratively by the clinician and the patient, that connects the patient's early experiences to their core schemas, their schema modes, their coping strategies, and their current difficulties. The Schema Map typically places the core schemas at the centre, with connecting lines to the developmental experiences that gave rise to them, to the current triggers that activate them, and to the coping modes through which they are maintained. The map makes visible, in a single visual representation, the pattern that has been running the patient's life: the connection between what happened to them, what they came to believe about themselves, and how those beliefs continue to generate the crises and relational difficulties that brought them into treatment. A detailed guide to constructing the Schema Map is provided in Chapter 12 of this manual, and a reproducible Schema Map Template is provided in Appendix C.

Section Three: 'The Future' — Stage 3: Functional Recovery and Identity Consolidation

Section Three is completed collaboratively with the patient at the transition from Stage 2 to Stage 3, and it captures the patient's own definition of recovery. This section represents a deliberate shift in the therapeutic conversation from understanding the past to building the future, from the question 'Why am I the way I am?' to the question 'Who do I want to become?'

Recovery Goals

This domain records the patient's personally defined recovery goals across four life domains: relationships (what kind of relationships do they want, and what does a healthy relationship look like to them?), occupation (what kind of work, study, or meaningful activity do they want to engage in?), identity (who do they want to be, and what qualities do they want to define them?), and daily life (what does a good day look like, and what routines and habits do they want to establish?). The goals are expressed in the patient's own language and are framed positively, in terms of what the patient wants to move towards rather than what they want to move away from.

Behavioural Experiments

This domain records the specific behavioural experiments designed to test the patient's capacity to engage in the activities, relationships, and roles specified in their recovery goals. Each experiment specifies the schema-generated prediction that is being tested, the experiment itself, the predicted outcome, and the actual outcome. For example, a patient with a Failure schema whose recovery goal is to return to education might design an experiment in which they attend a taster session at a local college, testing the prediction 'I will not be able to cope and everyone will see that I am stupid' against the possibility that they will manage the session and find it interesting.

Social Capital and Community Resources

This domain records the patient's existing and developing social networks, community connections, and sources of support outside the therapeutic relationship. It includes named individuals who provide support, community organisations in which the patient is or could become involved, peer support networks, and any other resources that contribute to the patient's social capital and reduce their dependence on the therapeutic relationship as their primary source of connection.

Relapse Prevention Plan

This domain records the patient's personalised relapse prevention plan, including identified early warning signs of schema reactivation and emotional dysregulation, vulnerability factors that increase the risk of relapse, specific coping strategies to be deployed at each level of risk, named support contacts, and the process for re-accessing the service if needed. The relapse prevention plan is a living document that is reviewed and updated throughout Stage 3 and that the patient retains after the end of formal treatment.

Neurodiversity Adaptation Checklist

When the patient has a co-occurring neurodevelopmental condition, the worksheet should be supplemented with a Neurodiversity Adaptation Checklist that documents the specific adaptations required across all three stages. This checklist records sensory regulation needs, including documented sensory sensitivities and the environmental adaptations required in the therapeutic setting; communication adaptations, including the patient's preferred communication style and any adjustments needed to the clinician's language, pacing, or use of visual aids; processing time requirements, including the need for additional silence during sessions that should not be interpreted as resistance or withdrawal; executive function support for patients with ADHD, including shorter sessions with breaks, written between-session reminders, and structured session agendas; masking fatigue assessment for Autistic patients, including strategies to reduce masking demands and encourage authentic engagement; and interoception adaptation for patients who struggle with awareness of internal body signals, including modifications to mindfulness and emotion identification exercises.

Worked Example: A Completed 'The Now' Section

The following worked example illustrates a completed Section One for a hypothetical patient, demonstrating the level of detail expected and the language in which the formulation is expressed. This example uses a composite patient who does not correspond to any actual individual.

IPTF FORMULATION WORKSHEET — SECTION ONE: 'THE NOW'	
Patient (pseudonym)	Emma, aged 32
ICD-11 Severity	Moderate Personality Disorder. Significant impairment in self-functioning (unstable identity, highly self-critical, difficulty setting and pursuing goals) and interpersonal functioning (pattern of intense, unstable relationships; difficulty tolerating perceived rejection; limited capacity for sustained trust). Emma describes herself as 'not knowing who I really am' and reports that her relationships follow a repeated pattern of intense closeness followed by explosive conflict and withdrawal.
Trait Profile	Prominent: Negative Affectivity, Disinhibition. Present but not prominent: Detachment. Borderline Pattern Specifier applied. Emma experiences frequent, intense emotional fluctuations that she describes as 'going from zero to a hundred in seconds', accompanied by impulsive behaviours including self-laceration, binge drinking, and reckless spending.
Life-Threatening Behaviours	Self-laceration to forearms using a razor, approximately 2–3 times per week, typically following arguments with partner or perceived rejection by friends. Function: emotional regulation ('it stops the noise in my head') and self-punishment ('I deserve it'). Most recent episode: 4 days ago. Two previous overdoses, most recent 8 months ago, described as impulsive during acute crisis rather than planned. Current suicidal ideation: passive ('I wish I could just not wake up') but no active plan or intent.
Adaptive Coping	Walking her dog ('the only thing that always calms me down'), listening to music, writing in her journal (intermittent), contact with her sister (the one person she trusts consistently).
Stage 1 Priority	Immediate priority: Distress Tolerance (TIP skills for acute crisis management, ACCEPTS for between-crisis periods). Secondary priority: Emotion Regulation (identifying and naming emotions, reducing vulnerability with ABC PLEASE). Emma will attend the Stage 1 skills group commencing Week 1, Block Two (Distress Tolerance), joining mid-cycle, with individual sessions focused on safety planning and behavioural chain analysis of self-harm episodes.

Chapter Summary

This chapter has presented the IPTF Formulation Worksheet in its fully developed form, with detailed guidance for completing each of its three sections, the relational stance required for its collaborative use, and a worked example illustrating a completed Section One. The worksheet is the organising framework for the entire IPTF treatment and should be completed collaboratively with the patient, updated at each stage transition, and used actively in sessions throughout the treatment. A full-size reproducible version of the worksheet is provided in Appendix B. The chapters that follow move from assessment and formulation into the delivery of treatment, beginning with the Stage 1 overview in Chapter 5.

PART II

Stage 1: Stabilisation and Safety

The Clinician's Guide

Chapter 5

Stage 1 Overview: Aims, Targets, and Delivery Structures

> *DBT is the engine room: it manages the heat so the machine does not explode. Without Stage 1, there is no Stage 2, because you cannot think clearly when you are on fire.*
>
> — Jayden Josh James, 2026

The Purpose of Stage 1

Stage 1 of the Integrated Personality Treatment Framework is the foundation upon which everything else rests. Its primary aim is to establish behavioural safety and emotional stabilisation, providing the patient with a functional repertoire of emotion regulation and distress tolerance skills that enables them to manage their distress without resorting to the life-threatening, therapy-interfering, and quality-of-life-interfering behaviours that have characterised their pre-treatment functioning. Stage 1 does not attempt to explore the developmental origins of the patient's difficulties, nor does it seek to modify their core beliefs or schemas. It focuses exclusively on the present: on equipping the patient with the practical skills and strategies they need to survive their crises, maintain their safety, and engage consistently with treatment.

The rationale for this exclusive focus on stabilisation is grounded in the neurobiological model described in Chapter 2 of this manual. When the patient's emotional arousal exceeds the threshold at which prefrontal regulatory capacity is compromised, typically represented by the 7/10 Arousal Rule, the reflective, mentalising, cognitively flexible engagement that Stage 2 requires is neurobiologically impossible. The amygdala-based threat detection system is activated, the prefrontal cortex is effectively offline, and the patient is operating from the survival-oriented, stimulus-response processing that generates the impulsive, crisis-driven behaviour the treatment seeks to address. Stage 1 calms the amygdala. It brings the arousal down to a level at which the prefrontal cortex can come back online, and at which the patient can begin to think about their experience rather than merely react to it. Without this stabilisation, the psychological exploration of Stage 2 is not merely difficult; it is contraindicated, because it risks activating emotionally charged material in a patient who does not yet possess the regulatory capacity to process it safely.

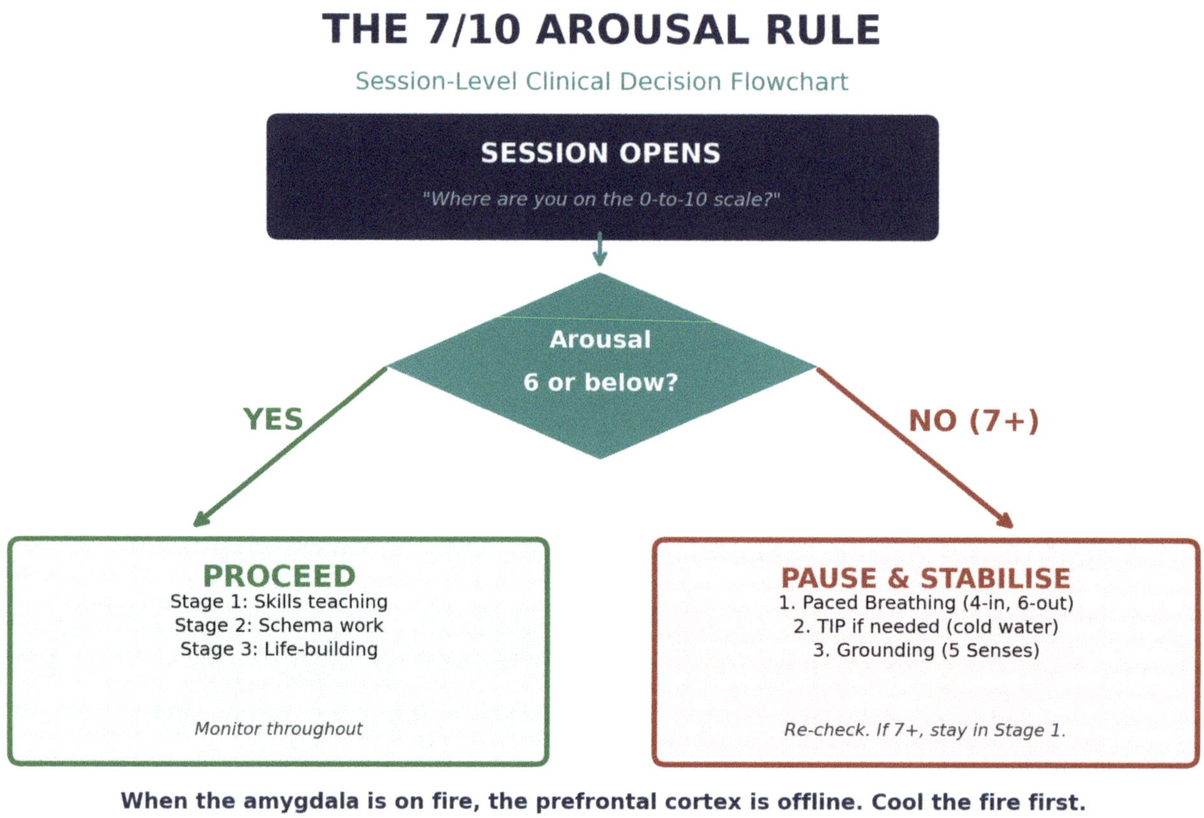

Figure 4. The 7/10 Arousal Rule: Session-level clinical decision flowchart.

The Treatment Hierarchy

The treatment targets of Stage 1 are organised in a strict hierarchy adapted from Linehan's (1993a) target hierarchy for standard DBT. The hierarchy determines the priority of clinical attention within every individual session and across the treatment as a whole. The hierarchy is not optional; it is the structural backbone of Stage 1 and the mechanism through which the IPTF ensures that the most dangerous behaviours are addressed before less dangerous but still clinically significant ones.

Target One: Life-Threatening Behaviours. These include suicidal behaviour, including suicidal ideation with plan or intent, suicide attempts, and preparatory acts; non-suicidal self-injury, including cutting, burning, hitting, overdose taken without suicidal intent, and other deliberate self-harm; and any other behaviour that places the patient at imminent risk of death or serious physical injury, including severe substance intoxication, dangerous impulsive acts, and refusal of life-sustaining medical treatment. Life-threatening behaviours always take priority in the session. If the patient has engaged in life-threatening behaviour since the previous session, or reports current suicidal ideation with plan or intent, the session must address this before any other content, regardless of the planned agenda.

Target Two: Therapy-Interfering Behaviours. These include behaviours by the patient that interfere with the delivery of effective treatment, such as non-attendance, persistent lateness, non-completion of between-session practice, emotional withdrawal or dissociation during sessions, hostility towards the therapist or group members, and violations of the treatment agreement. They also include behaviours by the therapist that interfere with the delivery of effective treatment, including inadequate preparation, failure to adhere to the treatment structure, excessive accommodation of avoidance, and failure to address ruptures in the therapeutic alliance. The inclusion of therapist behaviours in the target hierarchy is a distinctive feature of the DBT model that the IPTF retains: the treatment holds both parties accountable for the therapeutic process.

Target Three: Quality-of-Life-Interfering Behaviours. These include behaviours and circumstances that significantly impair the patient's quality of life and capacity for recovery, such as substance misuse, housing instability, financial crisis, unemployment, social isolation, involvement with the criminal justice system, and engagement in abusive or exploitative relationships. Quality-of-life targets are addressed when the first two target levels are under sufficient control, and they are typically the focus of the individual therapy sessions rather than the skills group.

◆ CLINICAL PEARL

At the start of every individual session, review the diary card and ask three questions in this order: (1) 'Have you harmed yourself or had strong urges to harm yourself since we last met?' (2) 'Is there anything that has made it harder for you to engage with the treatment this week?' (3) 'What else has been going on that has affected your quality of life?' This three-question structure enacts the target hierarchy and ensures that life-threatening behaviours are never overlooked because the patient or the therapist is drawn to discuss a less urgent but more interesting topic.

Delivery Structures: Adapting Stage 1 to Resource Levels

One of the IPTF's design principles is that its modular structure permits adaptation to different resource levels without sacrificing the core mechanisms of change. Stage 1 can be delivered in three configurations, each appropriate to a different service context.

Configuration One: Full Intensive Programme

The full intensive configuration is the optimal delivery model and is recommended for specialist personality disorder services with dedicated DBT-trained staff. It includes a weekly skills training group of two to two and a half hours, delivered by two co-facilitators to a group of six to ten patients; weekly individual therapy of fifty to sixty minutes with a designated IPTF therapist; between-session telephone coaching, available from the individual therapist during agreed hours for the purpose of skills generalisation in real-time crises; and a weekly therapist consultation team meeting of sixty to ninety minutes, during which the clinical team reviews cases, addresses therapist burnout and countertransference, and maintains treatment fidelity. This configuration mirrors standard DBT's four modes of delivery and provides the most comprehensive support for patients at the severe end of the personality disorder spectrum.

Configuration Two: Skills-Focused Programme

The skills-focused configuration is designed for community mental health teams and Complex Emotional Needs pathways that cannot resource the full intensive model. It includes a weekly skills training group of ninety minutes to two hours, delivered by two co-facilitators; individual support sessions of thirty to forty-five minutes with the patient's existing care coordinator or allocated keyworker, focused on skills application to the patient's specific circumstances and on diary card review; and team supervision, in which the skills group facilitators receive fortnightly supervision from a clinician with DBT or IPTF training. This configuration delivers the most evidence-supported component of DBT, the skills training group, which has been shown in meta-analytic research to produce significant reductions in self-harm and emotional dysregulation even when delivered as a standalone intervention without the other three modes of standard DBT (Valentine, Bankoff, Poulin, Reidler, and Pantalone, 2015).

Configuration Three: Community-Adapted Programme

The community-adapted configuration is designed for primary care settings, third-sector organisations, and services working with individuals at the milder end of the personality disorder spectrum or with sub-threshold Personality Difficulty. It includes a structured psychoeducation and skills group of sixty to ninety minutes, delivered weekly for twelve to sixteen weeks, covering core mindfulness, distress tolerance, and emotion regulation skills; and individual review sessions at the beginning, midpoint, and end of the programme. This configuration is not intended as a standalone treatment for moderate to severe personality disorder but may serve as a preparatory or maintenance intervention, or as a sufficient intervention for individuals whose personality difficulties are less severe.

● NICE vs. REALITY

NICE CG78 recommends that people with borderline personality disorder should have access to comprehensive DBT programmes lasting at least twelve months. In reality, fewer than 30 per cent of NHS trusts in England provide a full standard DBT service, and waiting times for specialist personality disorder treatment commonly exceed twelve months. The IPTF's skills-focused configuration (Configuration Two) is designed to bridge this gap: it delivers the core evidence-based component of DBT within a resource envelope that community mental health teams can actually achieve, whilst maintaining the essential structural elements, including the skills group format, the diary card, and the treatment hierarchy, that make the intervention effective rather than merely educational.

The Stage 1 Treatment Agreement

Before Stage 1 begins, the clinician and the patient collaboratively agree a written Treatment Agreement that specifies the commitments of both parties. The Treatment Agreement is not a behavioural contract; it is a collaborative document that clarifies mutual expectations, reduces ambiguity, and provides a shared reference point for addressing therapy-interfering behaviours when they occur. The agreement should cover the following domains: attendance expectations, including the minimum attendance rate required to remain in the programme, typically 75 to 80 per cent of sessions, and the process for communicating absences; the diary card, including the expectation that the patient will complete the diary card daily and bring it to each session; between-session practice, including the expectation that the patient will attempt the practice assignments and bring the completed worksheets to the group; confidentiality, including the rules for confidentiality within the group and the limits of confidentiality with respect to safeguarding concerns; self-harm during treatment, including the expectation that the patient will attempt to use skills before engaging in self-harm and will report any self-harm to the clinician at the next session; substance use, including the expectation that the patient will not attend sessions under the influence of substances; and the duration and review process, including the anticipated length of Stage 1 and the process for reviewing progress and assessing readiness for Stage 2.

> **◆ CLINICAL PEARL**
> The Treatment Agreement should be discussed, not handed over. Sit alongside the patient, go through each point together, invite questions, and check that the patient understands and genuinely consents to each commitment. If the patient expresses reluctance about any element, explore the reluctance with curiosity rather than insistence: 'I notice you paused when we talked about the diary card. Can you tell me what came up for you?' The way you negotiate the agreement communicates what kind of therapeutic relationship this will be.

The Diary Card

The diary card is the primary self-monitoring tool used throughout Stage 1. It is completed daily by the patient and reviewed at the start of each individual session and, where applicable, at the start of each skills group. The IPTF diary card is adapted from the standard DBT diary card and includes the following domains: a daily rating of emotional distress on a 0 to 10 scale; a daily record of urges to self-harm on a 0 to 5 scale, with 0 indicating no urge and 5 indicating the strongest urge imaginable; a record of any self-harm episodes, including the method and the function; a record of any substance use; a record of the specific skills used that day, selected from the checklist of skills taught in the current block; and a brief note about the day's most significant emotional event. The diary card is not a test; it is a learning tool. The clinician reviews the card with the patient not to evaluate their performance but to identify patterns, to celebrate skill use, and to analyse the chains of events that led to target behaviours.

The Consultation Team

The IPTF, following the DBT model, specifies that clinicians delivering Stage 1 should participate in a regular consultation team. The consultation team serves the same function for the clinician that the treatment serves for the patient: it provides structure, validation, skills training, and a relational context within which difficult clinical experiences can be processed without the clinician having to manage them alone. The consultation team meets weekly in the full intensive configuration and fortnightly in the skills-focused configuration, for sixty to ninety minutes. The consultation team has four functions: to review current cases, with particular attention to patients who are at elevated risk or who are presenting with therapy-interfering behaviours; to maintain treatment fidelity, ensuring that the IPTF's staged structure, treatment hierarchy, and five active ingredients are being consistently applied; to address therapist wellbeing, providing a space for clinicians to discuss the emotional impact of working with personality disorder presentations and to receive validation and support from colleagues; and to problem-solve clinical dilemmas, drawing upon the collective expertise of the team to address situations in which the individual clinician feels stuck, frustrated, or uncertain.

The consultation team operates according to a set of agreements adapted from Linehan's (1993a) consultation team agreements. These include the dialectical agreement, which holds that there is no absolute truth and that the team seeks to find the synthesis between opposing positions; the consultation-to-the-patient agreement, which holds that the team does not intervene directly with the patient on behalf of the therapist but instead helps the therapist to develop their own approach; and the fallibility agreement, which holds that all team members, including the most experienced, are fallible and that mistakes are opportunities for learning rather than grounds for blame.

Chapter Summary

This chapter has provided the operational overview of Stage 1, covering its aims and neurobiological rationale, the treatment hierarchy that structures clinical attention, the three delivery configurations appropriate to different resource levels, the Treatment Agreement, the diary card, and the consultation team. The chapter that follows provides the detailed session-by-session facilitator's guide for the Stage 1 skills group curriculum.

Chapter 6

The Stage 1 Skills Curriculum: Session-by-Session Group Facilitator's Guide

> *The skills group is not a lecture. It is a laboratory in which patients experiment with new ways of responding to their emotional experience, in the company of others who understand what that experience is like.*
>
> — Jayden Josh James, 2026

How to Use This Chapter

This chapter provides a detailed session plan for each of the thirty-two skills group sessions that comprise the Stage 1 curriculum. Each session plan includes the session aims and objectives, the key teaching content, an experiential exercise with full facilitator instructions, and the between-session practice assignment. The sessions are organised into four blocks of eight sessions each, corresponding to the four DBT skills modules: Block One (Mindfulness and Orientation), Block Two (Distress Tolerance), Block Three (Emotion Regulation), and Block Four (Interpersonal Effectiveness). Most IPTF programmes deliver two full cycles of the curriculum, allowing patients to join the group at the start of any block and to complete both cycles over a twelve to sixteen month period.

Each session follows a standard structure that should be maintained consistently throughout the programme. The standard session structure for a two-hour session is as follows: opening mindfulness exercise (ten minutes); diary card review and homework review (twenty minutes); teaching new skill (forty minutes); break (ten minutes); experiential exercise and practice (thirty minutes); and wind-down and between-session practice assignment (ten minutes). The consistency of this structure is itself a therapeutic intervention, providing the predictability and reliability that constitutes the first of the five active ingredients: structure and consistency.

◆ CLINICAL PEARL

The most common mistake made by new skills group facilitators is to spend too long on the teaching component and to leave insufficient time for the experiential exercise. The experiential exercise is not optional; it is the mechanism through which declarative knowledge ('I know what paced breathing is') becomes procedural knowledge ('I can do paced breathing when I am distressed'). If you are running over time, cut the teaching content, never the exercise. The patient who has practised paced breathing ten times in the group is better equipped than the patient who can define paced breathing but has never done it.

General Facilitation Guidance

Skills groups should be co-facilitated by two clinicians wherever possible, one taking the lead on content delivery whilst the other monitors group dynamics, attends to individual patients who appear distressed, and models engaged participation. Both facilitators should have completed training in DBT skills or equivalent IPTF training and should receive regular supervision.

The therapeutic stance in the skills group combines warmth and validation with clear structure and gentle accountability. The facilitator validates the difficulty of learning new skills, normalises setbacks and non-completion of homework, and celebrates all attempts at skill use regardless of outcome. At the same time, the facilitator maintains the session structure, redirects tangential discussions, and gently holds the boundary between the skills group and individual therapy: the group is the place to learn skills, not the place to process trauma or explore developmental history. When patients begin to share distressing personal material in the group, the facilitator validates the emotion, acknowledges the courage it takes to share, and redirects to the skill: 'Thank you for sharing that, and I can hear how painful it is. Let us see if we can use what you have just described as a real-life example of where the skill we are learning today might be useful.'

Block One: Mindfulness and Orientation (Sessions 1 to 8)

The Mindfulness block serves a dual purpose: it introduces the foundational mindfulness skills that underpin all subsequent modules, and it orients new patients to the programme, the group format, and the treatment expectations. Mindfulness is revisited at the opening of every subsequent session throughout the programme, reinforcing it as the bedrock skill upon which all others are built.

Session 1: Welcome, Orientation, and Introduction to Wise Mind

Session Aims: To orient patients to the skills group programme; to introduce the concept of Wise Mind as the synthesis of Emotion Mind and Reasonable Mind; to establish group norms and expectations.

The session opens with facilitator introductions and a brief overview of the programme structure, including the four blocks, the session format, and the treatment agreement. Facilitators explain that the group is a skills-learning space rather than a processing space, and that the skills taught here have a strong evidence base for helping people manage intense emotions and build more stable lives. The concept of Wise Mind is then introduced using the three-circle Venn diagram: Emotion Mind, which is driven entirely by feelings and urges; Reasonable Mind, which is driven entirely by logic and facts; and Wise Mind, which integrates both, incorporating intuition, values, and considered judgement. The facilitator uses everyday examples to illustrate each state: Emotion Mind is sending the angry text message at two in the morning; Reasonable Mind is making a list of pros and cons about whether to send it; Wise Mind is recognising the anger, understanding what it is telling you, and deciding how to respond in a way that serves your long-term interests. Patients are invited to share examples from their own experience of each mind state, with the facilitator validating each contribution.

Experiential Exercise: The Stone in the Lake Meditation. Facilitators guide a five-minute visualisation in which patients imagine themselves as a lake. Thoughts and feelings are pebbles that fall into the water, creating ripples on the surface, but the depths of the lake remain still. Patients are invited to notice what is at the bottom of the lake, beneath the surface turbulence. This represents Wise Mind: the deeper knowing that is always present, even when the surface is disturbed. After the exercise, facilitators invite brief sharing about the experience, normalising any difficulty with the practice.

Between-Session Practice: Patients are asked to notice at least one moment each day when they can identify which mind state they are in (Emotion Mind, Reasonable Mind, or Wise Mind) and to record this on their diary card.

◆ CLINICAL PEARL: De-escalation Scripts for Stage 1 Sessions

Stage 1 sessions, particularly those in the early weeks of Block One, frequently encounter acute emotional escalation in individual group members or, less commonly, across the group as a whole. The following three scripts provide facilitators with a structured verbal response to the three most common escalation scenarios encountered in the Stage 1 skills group context. Each script is designed to validate, contain, and redirect, in that order, without departing from the group format or reinforcing avoidance of distress.

Script 1: Emotional Overwhelm in Session

Scenario: A group member becomes visibly distressed during the session content, begins to cry significantly, or dissociates.

Facilitator: "I can see that something is coming up for you right now, and I want you to know that is completely okay. You are in a safe place. [Pause.] I wonder if we can try something together for just a moment. Can you feel your feet on the floor? Good. Press them down, just a little. [Pause.] And take a slow breath with me — in through the nose, and out through the mouth. [Pause.] That is your Wise Mind, right there. [Pause.] We are going to carry on with the group, and I want you to know you can just sit with whatever is coming up — you do not have to do anything with it right now. If you need a few minutes outside with [second facilitator's name], that is completely fine. What would be most helpful for you?"

Clinical note: The co-facilitator should remain with the group whilst the lead facilitator briefly attends to the distressed patient if they leave the room. Do not suspend the session for the group. This models that distress can be contained without derailing the system.

Script 2: Therapy-Interfering Avoidance

Scenario: A group member refuses to participate in an exercise, becomes dismissive or sarcastic, or attempts to derail the session with off-topic content.

Facilitator: "I notice you seem to be finding this exercise a bit tricky to connect with today, and that is okay — it does not mean the skills are not working. Sometimes when something feels awkward or a bit pointless, it can actually be a signal that it is touching something important. You do not have to do the exercise today — you are welcome to just observe. But I'd love it if you could stay with us, because what you bring to this group matters. Is there something about this exercise that is not sitting right for you? Sometimes we can adjust the approach." [If the behaviour continues:] "I am going to need us to keep the group space safe and focused for everyone here. Can we agree to talk about this more at the end, or I can check in with you in your individual session this week?"

Clinical note: Persistent therapy-interfering behaviour in the group context should be addressed in the patient's individual Stage 1 session using a behavioural chain analysis. Facilitators should not engage in extended negotiations within the group session, as this inadvertently reinforces the avoidance behaviour.

Script 3: Crisis Escalation in Session

Scenario: A group member discloses active suicidal ideation or intention, or reports that they have self-harmed immediately prior to or during the session.

Facilitator: "Thank you for telling me that. That took courage, and I am really glad you said something. I am going to ask [co-facilitator's name] to stay with the group for a few minutes whilst you and I step outside together. [To the group:] We are going to take a short break. [Outside with the patient:] I want to make sure you are safe right now. Can you tell me a little more about what is happening for you? [Conduct a brief risk assessment per your service protocol. If immediate risk is present:] I need to make sure we have the right support in place for you today. That means I am going to contact [care coordinator / crisis team / on-call clinician] so that we can keep you safe. I am going to be with you whilst we do that. You are not in trouble — this is exactly what the safety plan is for."

Clinical note: Following any in-session crisis disclosure, the facilitator must complete a contemporaneous record in the patient's notes, notify the responsible clinician, and review the patient's safety plan at the start of their next individual session. The group should be supported to process the interruption at the start of the following session using a brief, non-disclosing group check-in.

Session 2: Mindfulness 'What' Skills: Observe

Session Aims: To introduce the first Mindfulness 'What' skill: Observing; to develop the capacity for non-reactive awareness of internal and external experience.

The facilitator explains that Mindfulness has two sets of skills: the 'What' skills (what you do) and the 'How' skills (how you do it). This session focuses on the first 'What' skill: Observe. Observing means noticing your experience, both internal (thoughts, feelings, bodily sensations, urges) and external (sights, sounds, smells, tastes, textures), without trying to change it, judge it, or react to it. The facilitator uses the metaphor of standing on a bridge watching traffic pass beneath: the cars are your thoughts and feelings, and your job is to notice them passing, not to jump down and chase them. The distinction between having a thought and being fused with a thought is explored: when you observe a thought, you create a small but critically important space between the thought and your response to it. This space is where choice lives. The facilitator normalises the difficulty of observing without reacting and emphasises that this is a practice, not a performance.

Experiential Exercise: The Five Senses Exercise. Patients are guided through a structured observation exercise in which they spend one minute attending to each of the five senses in turn: sight (name five things you can see), hearing (name four things you can hear), touch (name three things you can feel), smell (name two things you can smell), and taste (name one thing you can taste). This exercise anchors awareness in the present moment through sensory observation and is a portable grounding tool that patients can use in moments of distress.

Between-Session Practice: Patients practise the Five Senses Exercise once daily, ideally at a routine time such as during their morning cup of tea, and record the experience briefly on their diary card.

Session 3: Mindfulness 'What' Skills: Describe

Session Aims: To introduce the second 'What' skill: Describing; to develop the capacity to put words to internal experience without interpretation or judgement.

The facilitator introduces Describing as the skill of putting words to what you observe, labelling your experience accurately and specifically without adding interpretation, evaluation, or judgement. The key teaching point is the distinction between description and interpretation. 'My chest feels tight and my heart is beating fast' is a description. 'I am having a panic attack' is an interpretation. 'I notice that I am having the thought that nobody likes me' is a description. 'Nobody likes me' is a fusion with the thought. The ability to describe internal experience accurately is a foundational capacity that supports all subsequent IPTF work: in Stage 1, it enables the patient to identify the specific emotion they are experiencing and to select the appropriate skill; in Stage 2, it supports the mentalising capacity that schema work requires. The facilitator demonstrates the describing skill using a series of images shown to the group, inviting patients to practise the distinction between observation, description, and interpretation.

Experiential Exercise: The Emotion Naming Exercise. Facilitators present a series of brief scenario descriptions and ask patients to identify and name the primary emotion using a specific emotion vocabulary list provided as a handout. The exercise begins with straightforward scenarios and progresses to more ambiguous ones that involve mixed or conflicting emotions, normalising the experience of feeling multiple things simultaneously.

Between-Session Practice: Patients are asked to practise describing their emotions at least twice daily using the format 'I notice I am feeling [emotion word]' and to record this on their diary card. They are given the Emotion Vocabulary Handout to support this practice.

Session 4: Mindfulness 'What' Skills: Participate

Session Aims: To introduce the third 'What' skill: Participating; to develop the capacity for full, unselfconscious engagement in the present moment.

The facilitator introduces Participating as the skill of throwing yourself completely into the current activity, becoming one with the experience rather than standing outside it observing or analysing. Participating is what happens when you are so absorbed in something that you lose track of time: a musician lost in the music, a footballer who makes the perfect pass without thinking about it, a child absorbed in play. For patients with personality disorder, who often experience a chronic sense of detachment, emptiness, or being 'outside looking in,' the experience of full participation can be both unfamiliar and profoundly connecting. The facilitator explores the barriers to participation that patients commonly experience, including self-consciousness, fear of judgement, fear of losing control, and the hypervigilance that comes from a history of threat, and normalises these barriers as understandable adaptations to past experience rather than personal failings.

Experiential Exercise: The Group Activity Exercise. The group engages in a simple, low-stakes activity together, such as a collaborative drawing exercise in which each person adds to a shared picture, or a structured movement exercise in which the group follows a series of increasingly playful instructions. The purpose is to create an experience of participation in which patients notice their internal commentary ('this is silly,' 'everyone is looking at me,' 'I can't do this') and practise letting it go in favour of simply doing the activity. The facilitator debriefs by asking: 'What did you notice happening in your mind whilst you were doing that? What happened when you let those thoughts go and just participated?'

Between-Session Practice: Patients identify one activity during the week that they can practise participating in fully, without multitasking, and record their experience on the diary card.

Session 5: Mindfulness 'How' Skills: Non-Judgementally

Session Aims: To introduce the first 'How' skill: Non-Judgementally; to develop the capacity to observe and describe experience without adding evaluative labels.

The facilitator introduces the 'How' skills as describing the quality or manner in which the 'What' skills are practised. Non-Judgementally is the practice of observing, describing, and participating without adding evaluative labels of 'good' or 'bad', 'right' or 'wrong', to your experience. This is perhaps the most difficult of all the mindfulness skills for patients with personality disorder, because many have internalised a Punitive Parent mode that relentlessly evaluates and condemns their experience. The facilitator makes a critical distinction: non-judgemental does not mean approving. It means describing the facts without adding the evaluation. 'I cut myself last night' is a non-judgemental description of a fact. 'I am disgusting for cutting myself last night' adds a judgement that is not factual but evaluative, and that increases shame, which increases distress, which increases the urge to cut. The facilitator acknowledges that judging is a deeply ingrained habit, particularly for people whose early environment was highly judgemental, and emphasises that the goal is not to eliminate judgement but to notice it, name it as a judgement, and let it go.

Experiential Exercise: The Judgement Jar Exercise. Each patient is given ten small tokens. Over a fifteen-minute period of group discussion on a neutral topic, patients are asked to place a token in a central jar each time they notice a judgemental thought arising in their mind. At the end of the exercise, the group counts the tokens together and discusses what they noticed. This exercise externalises and normalises the ubiquity of judgemental thinking and reduces the shame associated with it.

Between-Session Practice: Patients practise noticing judgemental thoughts throughout the day, silently labelling them ('that is a judgement') and recording the frequency on their diary card. They are encouraged to notice judgements about themselves, about others, and about situations.

Session 6: Mindfulness 'How' Skills: One-Mindfully

Session Aims: To introduce the second 'How' skill: One-Mindfully; to develop the capacity for single-pointed attention in the present moment.

The facilitator introduces One-Mindfully as the practice of doing one thing at a time, with your full attention, in the present moment. For patients with personality disorder, whose experience is often characterised by rumination about the past, anxiety about the future, and chronic multitasking driven by the sense that there is never enough time, One-Mindfully offers a radically different way of engaging with daily life. The facilitator explores the connection between multi-tasking and emotional dysregulation: when attention is scattered across multiple concerns simultaneously, the nervous system is in a state of chronic low-level activation that makes it harder to regulate emotional responses. By contrast, when attention is focused on a single task, the nervous system can settle, and the prefrontal regulatory capacity has a better chance of maintaining control. The facilitator uses practical examples: eating a meal without looking at your phone, walking without planning what you will say when you arrive, listening to someone without rehearsing your reply.

Experiential Exercise: The Mindful Eating Exercise. Each patient is given a single raisin or small piece of chocolate. The facilitator guides a five-minute exercise in which patients observe the object's visual appearance, texture, weight, smell, and finally taste, chewing slowly and attending to the full sensory experience. This classic mindfulness exercise illustrates the richness of experience that becomes available when attention is fully focused on a single activity.

Between-Session Practice: Patients choose one routine daily activity, such as brushing their teeth, making a cup of tea, or walking to the bus stop, and practise doing it one-mindfully, with full attention, every day during the coming week.

Session 7: Mindfulness 'How' Skills: Effectively

Session Aims: To introduce the third 'How' skill: Effectively; to develop the capacity to focus on what works rather than what is 'fair' or 'right.'

The facilitator introduces Effectively as the practice of focusing on what works in the current situation, rather than on what should work, what is fair, or what you have the right to do. For patients with personality disorder, who have often experienced profound injustice and invalidation, the concept of acting effectively rather than being right can be challenging. The facilitator validates this difficulty explicitly: 'You have every right to be angry about what happened to you, and your anger is completely understandable. The question Effectively asks is not whether your anger is justified, because it almost certainly is, but whether acting on it right now will get you closer to what you actually want. Sometimes the effective thing to do is the thing that feels unfair, because the alternative is a short-term satisfaction that costs you something more important in the long term.' The facilitator uses clinical examples: the patient who was right to be angry at the housing officer but whose angry outburst resulted in being banned from the office and losing access to the help they needed; the patient who was justified in confronting their friend but whose confrontation ended the friendship they valued.

Experiential Exercise: The Effectiveness Dilemma Discussion. The facilitator presents two brief vignettes describing interpersonal dilemmas in which the 'right' course of action and the 'effective' course of action diverge, and the group discusses what Effectively would look like in each scenario. The exercise highlights the dialectical tension between acceptance and change that runs through all of DBT.

Between-Session Practice: Patients are asked to identify one situation during the week in which they chose to act effectively rather than acting on their immediate emotional impulse, and to record the situation and the outcome on their diary card.

Session 8: Mindfulness Integration and Block One Review

Session Aims: To integrate all six mindfulness skills through application to a personally meaningful situation; to review Block One learning and consolidate skills; to prepare for Block Two.

The final session of Block One brings all six mindfulness skills together through a structured integration exercise. The facilitator reviews each skill briefly, using patient examples from the preceding weeks wherever possible, and then guides the group through a comprehensive exercise that applies all six skills in sequence. The session also includes a formal review of Block One, in which each patient identifies the mindfulness skill they found most useful and the one they found most challenging, and a brief orientation to Block Two, which will focus on Distress Tolerance. The facilitator normalises any anxiety about moving to a new module and emphasises that mindfulness practice will continue throughout the programme as the opening exercise of every session.

Experiential Exercise: The Personal Application Exercise. Each patient identifies a recurring difficult situation in their life, something that happens regularly and that typically triggers emotional distress. Working individually and then sharing with the group, each patient applies the six mindfulness skills to this situation in sequence: Observe (what do I notice happening in my body and mind?), Describe (what emotion am I experiencing?), Participate (can I engage with the situation rather than withdrawing?), Non-Judgementally (can I drop the evaluative labels?), One-Mindfully (can I focus on one thing at a time?), and Effectively (what response will serve my long-term interests?).

Between-Session Practice: Patients continue daily mindfulness practice using whichever technique they found most helpful, and complete a Block One Reflection Sheet identifying their key learning, their strongest skill, and their area for continued development.

Block Two: Distress Tolerance (Sessions 9 to 16)

The Distress Tolerance block teaches skills for surviving acute emotional crises without making the situation worse. These skills are not designed to solve the problem or to change the emotion; they are designed to get the patient through the crisis alive and without engaging in target behaviours. The distinction between distress tolerance and emotion regulation is critical: distress tolerance is for the acute emergency, the moment when the emotion is so intense that you cannot think straight and your only goal is to survive the next hour; emotion regulation is for the longer-term work of understanding and modulating your emotional patterns. Distress tolerance is the fire extinguisher; emotion regulation is the fire prevention system.

> ▶ **PATIENT PERSPECTIVE:** *'Before I learned TIP, my only option when the pain got too much was to cut. I literally did not know there was anything else I could do. The first time I used paced breathing instead of cutting, I could not believe it actually worked. It did not make the pain go away, but it brought it down enough that I could think. That was the moment everything started to change.' — Composite patient testimony*

Session 9: Introduction to Distress Tolerance and the TIP Skill: Temperature

Session Aims: To introduce the Distress Tolerance module and its rationale; to teach the first TIP skill: Temperature (cold water application for rapid physiological regulation via the mammalian dive reflex).

The facilitator opens with psychoeducation about the body's physiological response to extreme emotional distress, explaining in accessible terms that when emotional arousal reaches a high level, the body enters a fight-or-flight state in which the heart rate accelerates, breathing becomes rapid and shallow, and the thinking brain effectively goes offline. The TIP skills work by directly intervening in this physiological process, bringing the body back from the survival state to a calmer state in which thinking and skill use become possible again. The first TIP skill, Temperature, works by activating the mammalian dive reflex: when cold water contacts the face, particularly the area around the eyes and temples, the vagus nerve is stimulated, the heart rate slows, and the body's arousal level drops. The facilitator explains the technique: fill a bowl with cold water, hold your breath, and immerse your face for fifteen to thirty seconds; alternatively, hold a zip-lock bag of ice water against your forehead and eyes. The facilitator demonstrates with a bowl of cold water and discusses practical adaptations for when a bowl is not available: splashing cold water on the face, holding ice cubes in the hands, or placing a cold flannel across the forehead.

Experiential Exercise: Each patient is invited to try the cold water technique using bowls provided by the facilitators. Patients rate their arousal before and after the exercise on a 0 to 10 scale. The facilitator processes the experience, noting that the technique is not pleasant but that pleasantness is not the point: the point is that it works.

Between-Session Practice: Patients practise the Temperature skill at least twice during the week, once during a period of low arousal (to learn the technique) and once during a period of moderate arousal (to test it under realistic conditions), and record the before-and-after arousal ratings on their diary card.

Session 10: TIP Skills: Intense Exercise and Paced Breathing

Session Aims: To teach the remaining TIP skills: Intense Exercise for metabolising stress hormones and Paced Breathing for vagal stimulation and parasympathetic activation.

The facilitator teaches two further TIP skills. Intense Exercise works by metabolising the adrenaline and cortisol that flood the body during the fight-or-flight response: twenty minutes of vigorous cardiovascular exercise, such as running, fast walking, cycling, or even running up and down stairs, can significantly reduce physiological arousal. The facilitator discusses practical options for exercise that are accessible regardless of fitness level, location, or time of day. Paced Breathing works by activating the parasympathetic nervous system through deliberate slowing and deepening of the breath. The facilitator teaches the specific technique: breathe in through the nose for four counts, hold for one count, and breathe out through the mouth for six to eight counts, ensuring that the exhale is longer than the inhale. The longer exhale activates the vagus nerve and promotes parasympathetic dominance. The facilitator also introduces Progressive Muscle Relaxation as a complementary physiological regulation technique, guiding the group through a brief sequence of tensing and releasing major muscle groups.

Experiential Exercise: Guided Paced Breathing Practice. The facilitator leads the group through five minutes of paced breathing, counting aloud to provide the rhythm. Patients rate their arousal before and after. The facilitator then asks patients to practise paced breathing for two minutes without the facilitator counting, building the capacity for self-directed practice.

Between-Session Practice: Patients practise paced breathing for five minutes daily, ideally at the same time each day, and practise intense exercise on at least two occasions during the week. They record their experience on the diary card.

Session 11: ACCEPTS: Distraction Skills for Crisis Survival

Session Aims: To teach the ACCEPTS distraction skill set for managing acute distress when TIP skills alone are insufficient.

The facilitator introduces the ACCEPTS acronym as a set of distraction strategies for surviving a crisis: Activities (engaging in an activity that requires concentration), Contributing (doing something for someone else to shift focus outward), Comparisons (comparing the current situation to a time when things were worse, to gain perspective), Emotions (generating a different emotional state through music, comedy, or other emotional stimuli), Pushing Away (mentally pushing the distressing situation aside, putting it in a box to deal with later), Thoughts (engaging the thinking mind through puzzles, counting, or mental games), and Sensations (using intense physical sensations such as holding ice or snapping a hair elastic to interrupt the emotional spiral). The facilitator emphasises that distraction is not avoidance: avoidance means pretending the problem does not exist; distraction means deliberately choosing to redirect attention temporarily so that you can return to the problem when you are in a calmer state. Each patient identifies two or three ACCEPTS strategies that appeal to them and notes them on their personal distress tolerance plan.

Experiential Exercise: The Crisis Toolkit Exercise. Each patient begins assembling a personalised Crisis Toolkit, a physical collection of objects that support their chosen distress tolerance strategies. The facilitator provides materials and guides patients in selecting items: a photograph that generates a positive emotion, a list of activities, a small puzzle or fidget item, a peppermint oil vial for strong sensory input, and a written card listing their TIP skill steps. Patients take their toolkit home.

Between-Session Practice: Patients use at least one ACCEPTS strategy during the week and add at least one new item to their crisis toolkit.

Session 12: Radical Acceptance: The Foundation of Reality Acceptance Skills

Session Aims: To introduce the concept of Radical Acceptance as the foundation of the reality acceptance skills; to explore the distinction between acceptance and approval.

The facilitator introduces Radical Acceptance as one of the most powerful and most misunderstood skills in the entire DBT repertoire. Radical Acceptance means fully and completely accepting reality as it is, in this moment, without fighting it, without judging it, and without insisting that it should be different from what it is. The facilitator immediately addresses the most common misunderstanding: acceptance is not approval. Accepting that something has happened does not mean you think it was right, fair, or acceptable. It means you acknowledge that it has happened, because fighting against a reality that has already occurred generates suffering on top of pain. Pain is inevitable; suffering is the product of non-acceptance. The facilitator uses the formula: Pain plus Non-Acceptance equals Suffering. The facilitator explores the specific relevance of Radical Acceptance for personality disorder patients, many of whom have experienced genuinely terrible things that should not have happened. The skill is not asking them to forgive their abusers or to approve of what was done to them; it is asking them to stop expending energy fighting the fact that it happened, because that fight is unwinnable and the energy it consumes is energy that could be directed towards building a different future.

Experiential Exercise: The Letting Go Visualisation. Patients close their eyes and bring to mind a situation they are currently struggling to accept, something that has happened that they cannot change. The facilitator guides them to notice where in their body they are holding the resistance: the clenched jaw, the tight shoulders, the knot in the stomach. The facilitator then guides them through a gradual softening: 'See if you can soften around the edges of that tension. You are not letting go of the feeling; you are letting go of the fight against the feeling. Allow it to be there, just for this moment.' The exercise is followed by a gentle debrief in which patients share one word describing their experience.

Between-Session Practice: Patients identify one small thing they are struggling to accept and practise saying to themselves, 'I cannot change the fact that this has happened. I can choose what I do next.' They record their practice on the diary card.

Session 13: Turning the Mind and Willingness

Session Aims: To teach Turning the Mind as the mechanism for practising Radical Acceptance repeatedly; to introduce Willingness as the alternative to Willfulness.

The facilitator explains that Radical Acceptance is not a one-time decision but a process that must be repeated, often many times, because the mind naturally returns to non-acceptance. Turning the Mind is the skill of noticing when you have slipped out of acceptance and gently turning your mind back towards it, like a compass needle returning to north. The facilitator normalises the need for repeated Turning the Mind: 'You may need to turn your mind back towards acceptance fifty times in a single day. That does not mean you are doing it wrong; it means you are doing it exactly right, because each time you notice and redirect, you are strengthening the acceptance muscle.' Willingness is then introduced as the stance of being open to engaging with reality as it is, doing what is needed in the current situation, even when you do not want to. Willfulness is its opposite: the stance of refusing to engage, of digging in your heels, of insisting that you will not participate in a reality you did not choose. The facilitator explores willfulness compassionately, as an understandable response to a history of powerlessness: 'Willfulness often comes from a place of deep pain: the feeling that you have been forced to accept too much already, that your consent has never been sought, and that accepting anything more would be surrender. The IPTF understands that history. And it asks you to consider whether willfulness is serving you now, or whether it is keeping you stuck in a battle you cannot win.'

Experiential Exercise: The Willingness Continuum Exercise. Patients rate their current level of willingness on a 0 to 10 scale across several life domains: treatment, relationships, work, and self-care. The group discusses what they notice about their patterns. Are they willing in some domains but willful in others? What might that tell them about what they are protecting?

Between-Session Practice: Patients practise Turning the Mind at least three times during the week, noticing when they have slipped into non-acceptance or willfulness and gently redirecting. They record each instance on the diary card.

Session 14: Pros and Cons of Tolerating Distress

Session Aims: To teach the Pros and Cons skill as a cognitive tool for crisis decision-making; to strengthen commitment to distress tolerance as a long-term strategy.

The facilitator introduces the Pros and Cons grid as a tool for pre-planning the decision to tolerate distress rather than acting on crisis urges. The grid has four quadrants: the pros of acting on the crisis urge (what you gain in the short term), the cons of acting on the crisis urge (what it costs you in the longer term), the pros of tolerating the distress (what you gain by riding it out), and the cons of tolerating the distress (what it costs you to endure the pain without relief). The critical teaching point is that this exercise should be completed in advance, when the patient is calm, not in the middle of a crisis. In the middle of a crisis, the thinking brain is offline and the patient will not be able to generate balanced pros and cons; they will be drawn to the immediate relief offered by the crisis urge. The completed grid is kept in the patient's crisis toolkit and consulted as a pre-prepared resource when urges arise.

Experiential Exercise: Each patient completes a personalised Pros and Cons grid for their primary target behaviour, whether that is self-harm, binge drinking, or another crisis urge. The facilitator guides the group through each quadrant, helping patients to be specific and honest about both the short-term benefits and the longer-term costs of their crisis behaviours.

Between-Session Practice: Patients place the completed Pros and Cons grid in their crisis toolkit and review it at least once during the week. If a crisis urge arises, they consult the grid before deciding how to respond.

Session 15: Half-Smiling, Willing Hands, and Body-Based Acceptance

Session Aims: To teach body-based acceptance skills that use physical posture to influence emotional state; to reinforce the mind-body connection in emotion regulation.

The facilitator introduces the concept that the body and the mind influence each other bidirectionally: just as emotions change your body (tight muscles, shallow breathing, clenched fists), changing your body can influence your emotions. Half-Smiling involves turning the corners of the mouth up very slightly, just enough to feel the change in the facial muscles but not enough to be visible to others. Research on the facial feedback hypothesis suggests that this subtle muscular change can reduce the intensity of negative emotion. Willing Hands involves unclenching the hands and turning the palms upward, either resting on the lap or at the sides, with fingers slightly apart. This open-palmed posture counteracts the clenched, defended posture that accompanies willfulness and distress, and it signals to the nervous system that there is no current threat requiring a defensive response. The facilitator combines both with Paced Breathing to create a integrated body-based acceptance practice: Half-Smile, Willing Hands, and slow, deep breathing, held for two to five minutes.

Experiential Exercise: Guided Body-Based Acceptance Practice. The facilitator leads the group through three minutes of combined Half-Smiling, Willing Hands, and Paced Breathing. Patients rate their emotional state before and after. The facilitator debriefs, noting that the technique may feel artificial or even silly at first, and that this is normal: the skill works on the body, not on the belief.

Between-Session Practice: Patients practise the combined technique once daily and deploy it at least once during the week in a situation of mild to moderate distress.

Session 16: Personal Distress Tolerance Plan and Block Two Review

Session Aims: To consolidate all Distress Tolerance skills into a personalised, hierarchical plan; to review Block Two learning; to prepare for Block Three.

The final session of Block Two is devoted to the construction of each patient's individualised Distress Tolerance Plan. The plan is a one-page document that lists the patient's distress tolerance skills in a personal hierarchy, ordered by the level of distress at which each skill is most useful. For low-level distress (3 to 4 out of 10), the patient might use mindfulness, Half-Smiling, or a gentle ACCEPTS distraction. For moderate distress (5 to 6 out of 10), the patient might use Paced Breathing, the Pros and Cons grid, or Radical Acceptance. For high-level distress (7 to 8 out of 10), the patient might use TIP Temperature or Intense Exercise. For extreme distress (9 to 10 out of 10), the patient uses TIP and contacts a support person or crisis service. The plan is written by the patient in their own words, laminated where possible, and kept in their crisis toolkit. The session concludes with a Block Two review and a brief orientation to Block Three.

Experiential Exercise: Each patient completes their Distress Tolerance Plan with facilitator guidance, shares it with the group, and receives feedback. The plan is photocopied so that the patient retains the original and the service holds a copy in the clinical record.

Between-Session Practice: Patients keep the Distress Tolerance Plan accessible at all times and use it as the first point of reference when distress arises during the week.

Block Three: Emotion Regulation (Sessions 17 to 24)

The Emotion Regulation block shifts the focus from crisis survival to the longer-term work of understanding and modulating emotional patterns. Where Distress Tolerance asks 'How do I survive this moment?', Emotion Regulation asks 'How do I reduce my vulnerability to emotional crises and increase my capacity to manage my emotions over time?' This block builds directly upon the mindfulness skills of Block One, particularly the Observe and Describe skills, which provide the self-monitoring capacity upon which emotion regulation depends.

Session 17: Understanding Emotions: Why We Have Them and How They Work

Session Aims: To provide psychoeducation about the function and nature of emotions; to challenge the belief that emotions are the enemy.

The facilitator opens with the most important message of the Emotion Regulation block: emotions are not the problem. Emotions are adaptive biological responses that have evolved to provide information about the environment and to motivate action. Fear tells you that there is a threat and motivates you to protect yourself. Anger tells you that a boundary has been violated and motivates you to assert yourself. Sadness tells you that you have lost something important and motivates you to seek comfort. The problem is not the emotions themselves but the strategies you use to manage them and the speed and intensity with which they arrive. For patients with personality disorder, whose early environments were characterised by emotional invalidation, this psychoeducation can be profoundly validating: 'Your emotions are not broken. They are doing exactly what they were designed to do. The difficulty is that your emotional system was calibrated in an environment of threat, and it is responding to the world as if the threat is still there, even when it is not.' The facilitator introduces the emotion model: an event triggers a thought, which triggers a body sensation, which triggers an emotion, which triggers an urge to act. Understanding this sequence is the foundation of emotion regulation, because it reveals the multiple points at which the sequence can be interrupted.

Experiential Exercise: The Emotion Timeline Exercise. Each patient selects a recent emotional episode and maps it onto the sequence: event, thought, body sensation, emotion, urge, action. The group discusses each step, and the facilitator highlights the points at which a different thought, a different body response, or a different action might have changed the outcome.

Between-Session Practice: Patients complete an Emotion Log daily, recording one significant emotional event using the sequence format. The Emotion Log handout is provided.

Session 18: Identifying and Naming Emotions

Session Aims: To develop the capacity to identify and accurately name primary emotions; to introduce the distinction between primary and secondary emotions.

The facilitator builds on the Describe skill from Block One, focusing specifically on the identification and naming of emotions. The session introduces the concept of primary and secondary emotions. A primary emotion is the initial, direct emotional response to an event: the flash of hurt when someone says something unkind. A secondary emotion is the emotion about the emotion: the anger at yourself for feeling hurt, or the shame about your anger. For patients with personality disorder, the secondary emotion is often more distressing than the primary emotion, and much of the emotional turmoil they experience is driven by secondary emotional reactions to primary feelings that are entirely appropriate. The facilitator uses the metaphor of layers: 'Your anger is often a coat covering a deeper feeling. If we can help you take off the coat and see what is underneath, whether it is hurt, fear, shame, or sadness, you can begin to address the real feeling rather than being controlled by the surface reaction.' The session includes a detailed exploration of the physical signatures of the basic emotions, because many patients with personality disorder have difficulty identifying their emotions by internal experience alone and need to learn to read their body's signals.

Experiential Exercise: The Emotion Faces Exercise. Using a set of photographs showing different emotional expressions, patients practise identifying emotions from facial cues and then mapping these onto their own physical experience: 'When I feel sad, my body does this; when I feel angry, my body does this.' This exercise develops both self-awareness and the beginnings of the empathic capacity that will be important in Stage 2.

Between-Session Practice: Patients continue the daily Emotion Log, adding a column for 'primary emotion' and 'secondary emotion' to develop the distinction.

Session 19: Reducing Vulnerability: ABC PLEASE

Session Aims: To teach the ABC PLEASE skills for reducing emotional vulnerability through lifestyle factors and positive experiences.

The facilitator introduces the concept that emotional vulnerability, the likelihood that you will experience intense emotional reactions, is influenced by physical and lifestyle factors that are within your control. The ABC PLEASE acronym addresses these factors. Accumulate Positive Experiences means deliberately building pleasant activities into daily life, both short-term (a walk, a favourite meal, a phone call to a friend) and long-term (working towards a meaningful goal). Build Mastery means engaging regularly in activities that produce a sense of competence and achievement, even small ones. Cope Ahead means anticipating difficult situations and mentally rehearsing how you will handle them, including which skills you will use. PhysicaL illness (treat it), Eating (balanced), Avoid mood-altering substances, Sleep (adequate), and Exercise (regular) address the physical foundations of emotional regulation. The facilitator discusses each component practically, acknowledging the barriers that patients face: the patient who cannot afford healthy food, the patient whose insomnia is resistant to sleep hygiene, the patient whose housing is too chaotic for routine. The discussion is grounded in the patient's real circumstances rather than in idealised prescriptions.

Experiential Exercise: The Pleasant Activities Scheduling Exercise. Each patient creates a weekly schedule that includes at least one pleasant activity per day and one Build Mastery activity per day. The activities must be specific, achievable, and genuinely pleasant to the individual patient, not activities prescribed by the facilitator.

Between-Session Practice: Patients follow their pleasant activities schedule during the week and record which activities they completed on their diary card.

Session 20: Opposite Action: Acting Against the Emotion's Urge

Session Aims: To teach the Opposite Action skill for changing unwanted emotions by acting in opposition to the emotion's action urge.

The facilitator introduces Opposite Action as one of the most powerful emotion regulation skills. The principle is simple: every emotion comes with an action urge, and acting on that urge maintains the emotion, whilst acting in opposition to that urge changes the emotion. Fear urges you to avoid: the opposite action is to approach. Sadness urges you to withdraw: the opposite action is to engage. Shame urges you to hide: the opposite action is to share. Anger urges you to attack: the opposite action is to be gentle. The critical teaching point is that Opposite Action is appropriate only when the emotion is not justified by the facts, or when acting on the emotion will not be effective. If you are afraid because someone is genuinely threatening you, the opposite action of approaching is not appropriate; the fear is giving you accurate information, and the appropriate response is to act on it. The skill requires the Check the Facts step: before deciding whether to use Opposite Action, you must check whether your emotion fits the facts of the situation.

Experiential Exercise: The Role-Play Exercise. In pairs, patients practise Opposite Action for three common emotion-urge pairs: shame urging hiding, fear urging avoidance, and anger urging attack. One patient describes a scenario, and the other coaches them through the opposite action. The facilitator debriefs each pair, highlighting effective coaching strategies.

Between-Session Practice: Patients identify one emotion during the week for which they practise Opposite Action, recording the emotion, the urge, the opposite action taken, and the result on their diary card.

Session 21: Check the Facts: Testing the Accuracy of Emotional Responses

Session Aims: To teach the Check the Facts skill for evaluating whether emotional responses are proportionate to the actual situation; to build the foundation for mentalising capacity in Stage 2.

The facilitator introduces Check the Facts as the skill that bridges emotion regulation and the cognitive work of Stage 2. The skill involves systematically checking whether your emotional response is proportionate to the actual facts of the situation, or whether it is being amplified by assumptions, interpretations, or schema-driven appraisals that may not be accurate. The facilitator walks through the Check the Facts sequence: What event triggered my emotion? What are my interpretations or assumptions about the event? What are the facts? Am I confusing my thoughts about the situation with the actual facts? Is my emotion proportionate to the facts, or is it responding to my interpretation? If my emotion is proportionate, I can act on it; if my interpretation is driving the intensity, I can use Opposite Action or mindfulness. The facilitator emphasises that Check the Facts is not about dismissing or invalidating the patient's emotional experience; it is about ensuring that the emotional response is serving the patient accurately, just as you would check a compass to make sure it is pointing north before following it.

Experiential Exercise: The Fact-Check Worksheet Exercise. Each patient selects a recent emotional event and works through a structured Fact-Check Worksheet, distinguishing between the triggering event, their assumptions and interpretations, the verifiable facts, and the resulting emotion with and without the assumptions. The group shares their worksheets and discusses the difference between facts and interpretations.

Between-Session Practice: Patients complete one Fact-Check Worksheet during the week for a situation in which their emotional response felt disproportionate to the situation.

Session 22: Building Mastery and Coping Ahead

Session Aims: To deepen practice of Build Mastery through graduated task engagement; to teach the Cope Ahead technique for anticipating and preparing for difficult situations.

The facilitator returns to the Build Mastery and Cope Ahead components of ABC PLEASE, providing deeper practical guidance. Build Mastery involves deliberately engaging in tasks that are slightly challenging but achievable, building competence and confidence incrementally. The facilitator guides patients in identifying their current 'stretch zone,' the range of difficulty at which tasks are challenging enough to build mastery but not so challenging that they trigger overwhelm and schema activation. Cope Ahead is then taught as a mental rehearsal technique: identify an upcoming situation that you anticipate will be difficult; imagine the situation as vividly as possible, including the emotional arousal you expect to experience; then mentally rehearse yourself coping effectively, deploying specific skills at specific moments of difficulty. The facilitator guides a group Cope Ahead exercise for a common challenging situation such as attending a social event or having a difficult conversation.

Experiential Exercise: Guided Cope Ahead Rehearsal. Each patient identifies an upcoming difficult situation in the coming week. The facilitator guides a ten-minute visualisation in which patients imagine themselves entering the situation, experiencing the anticipated distress, and successfully deploying specific skills. Patients write down their Cope Ahead plan specifying the situation, the anticipated challenges, and the skills they will use.

Between-Session Practice: Patients complete one Cope Ahead rehearsal before the anticipated difficult situation and record the outcome on their diary card.

Session 23: Understanding Emotional Patterns and Vulnerability Chains

Session Aims: To develop awareness of recurring emotional patterns and the vulnerability factors that contribute to emotional crises; to build upon Check the Facts with a longitudinal perspective.

The facilitator shifts from individual emotion episodes to the identification of recurring emotional patterns. Using the Emotion Logs that patients have been completing throughout Block Three, the facilitator guides patients in identifying themes: Are there particular times of day, days of the week, or situations that consistently trigger intense emotions? Are there vulnerability factors, such as poor sleep, hunger, alcohol, or interpersonal conflict, that reliably precede emotional crises? Are there patterns in the secondary emotions: does hurt consistently trigger anger, does fear consistently trigger shame? The identification of these patterns represents a significant step in the patient's development, because it marks the transition from being buffeted by emotional storms that appear to come from nowhere to recognising the conditions under which storms are likely to arise and the early warning signs that one is approaching. This pattern-recognition capacity is the bridge to Stage 2, where patterns will be traced back to their developmental origins.

Experiential Exercise: The Personal Pattern Map Exercise. Each patient constructs a simple visual map of their most common emotional pattern, tracing the sequence from vulnerability factor to trigger to emotion to urge to action. The group discusses each map, with the facilitator highlighting the choice points at which skills could be deployed to interrupt the pattern.

Between-Session Practice: Patients continue the Emotion Log, adding a column for 'vulnerability factors present today,' building the longitudinal dataset that will support the transition to Stage 2.

Session 24: Emotion Regulation Integration and Block Three Review

Session Aims: To integrate all Emotion Regulation skills through application to a complex scenario; to review Block Three learning; to prepare for Block Four.

The final session of Block Three consolidates the emotion regulation skills through a comprehensive integration exercise. The facilitator presents a detailed clinical vignette describing a multi-step emotional escalation, and the group works together to identify the points at which each emotion regulation skill could have been deployed. The session concludes with a Block Three review in which each patient identifies the skill they found most transformative and the area where they need continued practice, and a brief orientation to Block Four, which will focus on Interpersonal Effectiveness.

Experiential Exercise: Group Case Formulation Exercise. The facilitator presents a fictional scenario in which a character experiences a series of escalating emotional challenges over the course of a day. Working as a group, patients map the character's experience onto the emotion sequence, identify the vulnerability factors, check the facts of each emotional response, determine where opposite action or distress tolerance would be appropriate, and construct a plan for how the character could have navigated the day differently using the skills learned in Blocks One to Three.

Between-Session Practice: Patients complete a Block Three Reflection Sheet and identify one emotion regulation skill to continue practising daily throughout Block Four.

Block Four: Interpersonal Effectiveness (Sessions 25 to 32)

The Interpersonal Effectiveness block addresses the relational dimension of personality disorder: the difficulties in communicating needs, setting boundaries, managing conflict, and maintaining relationships that are among the most pervasive and most distressing features of the condition. This block is the natural bridge to Stage 2, because the interpersonal patterns explored here, the tendency to avoid asserting needs, the tendency to prioritise the other person's feelings at the expense of one's own, the tendency to oscillate between passive compliance and explosive confrontation, are the behavioural manifestations of the schemas and internal working models that Stage 2 will address at the cognitive level.

Session 25: Introduction to Interpersonal Effectiveness: Goals and Barriers

Session Aims: To introduce the Interpersonal Effectiveness module and its three priority areas; to identify personal interpersonal goals and the barriers to achieving them.

The facilitator introduces Interpersonal Effectiveness by explaining that every interpersonal interaction involves three potential goals: the objective goal (what you want from the interaction, the specific outcome you are seeking), the relationship goal (how you want the other person to feel about you after the interaction, and how you want the relationship to be), and the self-respect goal (how you want to feel about yourself after the interaction, maintaining your values and self-respect). Different situations require different prioritisations: sometimes the objective is most important and you are willing to accept some relational cost; sometimes the relationship is most important and you are willing to compromise on the objective; sometimes self-respect is the overriding priority. The facilitator explores the common barriers that patients with personality disorder face in interpersonal situations: not knowing what they want, believing they do not deserve to ask, fearing rejection or abandonment if they assert themselves, lacking the skills to communicate effectively, or having overwhelming emotions that derail the interaction.

Experiential Exercise: The Priority Assessment Exercise. Each patient identifies a current interpersonal situation they find difficult and determines which of the three goals is their highest priority in that situation. The group discusses how the prioritisation affects the approach taken.

Between-Session Practice: Patients observe their interpersonal interactions during the week and note, for two interactions, which priority (objective, relationship, or self-respect) they were pursuing and how effectively they pursued it.

Session 26: DEAR MAN: Getting What You Want Effectively

Session Aims: To teach the DEAR MAN skill for assertive communication focused on achieving an objective goal.

The facilitator introduces DEAR MAN as the primary assertiveness skill for situations in which the objective goal is the priority. The acronym stands for: Describe the situation factually without judgement ('When I do not receive a reply to my messages for several days...'), Express your feelings about the situation using 'I' statements ('...I feel anxious and unimportant'), Assert what you want clearly and specifically ('I would like us to agree to reply to each other within twenty-four hours'), Reinforce the positive consequences of the other person giving you what you are asking for ('If we can agree to this, I think it would help me feel more secure in our friendship and I would worry less'), stay Mindful by keeping your focus on the goal and not being distracted by tangential issues, Appear confident through your posture, eye contact, and tone of voice even if you do not feel confident internally, and Negotiate if necessary by being willing to give to get. The facilitator demonstrates each step using a clinical example, then guides the group through a step-by-step construction of a DEAR MAN script for a common situation.

Experiential Exercise: Paired Role-Play. Each patient writes a DEAR MAN script for a real situation in their life and practises delivering it to a partner, who role-plays the other person. The partner provides feedback on clarity, assertiveness, and effectiveness. The facilitator coaches each pair, paying particular attention to the elements that patients find most difficult: typically, the Assert and Appear Confident steps.

Between-Session Practice: Patients identify one real-life situation during the week in which they use the DEAR MAN skill, either in full or in part, and record the experience on their diary card.

Session 27: GIVE: Keeping the Relationship

Session Aims: To teach the GIVE skill for maintaining and strengthening relationships in interpersonal interactions.

The facilitator introduces GIVE as the skill for situations in which the relationship goal is the priority: when what matters most is that the other person feels respected, valued, and cared for, even if it means compromising on the objective. The acronym stands for: be Gentle, avoiding threats, attacks, judgements, and condescension; act Interested in the other person's perspective, listening actively and asking genuine questions; Validate the other person's feelings and point of view, even if you disagree with their conclusions; use an Easy manner, employing humour and lightness where appropriate. The facilitator explores the particular challenges of GIVE for personality disorder patients: the difficulty of being gentle when you feel angry, the difficulty of validating someone whose behaviour has hurt you, the difficulty of maintaining an easy manner when internal distress is intense. The session connects GIVE to the broader IPTF model: the capacity to validate another person's perspective, even when it differs from your own, is a form of mentalising that will be developed further in Stage 2.

Experiential Exercise: The Validation Practice. In pairs, one patient describes a recent frustrating situation whilst the other practises the GIVE skills, focusing particularly on validation. The listener's task is to reflect back the speaker's feelings without problem-solving, advising, or dismissing. The exercise is then reversed. The facilitator debriefs, highlighting effective examples of validation and discussing the difference between validation and agreement.

Between-Session Practice: Patients practise using at least one element of GIVE in a relationship interaction during the week and record the experience on the diary card.

Session 28: FAST: Maintaining Self-Respect

Session Aims: To teach the FAST skill for maintaining self-respect and personal values in interpersonal interactions.

The facilitator introduces FAST as the skill for situations in which the self-respect goal is the priority: when what matters most is that you act in accordance with your values and maintain your sense of integrity, even if it costs you the objective or strains the relationship. The acronym stands for: be Fair to both yourself and the other person; no Apologies for making a reasonable request, having an opinion, or disagreeing; Stick to your values rather than compromising them to please others; and be Truthful, avoiding lies, exaggeration, or helplessness that would undermine your credibility and self-respect. The facilitator explores the particular significance of FAST for patients with personality disorder, many of whom have internalised a Subjugation schema that leads them to chronically prioritise others' needs at the expense of their own, apologise excessively for their existence, and abandon their values in order to avoid conflict or abandonment.

Experiential Exercise: The Self-Respect Audit. Each patient reflects on a recent interaction in which they compromised their self-respect and identifies which element of FAST was missing. The group discusses the costs of chronic self-respect deficits and the relationship between self-respect and the Defectiveness schema that many patients carry.

Between-Session Practice: Patients identify one situation during the week in which they practise maintaining self-respect using the FAST skill and record the experience on the diary card.

Session 29: Saying No: Setting Boundaries Effectively

Session Aims: To teach skills for declining requests, setting limits, and maintaining boundaries in relationships.

The facilitator addresses one of the most practically important interpersonal skills for personality disorder patients: the ability to say no. Many patients have never learned to set boundaries effectively because their early environments punished boundary-setting, because their Subjugation or Self-Sacrifice schemas generate overwhelming guilt when they attempt to prioritise their own needs, or because they fear that saying no will lead to abandonment. The facilitator teaches a structured approach to declining requests: acknowledge the request and the person's feelings ('I understand that this is important to you'), state your decision clearly and without excessive apology ('I am not able to do that this time'), offer an alternative if appropriate ('What I could do instead is...'), and hold the boundary if the person pushes back ('I hear that you are disappointed, and I understand, but my answer has to be no on this occasion'). The facilitator uses role-play to practise boundary-setting in progressively more challenging scenarios, from declining a minor request to setting a boundary with someone who responds with guilt-tripping or anger.

Experiential Exercise: Progressive Role-Play. The facilitator sets up three scenarios of increasing interpersonal difficulty. In each, one patient practises saying no whilst the other patient, coached by the facilitator, escalates the pressure. The group discusses the emotional experience of maintaining the boundary under pressure and the skills used to manage the internal distress.

Between-Session Practice: Patients practise saying no to at least one request during the week, recording the situation, their emotional response, and the outcome.

Session 30: Building Relationships and Ending Destructive Ones

Session Aims: To teach skills for initiating and building positive relationships; to address the challenge of recognising and exiting destructive relationships.

The facilitator addresses two complementary interpersonal challenges. Building Relationships involves the skills of finding and approaching potential friends, maintaining contact through regular initiation, managing the vulnerability of self-disclosure, and tolerating the uncertainty of new relationships. The facilitator discusses the particular barriers that personality disorder patients face: the Mistrust/Abuse schema that interprets overtures as threats, the Defectiveness schema that generates the belief that nobody would want to be their friend, and the Social Isolation schema that has normalised loneliness. Ending Destructive Relationships involves recognising when a relationship is causing more harm than benefit, making the decision to end or limit it, and managing the grief and guilt that follow. The facilitator distinguishes between relationships that are temporarily difficult and relationships that are structurally destructive, providing criteria for the distinction. The session also addresses the particular challenge of relationships with family members whose behaviour is harmful but from whom complete separation may not be feasible or desired.

Experiential Exercise: The Relationship Map Exercise. Each patient draws a visual map of their current relationships, placing themselves at the centre and positioning others at distances that reflect the emotional closeness of the relationship. Patients identify relationships they wish to build, relationships they wish to maintain, and relationships they need to limit or end. The exercise provides the starting point for the social recovery work of Stage 3.

Between-Session Practice: Patients identify one specific action they will take during the week to invest in a positive relationship, such as initiating contact, suggesting an activity, or expressing appreciation.

Session 31: Managing Interpersonal Conflict Without Rupture

Session Aims: To teach skills for navigating conflict in relationships without destroying the relationship; to introduce the concept of rupture and repair as a Stage 2 theme.

The facilitator addresses the challenge that many personality disorder patients find most difficult: managing conflict without either withdrawing entirely or escalating to the point of relationship destruction. The session integrates skills from across the programme: using TIP and Paced Breathing to manage the physiological arousal that conflict triggers; using Check the Facts to evaluate whether the perceived slight is accurate; using DEAR MAN to communicate the grievance assertively rather than aggressively; using GIVE to maintain respect for the other person; and using FAST to maintain self-respect. The facilitator introduces the concept of rupture and repair, which will become a central therapeutic mechanism in Stage 2: the idea that conflict in relationships is not a catastrophe but a normal and potentially strengthening experience, provided that the rupture is acknowledged and repaired. For patients whose early experiences taught them that conflict leads to abandonment, punishment, or violence, the possibility that a relationship can survive conflict and emerge stronger is a genuinely novel concept.

Experiential Exercise: The Conflict Resolution Role-Play. In pairs, patients role-play a conflict scenario using the integrated skill set. The scenario involves a realistic interpersonal disagreement in which both parties have legitimate perspectives. After the initial role-play, the pair practises the repair process: acknowledging the rupture, expressing understanding of the other person's perspective, and collaboratively finding a resolution. The facilitator debriefs, highlighting effective integration of skills.

Between-Session Practice: Patients identify one interpersonal conflict during the week in which they consciously deploy the integrated skill set and record the experience, including any repair process, on the diary card.

Session 32: Interpersonal Effectiveness Integration, Block Four Review, and Stage 1 Completion

Session Aims: To integrate all Interpersonal Effectiveness skills; to conduct a comprehensive Stage 1 review; to prepare patients for the assessment of readiness for Stage 2.

The final session of the Stage 1 curriculum serves three functions. First, it integrates the Interpersonal Effectiveness skills through a comprehensive exercise. Second, it provides a formal review of the entire Stage 1 programme, allowing patients to reflect on their progress, identify their strongest and weakest skill areas, and celebrate their achievements. Third, it prepares patients for the transition assessment that will determine their readiness for Stage 2. The facilitator explains that over the coming weeks, each patient will have an individual meeting with their therapist to assess whether they are ready to move to Stage 2 or whether a second cycle of Stage 1 is recommended, and reassures patients that a second cycle is not a failure but an opportunity for consolidation. The session concludes with a structured feedback process and a celebration of the group's work, which may include certificates of completion.

Experiential Exercise: The Skills Integration Challenge. The facilitator presents a complex interpersonal scenario that requires the integrated use of mindfulness, distress tolerance, emotion regulation, and interpersonal effectiveness skills. Working as a group, patients identify which skills are needed at each point in the scenario and role-play the effective response. This exercise demonstrates the cumulative power of the skill set and builds confidence for the transition to Stage 2.

Between-Session Practice: Patients complete a comprehensive Stage 1 Self-Assessment Worksheet, rating their confidence in each skill on a 0 to 10 scale and identifying their priority areas for continued practice. This worksheet is brought to the Stage 2 readiness assessment session.

Chapter 7

The Stage 1 Individual Therapy Component

Purpose and Function of Individual Therapy in Stage 1

Alongside the skills group, individual therapy is the second mode of delivery in Stage 1 of the IPTF. Where the skills group provides a structured psychoeducational environment in which patients learn new skills in the company of peers, the individual therapy sessions provide the relational context within which those skills are personalised, applied, and integrated into the patient's specific life circumstances. The individual therapy component serves three primary functions.

The first function is the translation of group-taught skills into the patient's specific context. A skill taught in the abstract, using generic examples, achieves its therapeutic potency only when it is applied to the patient's actual life situations. The individual therapist works with the patient to identify the specific situations in which each skill is most relevant and to rehearse its application in those specific contexts, using role-play, mental rehearsal, and between-session experiments.

The second function is the management of the treatment hierarchy through behavioural chain analysis. When the patient has engaged in a target behaviour since the previous session, the individual therapy session is devoted to a systematic analysis of the chain of events, thoughts, emotions, urges, and behaviours that led to the target behaviour, with the aim of identifying the specific points in the chain at which a skill could have been deployed to produce a different outcome. The chain analysis is not a punishment for engaging in target behaviour; it is a learning tool that builds the patient's understanding of their own patterns and increases their capacity to intervene earlier in the chain on future occasions.

The third function is the provision of the relational context for therapeutic alliance development. The therapeutic alliance is the third of the IPTF's five active ingredients, and the individual therapy relationship is the primary vehicle through which it is cultivated. For patients whose attachment history is characterised by disorganisation, unpredictability, and the absence of a reliable secure base, the experience of a consistent, predictable, boundaried, and caring therapeutic relationship is a corrective relational experience of profound significance. This relational function of individual therapy is not separate from the skills work; it is integral to it. The patient who trusts their therapist enough to be honest about their self-harm is the patient who will receive an effective chain analysis. The patient who does not trust their therapist will minimise, deny, or avoid discussing their target behaviours, rendering the chain analysis impossible.

Session Structure for Stage 1 Individual Therapy

Each Stage 1 individual therapy session follows a standard structure that enacts the treatment hierarchy. The session opens with a diary card review, during which the therapist and patient review the week's diary card together, identifying any instances of target behaviours, any instances of skill use, and any significant emotional events. The diary card review takes approximately ten to fifteen minutes and serves as the agenda-setting mechanism for the session: if the diary card reveals a target behaviour, the session will focus on chain analysis; if the diary card reveals no target behaviours but significant emotional events, the session will focus on skills application and generalisation; if the diary card reveals a stable week with consistent skill use, the session may focus on a specific skill area that the patient wishes to develop further, or on preparation for upcoming challenges.

Behavioural Chain Analysis: A Detailed Protocol

The behavioural chain analysis is the primary analytical tool of Stage 1 individual therapy. It is conducted whenever the patient has engaged in a life-threatening or therapy-interfering behaviour since the previous session, and it may also be used for quality-of-life-interfering behaviours when the first two target levels are stable. The chain analysis follows a structured sequence that traces the entire causal chain from vulnerability factors through to the consequences of the target behaviour, identifying the links in the chain at which a skill could have been deployed to produce a different outcome.

The chain analysis begins with the identification of the target behaviour itself, described in specific, behavioural terms: what did you do, when did you do it, how severe was it, and what was the function it served? The therapist then works backwards to identify the prompting event: the specific event that set the chain in motion. The chain then traces forward from the prompting event through the sequence of links: the thoughts that arose in response to the event, the body sensations that accompanied the thoughts, the emotions that emerged, the urges that followed the emotions, and the actions taken, culminating in the target behaviour. For each link, the therapist and patient identify what the patient was feeling, what they were thinking, and what they did. The therapist then identifies the vulnerability factors that were present before the prompting event: had the patient slept poorly, missed meals, used substances, been in conflict with someone, or been triggered by an anniversary or reminder? Finally, the therapist and patient examine the consequences of the target behaviour: what happened afterwards, both immediately and in the longer term?

Once the chain is mapped, the therapist and patient work together to identify the solution analysis: the specific points in the chain at which a different response could have produced a different outcome. For each identified point, the therapist asks: 'What skill could you have used here? What would have happened if you had used Paced Breathing at this point? What if you had used Check the Facts when that thought arose? What if you had called your sister when the urge first appeared?' The solution analysis is not prescriptive; it is collaborative and curious, honouring the patient's autonomy whilst building their repertoire of alternative responses.

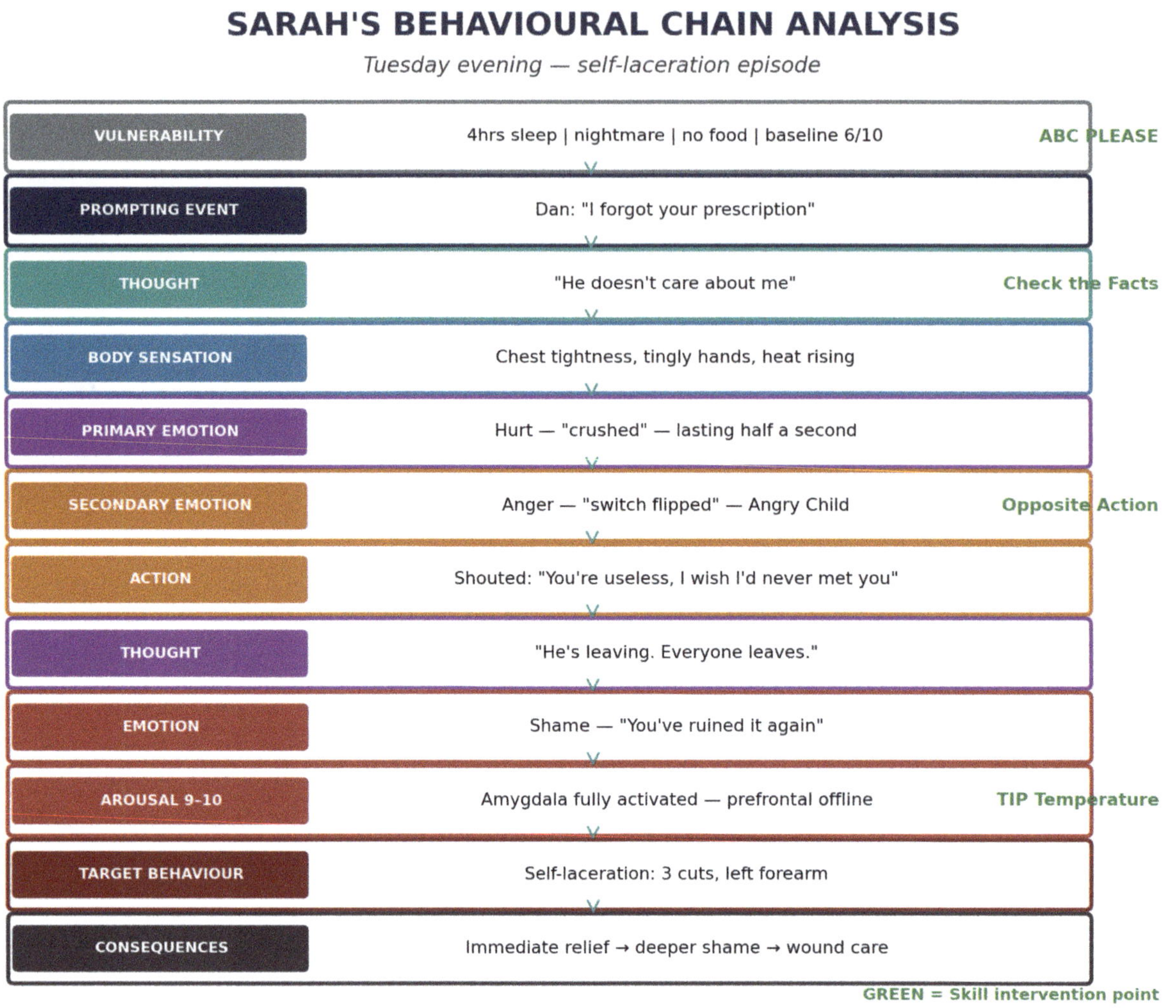

Figure 3. Sarah's Behavioural Chain Analysis with skill intervention points.

◆ CLINICAL PEARL

The chain analysis should take approximately thirty to forty minutes of the session. Common errors include spending too long on the prompting event and not enough time on the solution analysis, or conducting the chain analysis in a tone that feels interrogative rather than collaborative. Remember that the patient who is sitting in front of you discussing their self-harm has already taken a courageous step by being honest about it. Your task is not to establish culpability but to build understanding. Approach the chain analysis with the same curiosity and warmth that you would bring to any other therapeutic exploration.

Between-Session Contact and Telephone Coaching

In the full intensive configuration, the individual therapist provides between-session telephone coaching for the purpose of skills generalisation. The telephone coaching follows specific guidelines adapted from standard DBT. Coaching calls should be brief, typically five to fifteen minutes, and focused on skills application rather than emotional processing. The patient calls when they are experiencing a crisis or a strong urge to engage in a target behaviour, and the therapist helps them to identify the appropriate skill and to apply it in real time. The therapist does not provide extended emotional support or therapy by telephone; the function of the call is coaching, not counselling. If the patient needs extended support, they are directed to the crisis team or to their next scheduled session.

In the skills-focused configuration, where dedicated telephone coaching is not available, the equivalent function is served by the patient's crisis plan, which specifies the support contacts and crisis services available outside session hours. The individual support worker or care coordinator may also be available for brief between-session contact, though this is negotiated on a service-specific basis.

A Detailed Guide to the Diary Card Review

The diary card review is the clinical heartbeat of Stage 1 individual therapy. It should not be rushed, skipped, or treated as an administrative task. The review takes ten to fifteen minutes and follows a consistent sequence. The therapist begins by asking the patient to place the diary card on the shared surface between them, maintaining the side-by-side relational stance. The therapist then scans the card silently for approximately thirty seconds, noting the overall pattern before engaging the patient in discussion. This silent scan communicates that the therapist is taking the diary card seriously, and it provides the therapist with a global picture before attending to specific episodes.

The therapist then reviews each column in order of the treatment hierarchy. First, the self-harm column: 'I can see that you recorded self-harm on Wednesday. We will come back to that in a moment, because it is the most important thing we need to look at today.' Second, the therapy-interfering column, if applicable. Third, the quality-of-life column. Fourth, and critically, the skills column: 'I can also see that you used Paced Breathing on Thursday and Friday, and that your distress was lower on those days. That is really important, Sarah. Can you tell me about that?' The consistent prioritisation of the treatment hierarchy within the diary card review communicates the framework's clinical logic to the patient and ensures that life-threatening behaviours are never overlooked because a less urgent but more engaging topic draws the conversation elsewhere.

Worked Example: A Solution Analysis in Practice

The following vignette illustrates how the solution analysis operates as a collaborative clinical conversation, not as a prescriptive exercise. The therapist and patient have completed the chain analysis and are now reviewing it together.

> **Therapist Script:** *So we have mapped the whole chain from your vulnerability factors through to the self-harm. I want us to look at it together and think about where things could have gone differently. Not to blame you — this is not about that. It is about giving you more options for next time. Looking at the chain, where do you think the first opportunity was?*

The patient identifies the vulnerability factors: poor sleep and no food. The therapist validates this and connects it to ABC PLEASE. The therapist then asks about the second opportunity: 'What about when the thought arrived — "he does not care"? Is there a skill that could have helped there?' The patient identifies Check the Facts. The therapist continues through each link, co-constructing a map of alternative responses that the patient could deploy at different points in the chain. The session concludes with the patient selecting two specific skills to practise during the coming week and a plan for how to use them.

> **◆ CLINICAL PEARL**
>
> The solution analysis should generate a minimum of three intervention points and a maximum of five. Fewer than three does not give the patient enough options; more than five becomes overwhelming and dilutes the sense that any single intervention could have made a difference. For each intervention point, specify the exact skill by name and describe what deploying it would have looked like in the specific context of this patient's chain. 'Use a skill' is not a solution analysis; 'Use Paced Breathing for two minutes before responding to the text message' is a solution analysis.

Chapter Summary

This chapter has described the three functions of Stage 1 individual therapy, the standard session structure, the detailed protocol for behavioural chain analysis and solution analysis, and the guidelines for between-session telephone coaching. Together with the skills group curriculum described in Chapter 6, the individual therapy component completes the two core modes of Stage 1 delivery. The chapter that follows addresses the specific clinical challenges of crisis management and safety planning within Stage 1.

Chapter 8

Crisis Management and Safety Planning Within Stage 1

The IPTF Approach to Crisis

Crisis is the defining clinical challenge of Stage 1. The patients who enter Stage 1 are, by definition, experiencing recurrent crises: repeated episodes of acute emotional distress that overwhelm their existing coping capacity and result in life-threatening behaviours such as self-harm, overdose, or suicidal acts, or in presentations to emergency services. The IPTF's approach to crisis management is grounded in three principles: that crises are opportunities for skill deployment rather than evidence of treatment failure; that the patient's capacity to manage crises will increase progressively over the course of Stage 1 as their skills repertoire grows; and that the therapeutic response to crisis should be compassionate but structured, validating the patient's distress whilst maintaining the expectation of skill use.

The Collaborative Safety Plan

The collaborative safety plan is the cornerstone of crisis management in Stage 1. It is developed during the assessment sessions and updated regularly throughout the treatment. The safety plan is structured as a hierarchical sequence of responses to escalating distress, organised so that the patient moves through the steps in order, deploying the least intensive intervention first and escalating only if the distress continues to increase. The structure is as follows.

Step One: Recognising Warning Signs. The patient identifies the personal early warning signs that indicate their distress is beginning to escalate: specific thoughts ('nobody cares about me'), specific feelings (a rising sense of panic, a sinking feeling of hopelessness), specific body sensations (chest tightness, stomach churning), and specific behavioural patterns (withdrawing from contact, pacing, checking their phone repeatedly). These warning signs are the patient's unique distress fingerprint and should be described in their own language.

Step Two: Internal Coping Strategies. The patient lists the specific skills from the Stage 1 curriculum that they can deploy independently without needing to involve another person. These should be ordered by intensity: mindfulness and

Paced Breathing for mild to moderate distress; TIP Temperature and Intense Exercise for moderate to high distress; ACCEPTS distraction for sustained distress; Radical Acceptance and Turning the Mind for situations that cannot be changed.

Step Three: Social Coping Strategies. The patient identifies named individuals whom they can contact for support, with specific contact details. For each person, the patient records what kind of support they provide: one friend might be good for distraction and cheerfulness; a sibling might be good for practical help; a fellow group member might be good for validation and shared understanding.

Step Four: Professional Contacts. The patient lists the professional contacts available to them, including their IPTF therapist during agreed hours, their care coordinator, the crisis team telephone number, and any other relevant services. The plan should specify the circumstances under which each contact is appropriate.

Step Five: Emergency Plan. The plan identifies the nearest accident and emergency department, the transport route to reach it, and the circumstances under which the patient should attend. The plan may also specify environmental safety measures, such as the removal or restricted access to means of self-harm.

> **◆ CLINICAL PEARL**
> The safety plan must be written in the patient's own language, not in clinical jargon. It must be physically accessible: laminated and kept in the patient's bag, pinned to the fridge, saved as a photograph on their phone. A safety plan that is filed in the clinical notes and cannot be accessed in a crisis is not a safety plan; it is a piece of documentation. At every individual session, ask the patient: 'Where is your safety plan right now? Can you show me?' If they do not have it with them, spend five minutes at the end of the session helping them to make it accessible.

Managing Self-Harm Within the IPTF Framework

The IPTF takes a risk enablement approach to self-harm management, consistent with the principles described in Chapter 15 of the parent textbook. This means that the treatment aims to increase the patient's capacity to manage their own risk over time, rather than to manage risk on the patient's behalf through external controls. The goal of Stage 1 is not the immediate and complete elimination of self-harm but the progressive reduction of its frequency and severity through the development of alternative coping strategies. Clinicians should be realistic with patients about the trajectory of change: self-harm that has been used as a coping strategy for years or decades will not disappear overnight, and episodes of self-harm during treatment should be expected, analysed through chain analysis, and used as learning opportunities rather than treated as crises of clinical confidence.

When a patient reports self-harm, the clinician's response should follow a consistent pattern: validate the distress that drove the behaviour, without validating the behaviour itself; conduct a chain analysis to understand the sequence of events; identify the skills that could have been deployed at each link in the chain; and update the safety plan if the episode reveals gaps in the existing plan. The clinician should avoid two common errors: excessive alarm that communicates to the patient that their self-harm has frightened the clinician into providing extra care, which inadvertently reinforces the behaviour; and excessive minimisation that communicates that the clinician does not take their distress seriously, which replicates the invalidation of their developmental history.

Managing Suicidal Crises

When a patient reports active suicidal ideation with plan and intent, or when the clinician assesses that the patient is at imminent risk of a suicidal act, the immediate priority is the safety of the patient. The clinician should conduct a structured risk assessment that evaluates the current level of ideation, the specificity of the plan, access to means, the patient's stated intent, the presence or absence of protective factors, and any recent changes in circumstances that may have increased risk. Based on this assessment, the clinician determines, in collaboration with the patient where possible, the appropriate level of response: this may range from an enhanced safety plan with increased monitoring and next-day follow-up, through contact with the crisis team for community-based crisis support, to an assessment for inpatient admission where the risk is assessed as imminently life-threatening and cannot be safely managed in the community.

The IPTF approach to inpatient admission during Stage 1 follows the principle of brief, planned, skills-focused admissions rather than extended containment. Where admission is necessary, it should be as brief as clinically appropriate, with a clear plan for discharge and return to the IPTF programme. During the admission, the inpatient team should be aware of the patient's IPTF treatment and should support continued skills practice where possible. Upon discharge, the IPTF therapist should arrange a prompt follow-up session to conduct a chain analysis of the events leading to the admission and to update the safety plan.

Worked Example: Collaborative Safety Planning

The following illustrates the collaborative construction of a safety plan with 'Emma,' a patient in Week 3 of Stage 1 who has a history of overdose during acute crises. The therapist sits alongside Emma with the blank safety plan template between them.

> **Therapist Script:** *We are going to build your safety plan together. This is your document — it belongs to you, and we will write it in your words. It is designed to give you a step-by-step guide for what to do when things get really bad. Shall we start with the warning signs — the things that tell you a crisis might be building?*

Emma identifies her personal warning signs: 'I stop answering my phone. I start thinking everyone would be better off without me. I get a tight feeling in my chest that will not go away.' The therapist writes these on the plan in Emma's exact words. They then move through each step: internal coping strategies (Emma chooses Paced Breathing, walking her dog, and putting ice on her wrists), social contacts (her sister Claire, her friend Jen from the skills group), professional contacts (her care coordinator, the crisis team number), and the emergency plan (nearest A&E, call 999). At each step, the therapist checks: 'Does this feel realistic? If you were at a 9 out of 10, could you actually do this?' The honesty of these reality checks is essential. A safety plan that looks good on paper but cannot be enacted in a crisis is not a safety plan.

> **◆ CLINICAL PEARL**
>
> After completing the safety plan, ask the patient to read it back to you from the beginning. This serves two purposes: it checks that the plan makes sense when read in sequence, and it gives the patient practice in using the plan before a crisis occurs. Then take a photograph of the plan on the patient's phone. Laminate the original if your service has the facilities. A safety plan that lives in a filing cabinet is useless. A safety plan in the patient's pocket saves lives.

Managing the Post-Self-Harm Session

When a patient reports self-harm, the clinician's emotional response in the first thirty seconds sets the tone for the entire session. Two responses are particularly damaging. The first is excessive alarm: the clinician's face registers shock, they lean forward urgently, their voice rises, and they immediately escalate to risk assessment questions. This communicates to the patient that their self-harm has frightened the clinician, which inadvertently reinforces the behaviour as a powerful interpersonal communication tool and confirms the patient's schema that they are too much for anyone to handle. The second is excessive minimisation: the clinician barely acknowledges the disclosure, continues with the planned agenda, or responds with a brisk 'Okay, we will add that to the chain analysis.' This replicates the invalidation of the patient's developmental history and communicates that their distress is not worthy of attention.

The effective response balances validation with structure. The clinician receives the disclosure with warmth and gravity without panic: 'Thank you for telling me about that. I know it is not easy to be honest about self-harm, and I appreciate that you trust me enough to share it. We are going to look at it together, because understanding what happened is how we build your alternatives. But first, let me check — have you attended to the wound? Is it healing properly? Do you need any medical attention?' This response validates the difficulty of disclosure, normalises honesty within the therapeutic relationship, signals that the self-harm will be addressed through chain analysis rather than through alarm, and attends to practical wound care before proceeding.

Chapter Summary

This chapter has described the IPTF approach to crisis management within Stage 1, including the collaborative safety plan protocol, the management of self-harm through the risk enablement approach, and the management of suicidal crises including the framework for inpatient admission. The chapter that follows completes Part II by providing the detailed protocol for assessing readiness for Stage 2.

Chapter 9

Assessing Readiness for Stage 2: The Transition Protocol

> *The transition from Stage 1 to Stage 2 is not a graduation. It is a collaborative assessment of whether the patient has acquired the skills they need to do the deeper, harder, more painful work that lies ahead. Moving too early is not ambition; it is recklessness. Moving too late is not caution; it is avoidance of the work that matters most.*
>
> — Jayden Josh James, 2026

The Five Transition Criteria

The transition from Stage 1 to Stage 2 is clinically determined, not session-count determined. The patient's readiness is assessed against five criteria, all of which should be substantially met before the transition is made. The assessment is conducted collaboratively between the clinician and the patient, using a structured Transition Assessment Meeting that reviews each criterion in turn.

Criterion One: Behavioural Safety

The patient has demonstrated a sustained period of at least eight weeks free from life-threatening behaviours, or, where complete elimination has not yet been achieved, a significant and sustained reduction in the frequency and severity of life-threatening behaviours accompanied by evidence that the patient is deploying skills to manage urges. The clinician reviews the diary cards and clinical records from the preceding eight weeks to evaluate this criterion. The emphasis is on the trajectory of change rather than on an absolute threshold: a patient who has reduced their self-harm from three times per week to once per month, and who can demonstrate that they used skills to manage urges on the occasions when they did not self-harm, may meet this criterion even though they have not achieved complete abstinence.

Criterion Two: Emotional Regulation Capacity

The patient can identify and name their primary emotional states with reasonable accuracy; they can deploy at least two distress tolerance skills effectively in real-time crises, as evidenced by diary card records and self-report; and they can return their arousal to a manageable level within sessions, typically below 7 out of 10, within a reasonable timeframe. This criterion is assessed through diary card review, clinical observation across sessions, and the patient's self-report. The key indicator is not the absence of emotional distress but the presence of a regulatory response: the patient still experiences intense emotions, but they now have strategies for managing those emotions that were not available to them before Stage 1.

Criterion Three: Therapeutic Alliance Stability

The therapeutic relationship has achieved a sufficient degree of mutual trust, collaborative engagement, and capacity to navigate ruptures without relationship breakdown. The clinician assesses this criterion through their own clinical judgement, informed by the history of the therapeutic relationship across Stage 1: have there been ruptures, and if so, were they repaired? Is the patient able to be honest with the clinician about their difficulties, including their target behaviours? Does the patient attend consistently and engage actively in sessions? Is the clinician able to deliver the treatment effectively without being significantly affected by countertransference reactions?

Criterion Four: Cognitive Readiness

The patient demonstrates the beginning of reflective thinking about their own mental states and those of others. This does not require full mentalising capacity, which is a goal of Stage 2 rather than a prerequisite for it, but it does require the basic ability to step back from an emotional reaction and consider that the reaction may not accurately represent external reality. The Check the Facts skill taught in Block Three is the primary indicator of cognitive readiness: a patient who can complete a Fact-Check Worksheet and can identify the distinction between their interpretation and the facts has demonstrated sufficient cognitive readiness for Stage 2. A patient who remains wholly fused with their emotional experience and unable to entertain the possibility that their perception of a situation might be inaccurate is not yet ready for the cognitive mapping work that Stage 2 requires.

Criterion Five: Informed Consent

The patient has been fully informed about what Stage 2 involves, including the exploration of developmental history, the identification and modification of core beliefs and schemas, and the potential for the therapeutic work to be emotionally activating, and has expressed their willingness to engage in this work. Informed consent is not a formality; it is an expression of the patient's agency and self-determination, the fifth of the IPTF's active ingredients. The clinician should be honest with the patient about the nature of Stage 2 work: it will involve looking at painful experiences from the past, it may be more emotionally demanding than Stage 1, and there may be periods during Stage 2 when the patient feels worse before they feel better. The patient's decision to proceed should be genuinely voluntary and based on an accurate understanding of what lies ahead.

The Transition Assessment Meeting

The Transition Assessment Meeting is a dedicated session, typically sixty to ninety minutes, in which the clinician and the patient review each of the five criteria collaboratively. The clinician prepares for the meeting by reviewing the patient's diary cards, clinical records, and progress notes from Stage 1. The meeting follows a structured agenda: for each criterion, the clinician shares their assessment, invites the patient's perspective, and they agree together whether the criterion is met, partially met, or not met. The outcome of the meeting is one of three decisions.

Decision One: Transition to Stage 2. All five criteria are substantially met, and both the clinician and the patient agree that the patient is ready for the cognitive mapping and schema work of Stage 2. The transition is planned, with a specific start date for Stage 2 and a brief orientation to what Stage 2 will involve.

Decision Two: Extended Stage 1. One or more criteria are not yet met, and the clinician and the patient agree that a further period of Stage 1 work, typically a second cycle of the skills group curriculum, is needed before the transition can be made. The specific areas requiring further work are identified and a plan for addressing them is agreed.

Decision Three: Modified Pathway. The assessment reveals that the patient's needs would be better served by a modified pathway, which might include a referral to a different service, a period of individual Stage 1 work without the group component, or an adapted Stage 2 that begins with a more gradual introduction to cognitive work. This decision is made collaboratively and with full transparency about the clinical reasoning.

◆ CLINICAL PEARL

The Transition Assessment Meeting is one of the most important sessions in the entire IPTF treatment. Prepare for it carefully. Bring the patient's diary cards, your notes, and the Stage 1 Completion Checklist. Share your thinking openly and honestly. If you believe the patient is not ready for Stage 2, explain why with compassion and specificity, and frame the decision as a positive one: 'I think spending more time consolidating your skills is the best investment we can make in your recovery, because the stronger your foundations, the more effective the next stage will be.' If the patient disagrees with your assessment, listen carefully to their perspective and be willing to be persuaded. The assessment is collaborative, not unilateral.

The Stage 1 Completion Checklist

The following checklist provides a structured tool for documenting the Transition Assessment. The clinician completes the checklist collaboratively with the patient during the Transition Assessment Meeting and retains a copy in the clinical record. The patient receives a copy for their own records.

Criterion	Met / Partially Met / Not Met	Evidence and Notes
1. Behavioural Safety: sustained period (8+ weeks) of significantly reduced life-threatening behaviours with evidence of skill deployment		
2. Emotional Regulation: can identify and name emotions; deploys 2+ distress tolerance skills in crises; returns arousal to <7/10 in sessions		
3. Alliance Stability: consistent attendance; honest disclosure; capacity to navigate ruptures; collaborative engagement		
4. Cognitive Readiness: can distinguish interpretation from fact; beginning of reflective		

capacity; can complete Fact-Check Worksheet		
5. Informed Consent: understands Stage 2 content and demands; has expressed genuine willingness to proceed		
OVERALL DECISION: Transition to Stage 2 / Extended Stage 1 / Modified Pathway		

Preparing for Stage 2: The Orientation Session

When the transition decision is made, the clinician conducts an Orientation Session that prepares the patient for the shift from Stage 1 to Stage 2. The Orientation Session covers the following. The focus of Stage 2: the shift from managing the present to understanding the past, from 'How do I survive this crisis?' to 'Why do I keep ending up in crisis?' The patient is told that Stage 2 will involve exploring their developmental history, identifying the beliefs and patterns that were formed in response to their early experiences, and working to modify those beliefs and patterns so that they no longer generate the crises that Stage 1 addressed. The therapeutic process of Stage 2: the patient is told that Stage 2 will involve talking about their past in ways that may be emotionally activating, and that the skills they learned in Stage 1, particularly the distress tolerance and emotion regulation skills, are the tools that will enable them to manage this activation safely. The 7/10 Arousal Rule: the patient is reminded that if their arousal rises above 7 during Stage 2 sessions, the therapist will pause the exploratory work and return to Stage 1 skills until the arousal is manageable. This reassurance is important because it communicates that the patient will not be pushed beyond their capacity, that the therapist is monitoring their emotional state, and that the safety of Stage 1 is always available as a fallback. The IPTF Formulation Worksheet Section Two: the patient is told that the first task of Stage 2 will be the collaborative completion of Section Two ('The Why') of the Formulation Worksheet, which will involve a detailed exploration of their developmental history and the construction of a visual Schema Map that connects their early experiences to their current difficulties.

Chapter Summary

This chapter has described the transition protocol from Stage 1 to Stage 2, including the five transition criteria, the Transition Assessment Meeting, the Stage 1 Completion Checklist, and the Orientation Session that prepares the patient for the cognitive mapping work of Stage 2. Part II of this manual is now complete. Part III provides the detailed clinician's guide to Stage 2: Cognitive Mapping and Schema Work.

PART III

Stage 2: Cognitive Mapping and Schema Work

The Clinician's Guide

Chapter 10

Stage 2 Overview: Aims, Therapeutic Stance, and Delivery Structures

> *CBT is the navigator: it looks at the map to see where the machine is going and why it keeps taking the wrong turns. MBT is the compass: it orients both clinician and patient towards understanding. Stage 2 brings navigator and compass together.*
>
> — Jayden Josh James, 2026

The Purpose of Stage 2

Stage 2 represents the therapeutic heart of the Integrated Personality Treatment Framework. Where Stage 1 addressed the question 'How do I survive this crisis?', Stage 2 addresses the deeper and more consequential question: 'Why do I keep ending up in crisis?' The focus shifts from the management of emotional heat to the understanding of the cognitive and relational patterns that generate that heat in the first place. Stage 2 is the stage at which the patient begins to make explicit, and therefore available for modification, the connections between their early relational experiences and the beliefs, schemas, and internal working models that continue to organise their perception of and response to the interpersonal world.

The primary aim of Stage 2 is to help the patient understand and modify the deep-seated cognitive and relational structures that maintain their personality dysfunction. These structures include Early Maladaptive Schemas, the pervasive, self-defeating patterns of cognition and affect that were formed in response to adverse childhood experience and that function as templates through which the adult patient interprets their current world; Schema Modes, the moment-to-moment emotional and behavioural states through which schemas are expressed and maintained; Core Beliefs, the central organising convictions about the self, others, and the world that generate the automatic thoughts and emotional reactions that drive the patient's day-to-day functioning; and Coping Strategies, the patterns of surrender, avoidance, and overcompensation through which the patient manages the pain of schema activation, and which, whilst providing short-term relief, serve to perpetuate the schemas over time.

The Mentalising Therapeutic Stance

All Stage 2 work is delivered within the mentalising therapeutic stance described in Chapter 17 of the parent textbook. Mentalising is the capacity to understand behaviour, one's own and other people's, in terms of underlying mental states: thoughts, feelings, desires, intentions, and beliefs. The mentalising stance is not a technique to be deployed at specific moments; it is a way of being in the therapeutic relationship that pervades every interaction, every question, and every intervention throughout Stage 2. The stance is characterised by four qualities.

Curiosity. The mentalising therapist approaches the patient's experience with genuine, open-ended curiosity, resisting the temptation to interpret, explain, or diagnose, and instead inviting the patient to explore their own mental states with the therapist as a companion in the enquiry. The therapist asks questions such as 'I wonder what was going on for you when that happened?' and 'What do you think she might have been feeling at that moment?' rather than providing interpretations such as 'Your anger was a defence against the underlying sadness.' The curiosity must be genuine, not performative: the patient with personality disorder, whose relational history has typically been characterised by adults who were not genuinely interested in their experience, will detect inauthenticity immediately.

Not-Knowing. The mentalising therapist adopts a position of principled uncertainty, acknowledging that mental states are opaque, that we can never be entirely certain what another person is thinking or feeling, and that even our understanding of our own mental states is partial and provisional. This not-knowing stance communicates epistemic humility and models the reflective uncertainty that is the hallmark of mature mentalising. It contrasts sharply with the pre-mentalising modes that characterise personality disorder: psychic equivalence, in which the patient treats their thoughts and feelings as direct reflections of external reality; teleological mode, in which mental states are only credited when expressed through physical action; and pretend mode, in which the patient talks about mental states in a disconnected, intellectualised manner that has no emotional resonance.

Marked Mirroring. The mentalising therapist reflects the patient's emotional state back to them in a manner that is contingent, meaning that it accurately matches the patient's experience, and marked, meaning that the reflection is clearly identified as the therapist's understanding of the patient's state rather than the therapist's own emotional experience. Marked mirroring communicates to the patient that their emotional state has been seen, understood, and contained by another mind, without that other mind being overwhelmed by it. The 'marking' is achieved through subtle vocal and facial cues that signal 'I understand that you are feeling this' rather than 'I am feeling this too.'

Holding the Dialectic. The mentalising therapist holds multiple perspectives simultaneously, acknowledging the validity of the patient's emotional experience whilst gently introducing the possibility that other perspectives exist. This is not a confrontation of the patient's view but an expansion of it: 'I can completely see why you felt rejected when she cancelled the dinner. I wonder whether there might also be other reasons why she cancelled, and what it might feel like to hold both possibilities at the same time?' This dialectical holding is the mentalising equivalent of the DBT dialectic of acceptance and change, and it directly supports the cognitive flexibility that the schema work of Stage 2 requires.

◆ CLINICAL PEARL

The mentalising stance is the most difficult aspect of Stage 2 for clinicians to learn, because it requires the therapist to resist their natural inclination to understand, to interpret, and to help, and instead to sit with uncertainty, to wonder aloud, and to allow the patient's understanding to emerge from the collaborative exploration rather than from the therapist's expertise. If you find yourself providing explanations more often than asking questions, you have probably moved out of the mentalising stance and into an expert position. The test is simple: who is doing more of the thinking in the session? If the answer is the therapist, something has gone wrong.

Stage 2 Session Structure

Stage 2 is delivered primarily through individual therapy, typically on a weekly basis for a duration of twelve to eighteen months. Each session follows a standard structure adapted from the CBT-PD session format. The session opens with an arousal check: the patient rates their current emotional arousal on a 0 to 10 scale. If the rating is 7 or above, the session begins with Stage 1 skills work until the arousal is manageable; if the rating is below 7, the session proceeds to Stage 2 content. Following the arousal check, the session reviews any between-session practice, including thought records, behavioural experiment outcomes, and imagery rescripting reflections. The main body of the session focuses on the current phase of Stage 2 work, whether that is developmental history exploration, schema mapping, experiential processing, or cognitive restructuring. The session closes with a summary, a between-session practice assignment, and a brief emotional check-out.

The Four Phases of Stage 2

Stage 2 is organised into four sequential phases, each serving a distinct function within the overall process of cognitive and relational modification. Phase One (Developmental History and Schema Identification) gathers the historical data and identifies the core schemas, typically over eight to ten sessions. Phase Two (Schema Mapping and Mode Identification) constructs the visual Schema Map and identifies the patient's predominant schema modes, typically over eight sessions. Phase Three (Experiential Processing and Cognitive Restructuring) involves the active modification of schemas through imagery rescripting, chair work, cognitive restructuring, and behavioural experiments, typically over fifteen to twenty sessions. Phase Four (Consolidation and Preparation for Stage 3) reviews and consolidates the therapeutic work and prepares the patient for the functional recovery phase, typically over six to eight sessions. The phases are presented as a sequential guide, but in practice the boundaries between them are fluid: a patient in Phase Three may return to Phase One material when a new schema emerges, or may move briefly to Phase Four consolidation work when a particular schema shows significant modification.

NHS Delivery Context

Stage 2 requires a clinician with training in schema-focused or cognitive-behavioural approaches to personality disorder, working within a specialist personality disorder service or a community mental health team with access to specialist personality disorder supervision. The duration of twelve to eighteen months reflects the depth and complexity of the work. In services where specialist staff are limited, Stage 2 may be delivered by a smaller number of trained clinicians who receive the Stage 1 patients from a broader pool of skills group facilitators, creating an efficient stepped-care pathway within the IPTF. Where group-based schema work is available, it can supplement individual therapy by providing opportunities for interpersonal schema activation and mentalisation practice in a relational context that individual therapy cannot replicate.

Chapter Summary

This chapter has provided the operational overview of Stage 2, covering its aims, the mentalising therapeutic stance that pervades all Stage 2 work, the standard session structure, the four-phase sequential framework, and the NHS delivery context. The chapters that follow provide the detailed clinical guide for each of the four phases, beginning with Phase One: Developmental History and Schema Identification.

Chapter 11

Phase One: Developmental History and Schema Identification

> *When I finally told someone the full story of what happened to me as a child, and they did not look away, did not change the subject, did not tell me to move on — that was the beginning of everything changing.*
>
> — Composite patient testimony

Overview of Phase One

Phase One is the opening movement of Stage 2, typically spanning eight to ten sessions. Its purpose is twofold: to gather the developmental history that will provide the raw material for the Schema Map constructed in Phase Two, and to identify the Early Maladaptive Schemas and core beliefs that organise the patient's experience and maintain their personality dysfunction. Phase One is not merely a data-gathering exercise; it is a deeply therapeutic process in which the patient, often for the first time, tells the full story of their early experience to a listener who receives it with curiosity, compassion, and clinical understanding. The act of narrating a painful history to a present, attentive, non-judgemental witness is itself a corrective relational experience, particularly for patients whose previous attempts to share their story were met with dismissal, disbelief, or indifference.

The Structured Developmental History Interview

The developmental history interview follows a chronological structure, beginning with the patient's earliest memories and moving through childhood, adolescence, and early adulthood. The interview is conducted across three to four sessions, with each session covering a developmental period and allowing sufficient time for emotional processing. The clinician should resist the temptation to rush through the history in order to get to the 'real' therapeutic work; the history is the real therapeutic work, because it is the foundation upon which all subsequent schema identification, mapping, and modification will rest.

Session One of Phase One: Early Childhood (Birth to Age Seven)

The first Phase One session focuses on the patient's earliest years, with particular attention to the primary attachment relationships. The clinician opens by explaining the purpose of the developmental exploration and by reassuring the patient that they are in control of the pace and depth of the sharing.

> **Therapist Script:** '*Over the next few sessions, I would like us to spend some time exploring your early life, the experiences that shaped you growing up, and the relationships that were most important to you as a child. I am interested in this because I believe that the difficulties you experience now did not come from nowhere; they developed for understandable reasons, in response to what happened to you, and understanding those reasons is the key to changing the patterns. I want you to know that you can share as much or as little as you feel comfortable with. If anything feels too much, we can slow down, take a break, or use the skills from Stage 1 to manage the distress. There is no rush. We have time.*'

The clinician explores the following domains: family composition and household structure in the early years; the quality of the patient's relationship with each primary caregiver, including their emotional availability, consistency, warmth, and capacity for attunement; the patient's earliest memories and the emotional tone of those memories; any adverse experiences, including abuse, neglect, loss, separation, and household dysfunction; and the emotional climate of the home, including how emotions were expressed, tolerated, and responded to within the family.

Throughout the interview, the clinician listens for emotional resonance: the moments when the patient's voice changes pitch, when they pause or look away, when their body tenses, when their narrative becomes vague or disconnected, or when they shift into a qualitatively different emotional state. These moments of resonance signal schema proximity, indicating that the narrative has touched upon an experience that is connected to an active schema. The clinician notes these moments without interrupting the patient's flow, returning to them later in the session or in a subsequent session when the patient has had time to process.

◆ CLINICAL PEARL

During the developmental history interview, keep a simple tracking sheet on which you note the key events, the attachment figures, the adverse experiences, and, critically, the moments of emotional resonance. These resonance points are the threads that you will follow into the schema identification process. A patient who describes their mother as 'she was fine, she did her best' in a flat, disconnected tone whilst their body language communicates tension and avoidance is telling you something important in the gap between content and affect. Do not confront this gap in Phase One; note it. In Phase Two, the Schema Map will make it visible.

Sessions Two and Three: Middle Childhood and Adolescence

The second and third sessions extend the developmental history through middle childhood (ages seven to twelve) and adolescence (ages thirteen to eighteen). The middle childhood period is explored with attention to the expansion of the relational world beyond the family: peer relationships, school experiences, the development of competence and self-efficacy, and any experiences of bullying, social exclusion, or academic difficulty that may have contributed to schemas of Defectiveness, Social Isolation, or Failure. Adolescence is explored with attention to the developmental tasks of identity formation, peer attachment, romantic relationships, and the negotiation of autonomy from the family, attending to the ways in which the patient's personality difficulties may have first become apparent during this period.

Session Four: Early Adulthood and Pattern Identification

The fourth session completes the chronological history by covering early adulthood, and then steps back to begin identifying the recurring patterns that emerge across the developmental narrative. The clinician invites the patient to notice the themes: 'As we look back over everything you have shared, what patterns do you notice? What keeps repeating?' The patient's capacity to identify these patterns varies: some patients will readily recognise the recurring themes of rejection, abandonment, or invalidation; others will need the clinician's gentle guidance to connect the dots. The output of this session is a preliminary list of candidate schemas, expressed in the patient's own language, that will be refined through formal assessment in the sessions that follow.

Schema Identification: The Assessment Process

Table 1. The Eighteen Early Maladaptive Schemas: Young's Taxonomy with Domain Classification and Core Belief Patterns

Schema Name	Domain	Core Belief Pattern
Abandonment / Instability	*Disconnection and Rejection*	"People I love will leave me, be unpredictable, or die. Stable, lasting connection is not available to me."
Mistrust / Abuse	*Disconnection and Rejection*	"Others will hurt, manipulate, humiliate, or betray me. I must protect myself because people cannot be trusted."
Emotional Deprivation	*Disconnection and Rejection*	"My emotional needs for nurture, empathy, and protection will never be adequately met by others. I am essentially alone in managing my inner world."
Defectiveness / Shame	*Disconnection and Rejection*	"I am fundamentally flawed, defective, or inferior. If others knew the real me, they would reject me. I am unlovable at my core."
Social Isolation / Alienation	*Disconnection and Rejection*	"I am fundamentally different from others. I do not fit in anywhere. I am an outsider looking in on a world to which I do not belong."
Dependence / Incompetence	*Impaired Autonomy and Performance*	"I am unable to handle everyday responsibilities competently without significant help from others. I am fundamentally incapable."
Vulnerability to Harm or Illness	*Impaired Autonomy and Performance*	"Catastrophe is imminent and I am unable to prevent it. The world is dangerous and I am not equipped to cope with what might happen."
Enmeshment / Undeveloped Self	*Impaired Autonomy and Performance*	"I do not have an identity separate from the significant people in my life. I cannot exist as an autonomous individual without their emotional support."
Failure to Achieve	*Impaired Autonomy and Performance*	"I am fundamentally less successful and less capable than my peers. Failure is inevitable and reflects an intrinsic inadequacy in me."
Entitlement / Grandiosity	*Impaired Limits*	"I am special and superior to others. I should not be subject to the rules that govern ordinary people. I deserve whatever I want."
Insufficient Self-Control / Self-Discipline	*Impaired Limits*	"I cannot tolerate frustration, discomfort, or boredom. I am unable to restrain my impulses or feelings sufficiently to complete tasks or reach goals."
Subjugation	*Other-Directedness*	"I must submit to the control of others or else they will retaliate, abandon, or punish me. My own needs and feelings must be suppressed."
Self-Sacrifice	*Other-Directedness*	"I must attend to the needs of others at the expense of my own. Prioritising myself is selfish, and selfishness is

		unacceptable."
Approval-Seeking / Recognition-Seeking	*Other-Directedness*	"My sense of worth is entirely contingent on the approval, attention, and admiration of others. Without external validation, I am nothing."
Negativity / Pessimism	*Overvigilance and Inhibition*	"Things will inevitably go wrong. The negative aspects of life deserve the most attention because anything positive is temporary and illusory."
Emotional Inhibition	*Overvigilance and Inhibition*	"Emotional expression is dangerous or shameful. I must suppress my impulses and emotions or others will disapprove, abandon, or embarrass me."
Unrelenting Standards / Hypercriticalness	*Overvigilance and Inhibition*	"I must meet very high, internalised standards of behaviour and performance. Falling short is catastrophic and unacceptable. Mistakes carry enormous consequences."
Punitiveness	*Overvigilance and Inhibition*	"People who make mistakes or fail to meet standards deserve to be harshly punished. There is no room for forgiveness, empathy, or allowance for human error."

Table 1 presents all eighteen Early Maladaptive Schemas as identified by Young, Klosko, and Weishaar (2003) in Schema Therapy: A Practitioner's Guide. Domain classifications follow Young's five-domain model. Core belief patterns are expressed in the first person to support patient identification exercises. Clinicians are directed to the YSQ-S3 (Young and Brown, 2005) for standardised assessment.

Following the developmental history, the clinician conducts a formal schema identification process, typically across two to three sessions, using a combination of the Young Schema Questionnaire (YSQ-S3; Young and Brown, 2005), the downward arrow technique from CBT-PD, and clinical interview. The YSQ-S3 is administered as a starting point: the patient completes the questionnaire and the clinician reviews the results collaboratively, discussing each elevated schema with the patient and exploring whether it resonates with their experience. The questionnaire results are treated as hypotheses, not diagnoses: the patient's experiential confirmation or disconfirmation of each schema is the final arbiter.

For each identified schema, the clinician records the following information on the IPTF Schema Identification Worksheet: the schema name and domain; the core belief expressed in the patient's own words, in the format 'I am...' (about self), 'Others are...' (about others), and 'The world is...' (about the world); the developmental experiences hypothesised to have given rise to the schema; the current situations that most commonly trigger the schema; the emotional, cognitive, and behavioural responses that occur when the schema is activated;

and the coping strategies, including surrender, avoidance, and overcompensation, that the patient uses to manage the pain of schema activation.

The Downward Arrow Technique

The downward arrow technique, drawn from CBT-PD and originally described by Burns (1980) and subsequently elaborated by Beck and colleagues in the context of schema-level belief identification, provides a complementary and often clinically superior method for identifying core beliefs when compared with self-report questionnaire formats alone. The technique begins with a specific automatic thought reported by the patient, typically one that arose in the context of a recent distressing event, and progressively drills down through successive layers of meaning until the underlying core belief or Early Maladaptive Schema is reached. Because the technique is anchored in a specific, emotionally alive experience rather than an abstract questionnaire item, it is particularly effective with patients who struggle with alexithymia, with patients whose schemas are highly ego-syntonic and therefore invisible to direct introspection, and with patients whose intellectual defences make questionnaire-based approaches feel manageable at a cognitive distance but clinically unproductive.

The Seven-Step Downward Arrow Protocol

The following seven-step protocol provides a structured approach to conducting the downward arrow technique within Phase One of Stage 2. The protocol is designed to be delivered across one to two sessions, depending upon the patient's pace and the emotional intensity generated by the material.

Step 1: Identify the Starting Thought. Begin by asking the patient to recall a recent situation in which they experienced a significant emotional reaction. The situation should be specific and recent, ideally within the past two weeks, so that the emotional memory is accessible. Ask the patient to describe the situation briefly and then to identify the thought that occurred to them at the moment of greatest distress. Record this thought verbatim. Therapist script: "I'd like to try something with you that can help us understand what was really going on for you in that moment. Can you tell me about a recent situation — something specific that happened in the past couple of weeks — where you had a strong emotional reaction? What was the thought that went through your mind at the worst moment?"

Step 2: Establish Hypothetical Acceptance. Before beginning the downward chain, it is essential to establish the hypothetical frame. This frame invites the patient to explore the meaning of the thought as if it were true, rather than to evaluate its accuracy. This distinction is clinically important: the downward arrow is not a cognitive challenging exercise; it is a meaning-mapping exercise. Therapist script: "I'm not asking whether this thought is true or fair — we can think about that later. For now, I want to explore what this thought means to you. So let's imagine, just for a moment, that this thought was true. If it were true, what would that mean to you?"

Step 3: Follow the Chain of Meaning. Once the first meaning response is elicited, apply the same hypothetical frame to the new thought. Continue following the chain downward, using the standard prompts: "And if that were true, what would that mean?" or "And if that were true, what would that say about you as a person?" The clinician should resist the temptation to interpret, challenge, or comment during this phase. The task is purely to follow the patient's own meaning chain without deflection. Most patients will reach a core schema level belief within four to six iterations. Record each step of the chain on paper, which can be shared with the patient at the end of the exercise.

Step 4: Recognise the Core Belief. The chain has reached the core belief level when one of the following markers is present: the patient's response shifts from a situational meaning ("she doesn't want to see me") to a global, unconditional statement about the self ("I am fundamentally unlovable"); the patient's emotional arousal increases markedly; the patient reports that the belief "just feels true" or "has always been there"; or the patient's responses begin to loop back upon themselves without generating new meaning. At this point, the clinician should name what has been uncovered with gentleness and with explicit normalisation. Therapist script: "So at the very bottom of all of that, there is this belief: 'I am fundamentally unlovable.' Does that resonate with you? Does that feel like something that has been around for a long time?"

Step 5: Check for Schema-Level Resonance. Once the core belief is named, the clinician should ask a series of follow-up questions to establish its schema-level characteristics: its developmental history ("When did you first have this belief about yourself?"); its cross-situational pervasiveness ("Does this belief tend to come up in other areas of your life, not just in this situation?"); its emotional charge ("When this belief is activated, what emotion comes with it?"); and its behavioural consequences ("When you believe this about yourself, what do you tend to do?"). The answers to these questions allow the clinician to begin mapping the belief onto the schema domains and to identify the coping strategies the patient has developed to manage the pain of schema activation.

Step 6: Provide Psychoeducation and Normalisation. Following the identification of the core belief, the clinician provides brief psychoeducation that normalises the belief as an understandable outcome of the patient's early experience rather than as an accurate reflection of reality. This psychoeducation is not a cognitive challenge; it is an empathic contextualisation. Therapist script: "This belief — 'I am fundamentally unlovable' — makes complete sense given what you experienced growing up. If the people who were supposed to love you were unavailable, or critical, or inconsistent, then that is exactly the conclusion a child would draw: 'There must be something wrong with me.' That is not a failure of your thinking; that is a completely logical response to an illogical situation. The belief developed to make sense of your experience. The work we are going to do together is about updating that belief in the light of new experience, including the experience of this therapeutic relationship."

Step 7: Record and Integrate into the Schema Profile. The complete downward arrow chain should be transcribed onto the IPTF Schema Identification Worksheet, with the starting thought at the top, each intermediate meaning-step recorded in sequence, and the core belief identified at the bottom. The relevant schema domain from Young's taxonomy should be noted alongside the core belief, and the worksheet should be cross-referenced with the patient's YSQ scores. The chain itself constitutes valuable clinical material that can be revisited in later phases of treatment, particularly during cognitive restructuring in Phase Three, where the clinician works backwards up the chain to challenge each meaning-step with evidence and alternative perspectives.

Worked Clinical Example: The Downward Arrow in Practice

The following example illustrates the downward arrow technique applied with a patient (referred to here as "Marcus," a composite clinical illustration) who presented with emotionally unstable personality disorder and a history of chronic interpersonal difficulties. The starting event was a message from a colleague that Marcus had interpreted as dismissive.

Step in the Chain	Content
Triggering Situation	My colleague replied to my email with just one word: "Fine."
Automatic Thought	He is angry with me and he doesn't want to work with me.
↓ Meaning Level 1	I have upset him without meaning to, and now things will never be right between us.
↓ Meaning Level 2	People always end up pushing me away. I can't maintain relationships.
↓ Meaning Level 3	There is something fundamentally wrong with me. I am too much for people.
Core Schema (Base)	**"I am defective and unlovable. I will always be abandoned by people who matter to me." [Defectiveness/Shame + Abandonment/Instability schemas]**

In this example, the clinician would note that the downward arrow has uncovered a cluster of two interconnected schemas — Defectiveness/Shame and Abandonment/Instability — which would both be recorded on the Schema Identification Worksheet and cross-referenced with Marcus's elevated YSQ subscale scores. The clinical significance of the convergence between questionnaire data and the experiential material generated by the downward arrow is that it provides the patient with a coherent, felt understanding of their schema profile, rather than merely an intellectual one.

◆ CLINICAL PEARL

Most patients with personality disorder have between two and four core schemas that do the heavy lifting. Resist the temptation to identify every elevated schema on the YSQ as a treatment target. The most therapeutically productive approach is to identify the two or three schemas that are most active, most distressing, and most closely connected to the patient's current difficulties, and to focus the Stage 2 work on these. Less prominent schemas may be addressed later, or they may resolve spontaneously as the core schemas are modified, because schemas are interconnected and a shift in one often produces ripple effects across the schema profile.

Phase One Summary and Transition to Phase Two

Phase One concludes when the clinician and patient have gathered a comprehensive developmental history, identified the core schemas through the combined assessment process, and begun to formulate the connections between early experience and current difficulties. The output of Phase One is a preliminary schema profile or core belief map, expressed in the patient's own words and confirmed by their experiential validation, that provides the raw material for the Schema Map construction in Phase Two.

Chapter 12

Phase Two: Schema Mapping and Mode Identification

> *The Schema Map is the moment when the chaos starts to make sense. When you can see, on a single piece of paper, the connection between what happened to you as a child and what keeps happening to you as an adult, something shifts. You stop asking 'What is wrong with me?' and start asking 'What happened to me, and how is it still running my life?'*
>
> — Jayden Josh James, 2026

Overview of Phase Two

Phase Two, spanning approximately eight sessions, transforms the raw material gathered in Phase One into a visual, coherent, collaboratively owned map that makes the patient's patterns visible and comprehensible. The Schema Map is the centrepiece of the IPTF Formulation Worksheet Section Two ('The Why'), and its construction is one of the most significant therapeutic events in the entire IPTF treatment. When the patient can see, on a single page, the connections between their childhood experiences, their core schemas, their coping modes, and their current difficulties, they achieve a level of understanding that years of talking about their problems in an unstructured manner could not provide. The map does not merely describe the pattern; it makes the pattern available for modification, because you cannot change what you cannot see.

Constructing the Schema Map: A Step-by-Step Guide

The Schema Map is constructed collaboratively over three to four sessions, using a large sheet of paper, a whiteboard, or a digital drawing tool, depending on the patient's preference and the clinical setting. The clinician sits alongside the patient, as the IPTF's relational stance requires, and both contribute to the map's construction. The following steps provide a structured guide to the mapping process.

Step One: Place the Core Schemas at the Centre

The clinician and patient begin by writing the patient's two to four core schemas in the centre of the map, each in a distinct box or circle. Each schema is expressed as a core belief in the patient's own words. For example, for a patient whose core schemas are Abandonment and Defectiveness/Shame, the centre of the map might contain two boxes: 'Everyone will leave me eventually' and 'I am damaged and worthless.' The use of the patient's own language is essential: the schema must feel true to the patient's experience, not like a clinical label imposed from outside.

Step Two: Connect to Developmental Origins

From each schema, the clinician draws connecting lines backwards to the developmental experiences identified in Phase One that gave rise to it. For the Abandonment schema, the connections might include: 'Father left when I was four and never came back,' 'Mother was emotionally absent due to her own depression,' 'Placed in foster care aged eleven.' For the Defectiveness schema, the connections might include: 'Stepfather told me I was stupid and worthless,' 'Bullied at school for my appearance,' 'Mother never praised me or showed affection.' These connections make explicit the causal logic that links early experience to current belief: the patient did not develop the conviction that they are worthless in a vacuum; they developed it because the people who were supposed to love them treated them as though they were worthless.

Step Three: Connect to Current Triggers

From each schema, the clinician draws connecting lines forwards to the current situations that most commonly trigger it. For the Abandonment schema, current triggers might include: 'Partner does not reply to a text within an hour,' 'Friend cancels plans,' 'Therapist takes annual leave.' For the Defectiveness schema, current triggers might include: 'Receiving feedback at work,' 'Seeing happy families on social media,' 'Looking in the mirror.' The identification of current triggers makes the patient aware of the situations in which their schemas are most likely to be activated, enabling them to anticipate and prepare for these situations using the Cope Ahead skill from Stage 1.

Step Four: Map the Coping Modes

From each schema, the clinician draws connecting lines outward to the coping strategies that the patient uses to manage the pain of schema activation. These are organised into three categories: surrender behaviours, in which the patient submits to the schema and acts as though the core belief is true (for example, the patient with a Defectiveness schema who accepts abusive treatment from a partner because they believe they deserve no better); avoidance behaviours, in which the patient avoids situations that might trigger the schema (for example, the patient with an Abandonment schema who avoids forming close relationships to prevent the pain of future loss); and overcompensation behaviours, in which the patient acts in opposition to the schema in an excessive, rigid manner (for example, the patient with a Defectiveness schema who pursues perfection compulsively to prove that they are not worthless). The mapping of coping modes is clinically important because it reveals the maintenance mechanisms that keep the schemas alive: the patient's coping strategies, however understandable, prevent the disconfirmation of the core beliefs and ensure that the schemas persist across time and situations.

Mode Identification and Mapping

Following the construction of the Schema Map, the clinician introduces the concept of schema modes: the moment-to-moment emotional and behavioural states through which schemas are expressed. Mode identification helps the patient to recognise what is happening to them in real time, rather than understanding their patterns only in retrospect. The five core schema modes relevant to personality disorder are as follows.

The Vulnerable Child. This mode represents the raw, unprocessed emotional pain of the patient's unmet childhood needs. When the patient is in Vulnerable Child mode, they experience the emotions that the child they once were could not safely express: fear, sadness, loneliness, shame, and helplessness. The Vulnerable Child is the emotional core of the schema, and it is the part of the patient that the schema work ultimately seeks to heal.

The Angry Child. This mode represents the protest against the injustice of the patient's early experience. When the patient is in Angry Child mode, they experience rage, indignation, and the impulse to fight back against real or perceived mistreatment. The Angry Child's anger is often legitimate, but its expression is typically disproportionate to the current situation because it carries the accumulated weight of historical grievance.

The Detached Protector. This mode represents the psychological defence against overwhelming emotional pain. When the patient is in Detached Protector mode, they cut off from their emotional experience, withdraw from interpersonal contact, and present a flat, disengaged, or compliant exterior that conceals the turmoil beneath. The Detached Protector was an adaptive survival strategy in the patient's early environment, where feeling too much was dangerous; in adult life, it prevents the patient from accessing the emotional material that therapy needs to work with.

The Punitive Parent. This mode represents the internalised critical voice of the patient's primary caregivers. When the patient is in Punitive Parent mode, they attack themselves with the same contempt, criticism, and cruelty that was directed at them in childhood. The Punitive Parent tells the patient that they are worthless, that they deserve their suffering, that they are stupid for believing things could be different. This mode is the internal engine of self-harm, self-sabotage, and self-hatred, and its modification is one of the most important therapeutic goals of Stage 2.

The Healthy Adult. This mode represents the patient's capacity for compassion, rationality, and flexible responding. When the patient is in Healthy Adult mode, they can observe their schemas and modes without being overwhelmed by them, can respond to distress with self-compassion rather than self-criticism, and can make choices that serve their long-term interests rather than their immediate emotional impulses. The Healthy Adult is the mode that the IPTF seeks to strengthen throughout Stage 2, and it is the mode from which the patient will increasingly operate as the treatment progresses.

The clinician teaches the patient to identify their modes through a combination of psychoeducation, in-session observation, and between-session self-monitoring. A Mode Monitoring Diary is introduced, in which the patient records the mode they recognise themselves as being in at several points during the day, along with the trigger, the associated emotion, and the behaviour. The therapeutic goal is mode awareness: the patient's capacity to observe themselves moving into a particular mode and to name it, 'I think I have just gone into Detached Protector,' rather than being embedded within it. This metacognitive capacity is a form of mentalising that directly supports the experiential work of Phase Three.

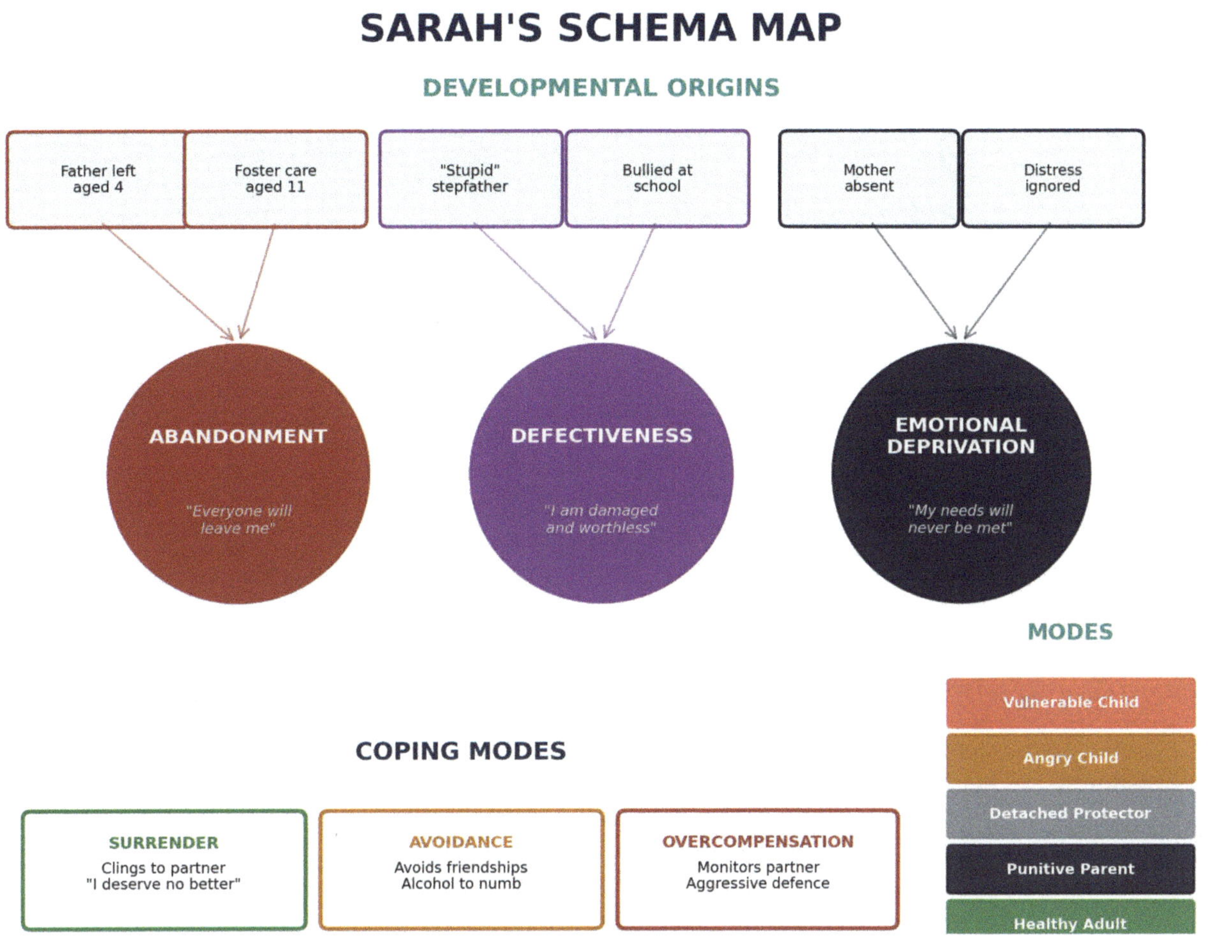

Figure 2. Sarah's Schema Map: Schemas, origins, triggers, coping modes, and modes.

◆ CLINICAL PEARL

When you introduce schema modes, use the patient's own language to name them. The Punitive Parent mode might be called 'the voice that tells me I am worthless' or 'my inner bully.' The Detached Protector might be called 'the wall' or 'the numb place.' When the patient can recognise and name their modes in their own words, the modes become objects of reflection rather than states of being, and this shift from subject to object is one of the most important developmental achievements of Stage 2.

Table 2. Clinical Markers for Schema Mode Identification

The following table provides clinicians with practical identification guidance for each of the five core schema modes. It should be used alongside the Mode Monitoring Diary as an observational framework during Phase Two sessions.

Mode	In-Session Behavioural Markers	Verbal Markers	Somatic / Affective Indicators	Recommended Therapeutic Response
Vulnerable Child	Shrinks posturally; avoids eye	"Nobody cares about me." "I always end up	Profound sadness; terror; shame;	Provide warm, attuned empathy. Name and validate the emotional

	contact; voice becomes small or childlike; may weep silently; clutches self or objects; appears younger than chronological age	alone." "I am scared." "I do not know what to do." "Please do not leave me."	loneliness; helplessness; constriction in chest or throat; urge to cry or hide; feeling very small	pain. Use limited reparenting: offer steady, compassionate presence. Avoid interpretation or challenge. The goal is emotional contact, not cognitive work.
Angry Child	Sudden shift in affect; raised voice or clenched jaw; leans forward or stands; interrupts; may become verbally aggressive; face flushes; rapid speech; may storm out	"This is completely unfair." "You do not understand at all." "I am sick of being treated this way." "Nobody ever listens to me."	Hot, pressurised rage; sense of profound injustice; physical heat and tension; adrenaline surge; urge to lash out verbally or physically; sometimes accompanied by shame	Acknowledge the anger as legitimate without reinforcing the behaviour. Validate the historical injustice whilst gently naming the mode: "The Angry Child is here right now." Do not attempt schema work whilst the patient is in this mode. Help them regulate first, then explore what triggered the mode.
Detached Protector	Flat affect; monotone voice; minimal eye contact; gives brief, factual answers; deflects with humour or intellectualisati on; appears compliant but unreachable; does not initiate; session feels like pulling teeth	"I do not know. I am fine." "I cannot really feel anything." "It does not really matter." "I am just getting on with it." Answers questions without elaborating	Emotional numbness; blankness; disconnection from bodily sensation; sense of floating or watching from outside; absence of distress where distress would be expected	Gently name the mode without confrontation. Use grounding and sensory anchoring to increase presence. Invite curiosity: "I notice you seem a little far away right now. I wonder if part of you is protecting itself. That makes complete sense. I am not going anywhere." Do not force emotional access — this mode exists to protect the patient from pain they felt unable to tolerate.
Punitive Parent	Tense, self-condemning posture; voice becomes harsh or cold when speaking about themselves; may engage in self-harm ideation during session; dismisses own progress; rejects therapist warmth	"I am pathetic." "I deserve what happens to me." "I am stupid for even trying." "I cannot believe I did that again." "You must be so tired of me."	Intense shame; self-disgust; heavy, crushing quality to the affect; cold contempt directed at self; sometimes accompanied by physical self-directed gestures such as digging nails into hands	Firmly but warmly challenge the punitive voice. Do not collude: "I want to push back on what that voice is telling you, because it is simply not accurate or fair." Use chair work to externalise the Punitive Parent. Explicitly take the side of the Healthy Adult. Assess self-harm risk. This mode requires the most active therapeutic stance of any of the five modes.
Healthy Adult	Stable posture; consistent eye contact; engaged and	"I can see what happened there." "I notice I am going into that	Calm, grounded affect; emotional accessibility without	Reinforce and amplify. Name and celebrate the mode explicitly: "Notice what you just

	curious affect; able to hold complexity; responds to therapist questions thoughtfully; can observe own reactions with some distance; does not catastrophise	pattern." "That is the old belief, not the current reality." "I handled that differently than I would have before."	overwhelm; sense of being present in the room; curiosity rather than dread; modest sense of efficacy	did there — that was your Healthy Adult speaking." Use this mode as the platform for all cognitive and experiential work. The Healthy Adult is the ally of the therapeutic process and must be actively cultivated from the earliest phase of Stage 2 onwards.

◆ CLINICAL PEARL

◆ SCHEMA MAP TEMPLATE: A GUIDE FOR CLINICIANS

The Schema Map is the central clinical document of Phase Two. This guidance supports clinicians in constructing a map that is visually coherent, clinically comprehensive, and therapeutically meaningful for the individual patient.

SECTION A: The Five Required Components

A complete IPTF Schema Map must contain all five of the following components. An incomplete map should be treated as a working document and completed across subsequent sessions rather than presented prematurely to the patient as a finished formulation.

Component 1: Core Schemas Identified. List each of the patient's two to four primary schemas at the centre of the map. Each schema should be named using the standard YSQ taxonomy alongside the patient's own language for the belief. The patient's language takes precedence in the visual display; the taxonomy label is recorded in parentheses. Domain colour-coding should be applied at this stage so that domain clustering is immediately visible on the map.

Component 2: Developmental Origins. For each schema, one or two key developmental experiences are connected by a labelled arrow from the origin to the schema box, using compassionate and non-blaming language. These are hypotheses held lightly, not diagnoses, and should be confirmed through the patient's own experiential recognition.

Component 3: Current Triggers. For each schema, two or three situational triggers that most reliably activate the schema in the patient's current life are listed and connected by arrows showing the activation pathway. Triggers may be interpersonal, environmental, or interoceptive. The specificity of trigger identification is directly proportional to the map's clinical utility as a platform for behavioural experiments in Phase Three.

Component 4: Coping Modes. For each schema, the patient's characteristic coping strategies across the three coping styles (Surrender, Avoidance, Overcompensation) are recorded behaviourally and connected by arrows. A curved arrow looping back to the schema labelled "maintains" makes the self-perpetuating cycle visible, which is the map's most important clinical teaching tool.

Component 5: Mode States, Colour-Coded. The five schema modes are represented as labelled state boxes around the periphery of the map, each colour-coded consistently (suggested: Vulnerable Child in blue; Angry Child in red; Detached Protector in grey; Punitive Parent in dark red; Healthy Adult in green). Arrows from schema boxes to mode states show activation pathways. The Healthy Adult should be positioned prominently with connections labelled "healing and updating," representing the direction of therapeutic travel.

SECTION B: Visual Conventions

Colour-coding by domain. Schema boxes belonging to the same domain should share the same background colour. Suggested domain colours: Disconnection and Rejection (blue); Impaired Autonomy and Performance (orange); Impaired Limits (yellow); Other-Directedness (purple); Overvigilance and Inhibition (grey). The colour key should appear in the map's legend.

Directional arrows showing activation pathways. Arrows should always indicate direction of causality or influence. Developmental origins connect to schemas with an inward arrow. Triggers connect to schemas rightward or inward. Schemas connect to coping modes outwardly. Coping modes loop back to schemas with a curved arrow labelled "maintains." Schemas connect to mode states diagonally. The Healthy Adult connects to schemas labelled "updates." Avoid crossing arrows by positioning elements systematically before adding connections.

Patient's own language for labels. All labels visible on the map should use the patient's own language wherever possible. Clinician technical terminology should appear only in the legend or as secondary labels in a smaller font. A map that the patient can read and recognise as their own story is a therapeutically active document. A map that reads as a clinical taxonomy is not.

SECTION C: Clinical Completion Notes

Complete collaboratively, across two to three sessions. The Schema Map should not be completed by the clinician outside sessions and presented to the patient as a finished product. It should be built collaboratively, with the clinician drawing in pencil or on screen and the patient contributing, correcting, and expanding at every stage. The process of building the map is itself therapeutic: it externalises the patient's internal experience, places it on paper between two people, and makes it discussable. Typical completion timeline: Session 1 covers core schemas and developmental origins; Session 2 covers triggers and coping modes; Session 3 covers mode states, connections, and a full review with the patient. Some patients will require additional sessions, particularly where developmental history is complex or where the mapping process evokes significant emotional distress.

Use A3 paper or a digital whiteboard for accessibility. The Schema Map contains a significant amount of information and benefits from generous physical space. A3 paper or a digital whiteboard application allows sufficient room for all five components without crowding. A3 maps can be laminated and given to the patient as a portable reference document. Digital maps can be exported as PDFs and shared securely. For patients with visual impairment, a tactile or audio-described version of the map may be appropriate; clinicians should consult their service's accessibility lead.

Photograph and include in the patient's clinical record. The completed Schema Map constitutes a formal clinical document and must be included in the patient's clinical record. For paper maps, a photograph or scan should be taken at the end of each session in which the map is amended, so that the clinical record captures the map's evolution over time. The final completed map should be scanned at high resolution and stored in the patient's electronic record alongside the IPTF Formulation Worksheet. The map should be referenced explicitly in clinical letters, transfer summaries, and any discharge documentation, to ensure continuity of formulation if the patient moves to a different clinician or service.

Reference: Young, J. E., Klosko, J. S., and Weishaar, M. E. (2003). Schema Therapy: A Practitioner's Guide. Guilford Press. The five-component map structure described here represents an IPTF adaptation of Young's original model, extended to incorporate explicit mode states and maintaining cycles in accordance with IPTF clinical governance guidance.

Chapter Summary

This chapter has provided the step-by-step guide to constructing the Schema Map and identifying schema modes. The Schema Map connects the patient's core schemas to their developmental origins, current triggers, and maintaining coping modes, providing a visual representation of the pattern that has been running the patient's life. Mode identification enables the patient to recognise, in real time, the emotional and behavioural states through which their schemas are expressed. The chapter that follows addresses Phase Three: the active modification of schemas through experiential processing and cognitive restructuring.

Chapter 13

Phase Three: Experiential Processing and Cognitive Restructuring

> *The schema does not change because you understand it. The schema changes because you experience something different. Understanding opens the door; experience walks through it.*
>
> — Jayden Josh James, 2026

Overview of Phase Three

Phase Three is the longest and most technically demanding phase of Stage 2, typically spanning fifteen to twenty sessions. It is the phase in which the schemas and modes identified in Phases One and Two are actively modified through a combination of experiential and cognitive techniques. The IPTF draws upon four primary therapeutic tools in Phase Three: imagery rescripting, the signature technique of Schema-Focused Therapy; chair work, also drawn from SFT; cognitive restructuring and Socratic questioning, drawn from CBT-PD; and behavioural experiments, also drawn from CBT-PD. The clinician selects and sequences these tools based on the patient's needs, schema content, mode presentation, and therapeutic readiness, moving flexibly between them rather than following a rigid protocol.

The integration of experiential and cognitive approaches is a distinctive feature of the IPTF. Experiential techniques, specifically imagery rescripting and chair work, access the emotional core of the schema: they reach the Vulnerable Child who carries the unprocessed pain of the early experience, and they provide a corrective emotional experience that modifies the schema at the affective level. Cognitive techniques, specifically Socratic questioning, evidence examination, and behavioural experiments, address the schema at the level of belief: they challenge the accuracy and utility of the core beliefs and provide rational and empirical evidence for alternative, more adaptive perspectives. Both levels of intervention are necessary for lasting change. A schema that has been modified at the emotional level through imagery rescripting but not challenged at the cognitive level may resurface when the patient encounters a situation that activates the old belief. A schema that has been challenged at the cognitive level through thought records but not processed at the emotional level may persist as an intellectually acknowledged but emotionally unchanged conviction: the patient knows the belief is irrational but still feels its truth.

Imagery Rescripting: A Detailed Clinical Protocol

Imagery rescripting is the signature experiential technique of Schema-Focused Therapy and one of the most powerful therapeutic interventions available for personality disorder treatment. It works by reactivating an early memory in which a schema was formed and introducing a new, corrective experience into the memory during the reconsolidation window, thereby modifying the emotional associations stored with the memory (Arntz and Jacob, 2013; Nader, Schafe, and Le Doux, 2000). The technique requires careful preparation, skilled facilitation, and thorough processing, and it should only be used by clinicians who have received specific training in imagery rescripting.

Contraindications and Precautions

Imagery rescripting should not be attempted if the patient's current emotional arousal is above 7 on the 0 to 10 scale; if the patient has not yet acquired a functional repertoire of Stage 1 skills; if the patient is actively dissociating or has a history of dissociative episodes during therapy; if the patient has not given informed consent after a full explanation of what the technique involves; or if the therapeutic alliance is not sufficiently stable to contain the emotional activation that the technique generates. For patients with a significant dissociative presentation, the clinician should introduce imagery rescripting gradually, beginning with less emotionally charged memories and building towards the core schema memories as the patient's capacity for grounded emotional processing develops.

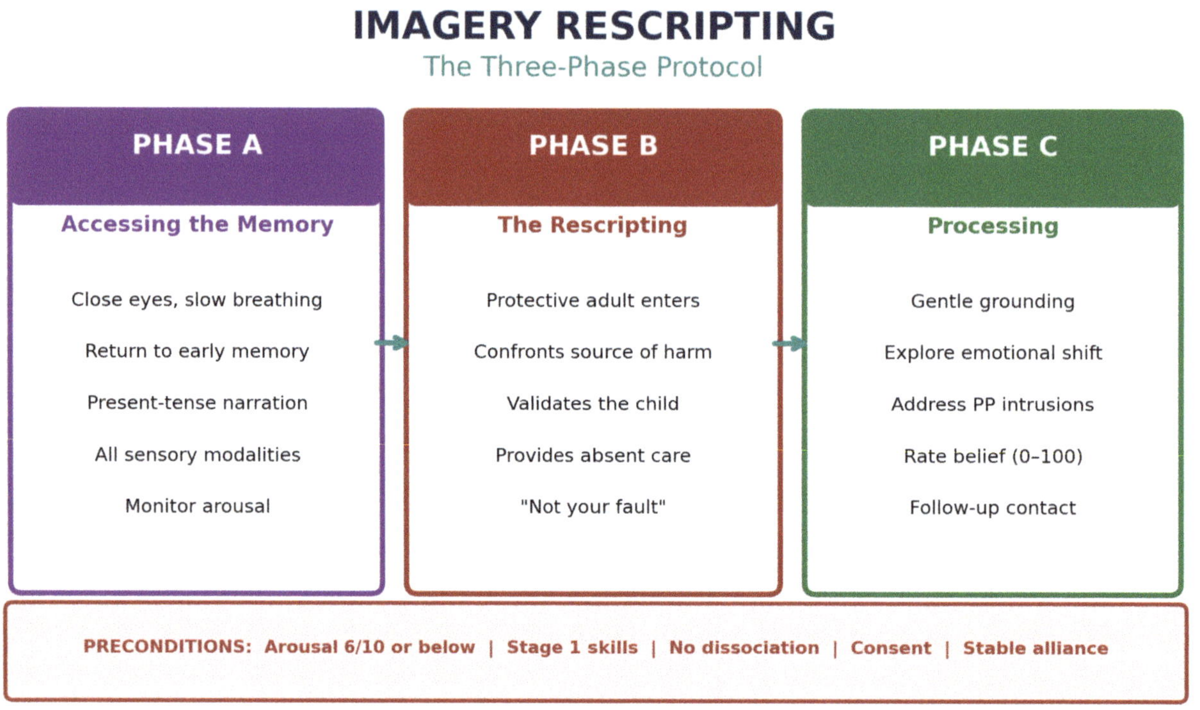

Figure 6. Imagery Rescripting: Three-phase protocol with preconditions.

The Three-Phase Imagery Rescripting Protocol

Phase A: Accessing the Memory. The clinician begins by inviting the patient to close their eyes, if they feel comfortable doing so, and to bring to mind an early memory that is connected to one of their core schemas. The clinician may suggest a specific memory identified during Phase One, or may invite the patient to let a memory arise spontaneously in response to the schema. The patient is asked to describe the memory in the present tense, as though it is happening now, attending to all sensory modalities: what they can see, hear, smell, feel, and taste. The present-tense narration activates the memory network more fully than past-tense recollection, making the emotional content of the memory available for processing. The clinician monitors the patient's arousal throughout, watching for signs of overwhelming distress or dissociation. If the patient's arousal approaches the upper limit of manageable distress, the clinician may use grounding techniques, including asking the patient to open their eyes briefly and name five things they can see in the room, before returning to the imagery.

> **Therapist Script:** '*I would like to invite you to close your eyes, and in your own time, let yourself drift back to a memory from your childhood that connects to the belief that you are worthless. There is no rush. Just let a memory come to mind. When you have it, tell*

> *me where you are. Describe it as though it is happening right now. What can you see?'*

Phase B: The Rescripting Intervention. Once the memory is activated and the patient is experiencing the emotional content, the clinician introduces the rescripting. There are two primary forms of rescripting. In therapist-led rescripting, the clinician enters the image as a protective adult figure and addresses the source of harm directly, expressing what the child needed to hear: 'Stop. You cannot treat this child this way. This child has done nothing wrong. What you are doing is abuse, and it needs to stop now.' The clinician then turns to the child in the image and provides the validation and care that were absent: 'You did not deserve that. None of this was your fault. You are a child, and you deserve to be safe and loved.' In patient-led rescripting, the patient's adult self enters the image and provides protection and care to the child self. The choice between these forms depends on the patient's readiness: therapist-led rescripting is typically used first, when the patient's Healthy Adult is not yet strong enough to provide the rescripting independently, and patient-led rescripting is introduced later as the patient's capacity grows.

> **Therapist Script:** *'Now I am going to come into this memory with you. I am the adult who should have been there to protect you. [Addressing the source of harm:] I want you to stop what you are doing right now. This child has done nothing to deserve this. What you are doing is wrong, and I am not going to allow it to continue. [Turning to the child:] I want you to know that none of this is your fault. You are not stupid. You are not worthless. You are a child who deserves to be safe and cared for, and what is happening to you should not be happening. I am here now, and I am going to make sure you are safe.'*

Phase C: Processing and Integration. After the rescripting, the clinician guides the patient back to the present moment through a gentle grounding exercise. The processing phase explores the patient's emotional experience: what they felt during the memory, what they felt when the rescripting occurred, whether anything shifted, and what the experience means to them. The clinician also explores any obstacles to the rescripting: did the patient find it difficult to believe the rescripting, and if so, what got in the way? Often, the Punitive Parent mode will intrude, telling the patient that they did deserve the abuse, that the rescripting is just pretend, or that nothing can really change. These intrusions are themselves valuable therapeutic material that can be addressed through chair work or cognitive restructuring in subsequent sessions.

◆ **CLINICAL PEARL**

The first imagery rescripting session is often the most emotionally intense session in the entire IPTF treatment. Prepare for it. Ensure the session is scheduled at a time when neither you nor the patient has a conflicting commitment immediately afterwards. Have the patient's crisis plan accessible. Arrange a follow-up contact, whether a brief telephone check-in or an early next session, within forty-eight hours. After the session, give yourself time to process your own emotional response, either in supervision or in your consultation team. Imagery rescripting activates the therapist's empathy system powerfully, and the vicarious exposure to the patient's trauma memories requires its own processing.

Chair Work: A Detailed Clinical Protocol

Chair work, developed within Schema-Focused Therapy by Arntz and Jacob (2013) and refined by Kellogg (2015), uses the physical act of sitting in different chairs to externalise different schema modes, enabling the patient to observe, dialogue with, and ultimately modify the relationships between their internal modes. The technique is particularly effective for addressing the Punitive Parent mode, because it enables the patient to hear the critical voice as coming from a specific chair, a specific mode, rather than experiencing it as the voice of reality, and to practise responding to it from the Healthy Adult chair.

The Two-Chair Technique for the Punitive Parent

The basic two-chair technique uses two chairs, one designated as the Punitive Parent chair and one as the Healthy Adult chair. The patient begins by sitting in the Punitive Parent chair and speaking the words of the critical voice aloud: the attacks, the condemnations, the shaming messages that the patient directs at themselves. The clinician encourages the patient to speak these words in the second person, as they were originally delivered: 'You are pathetic. You will never amount to anything. Nobody could ever love you.' The act of voicing these attacks aloud, from a specific chair, creates a powerful externalisation: the patient hears the words as coming from outside themselves, from a chair that represents a specific mode rather than from an undifferentiated inner experience. The patient then moves to the Healthy Adult chair and is coached by the clinician to respond to the Punitive Parent with compassion, assertion, and rationality: 'That is not true. I am not pathetic. I am someone who survived terrible things, and I deserve compassion, not contempt.' The clinician may model the Healthy Adult response first, particularly in early sessions when the patient's Healthy Adult is not yet strong enough to challenge the Punitive Parent independently.

The Three-Chair Technique: Adding the Vulnerable Child

The three-chair technique adds a third chair, the Vulnerable Child chair, to the two-chair exercise. In this format, the Punitive Parent attacks the Vulnerable Child, and the Healthy Adult intervenes to protect and comfort the child. The patient moves between all three chairs, experiencing each mode in turn. The three-chair technique is particularly powerful because it gives the patient the experience of the Healthy Adult defending the Vulnerable Child, which directly parallels the therapist-led imagery rescripting in which the protective adult defends the child in the memory. Over time, the patient's capacity to access the Healthy Adult mode and to deploy it in defence of the Vulnerable Child strengthens, and this capacity generalises beyond the consulting room into the patient's daily life.

CBT-PD in Phase Three: A Detailed Clinical Protocol

Cognitive Behavioural Therapy for Personality Disorder, as developed and systematised by Kate Davidson (2007) and elaborated within the British clinical psychology tradition, represents the IPTF's primary tool for addressing the belief-level architecture that maintains schemas between and beyond the emotional work of imagery rescripting and chair work. If SFT's experiential techniques reach the Vulnerable Child who carries the unprocessed pain of early experience, CBT-PD's cognitive tools address the intellectual fortress that the adult has constructed around that pain: the conditional assumptions, compensatory strategies, and core beliefs that have accumulated into a worldview as automatic as breathing and as invisible to examination as the air. Where imagery rescripting and chair work access the schema at its affective root, CBT-PD disciplines the belief system that the schema has generated, testing it against evidence, examining its historical origins, and constructing alternative beliefs that are not merely intellectually affirmed but lived and practised into conviction. Both levels of intervention are necessary for durable change. The IPTF clinician therefore deploys CBT-PD not as an alternative to the experiential work but as its cognitive complement, sequencing and interweaving the two approaches in accordance with the patient's readiness and the schema's current temperature.

The CBT-PD Conceptualisation in Phase Three

CBT-PD organises the belief system across three levels that correspond closely to the SFT schema model and that, in the IPTF, are understood as mutually illuminating rather than competing accounts of the same underlying structure. At the deepest level sit the Core Beliefs: the absolute, unconditional statements about the self, others, and the world that correspond directly to the Early Maladaptive Schemas identified through the Phase One and Two work ('I am fundamentally defective', 'People will always abandon me', 'The world is dangerous'). These core beliefs are not conclusions drawn from evidence; they are the lens through which all subsequent experience is perceived and interpreted. At the intermediate level sit the Conditional Assumptions: the if-then rules and should-must imperatives through which the individual has constructed an adaptive strategy to manage the terror of the core belief ('If I never let anyone close, I cannot be abandoned', 'If I am perfect, nobody can criticise me'). At the surface level sit the Compensatory Strategies: the behavioural patterns, coping modes, and interpersonal strategies that the individual enacts moment to moment in the service of the conditional assumptions (social withdrawal, overachievement, emotional suppression, aggression). In CBT-PD, therapeutic change is achieved by working systematically across all three levels, and in the IPTF this work is integrated with the SFT mode map so that the conceptualisation at both levels enriches and deepens the other.

The Downward Arrow Technique

The downward arrow technique is one of the most clinically efficient tools in the CBT-PD repertoire and one of the most important bridges between the day-to-day cognitive work and the deeper schema material of Phase Three. It is used to excavate the belief hierarchy from a current automatic thought downwards to the core belief that drives it, making explicit the chain of meaning that connects the surface cognition to the deep schema. The technique is particularly valuable early in Phase Three, when the clinician is moving from Phase Two's schema mapping work into the active modification phase, because it anchors the cognitive work directly in the patient's live experience rather than in abstract conceptualisation.

The procedure begins by identifying a specific automatic thought connected to a recent emotionally significant situation. The clinician then asks, in response to each answer, 'And if that were true, what would that mean about you?' or 'And if that happened, what would be the worst thing about it?' This repeated questioning drives progressively deeper into the belief system, revealing the conditional assumptions that connect the surface thought to the core belief. The sequence continues until the patient arrives at an absolute, generalised statement that has the character of a core belief: a statement that cannot be driven deeper because it represents a bedrock assumption about the self rather than a contingent interpretation of a situation.

Therapist Script — Downward Arrow: 'You said that when your manager did not reply to your email today, you felt a strong wave of dread. What did you think was happening?' [Patient: 'That she was annoyed with me.'] 'And if she were annoyed with you, what would that mean?' [Patient: 'That I had done something wrong.'] 'And if you had done something wrong, what would that mean about you?' [Patient: 'That I am incompetent.'] 'And if you were incompetent — really incompetent, in the way that feels true right now — what is the worst thing that would mean about you as a person?' [Patient, after a pause: 'That I am not worth anything. That I should not be here.'] 'There it is. That is the belief we need to look at — not the email, not your manager, but that deep conviction that you are not worth anything. Can you see how that connects to the Defectiveness schema we have been working on?'

Socratic Questioning and Evidence Examination

Socratic questioning is the cognitive clinician's most versatile tool: a method of guided discovery in which carefully sequenced questions lead the patient towards examining and revising their beliefs through their own reasoning rather than through the therapist's assertion. In personality disorder work it requires particular skill, because the core beliefs are not merely thoughts that have been held in error but deep structures that have served a survival function, and challenging them without adequate validation and relational safety risks replicating the dismissiveness of the original invalidating environment. The Socratic process within the IPTF therefore always begins with empathic acknowledgement of why the belief arose and what function it served, before moving to its examination.

The Socratic sequence in CBT-PD for personality disorder follows six movements. The clinician begins by naming and validating: 'So the belief we are working with is "I am fundamentally unlovable." I want you to know that I completely understand why you came to believe that, given what you went through. Today I would like to look at it with you.' The clinician then examines the evidence for the belief, attending especially to the quality of the evidence: does it genuinely support the belief in its absolute form, or does it support a more conditional version? Evidence examination for personality disorder must attend to the common cognitive processing errors that characterise schema-driven thinking — overgeneralisation from selected instances, dismissal of disconfirming evidence, and the attribution of positive events to luck or performance rather than to self-worth. The clinician explores the evidence against the belief, drawing on recent experiences, other people's responses, and evidence that the patient has tended to discount. The clinician then examines the belief through alternative frames: 'If a close friend held this belief about themselves, would you agree with them? What would you want them to understand?' The clinician explores the consequences of the belief — 'What does holding this belief cost you? How does it shape your decisions and your relationships?' — and finally invites the patient to construct an alternative belief that is honest about the history whilst not totalising: 'If the absolute belief is not completely true, and if the evidence does not fully support it, what would be a more accurate statement about who you are?'

Evidence examination uses a structured Evidence For and Against Worksheet to make this process systematic and portable beyond the session. The patient records the core belief at the top of the worksheet and then identifies specific life experiences that appear to support it and specific experiences that appear to contradict it. For most patients with personality disorder, this exercise reveals a striking temporal asymmetry: the evidence that is recruited in support of the belief is drawn almost exclusively from the early developmental period and from experiences in which the patient was powerless, frightened, or dependent, whilst the evidence that contradicts the belief — often more abundant and more recent — has been systematically filtered out by the schema's selective attention. Making this asymmetry visible and discussing the mechanism by which the schema perpetuates itself through selective perception is itself a powerful therapeutic intervention. It shifts the patient from experiencing the belief as an empirical fact established by accumulated evidence to understanding it as a hypothesis generated by a cognitive system calibrated in adverse developmental conditions.

The Historical Review Method

The Historical Review Method, developed within the CBT for persistent belief change tradition (Padesky, 1994), is one of the most effective CBT-PD techniques for addressing the deeply entrenched core beliefs that characterise personality disorder, and it is particularly well-suited to Phase Three because it builds directly upon the developmental history gathered in Phase One. The technique takes the patient back through their life history, decade by decade from the earliest childhood memories, reexamining the evidence that was originally used to construct the core belief. Its power lies in a fundamental challenge to the belief's evidentiary status: the clinician and patient examine together whether the experiences that the patient has cited as evidence for the belief ('I was abandoned as a child, therefore I am unlovable') actually constitute valid evidence for the belief, or whether an alternative explanation — one that is about the limitations or failures of the people in the patient's environment rather than about an intrinsic quality of the patient — would fit the evidence equally well or better.

The procedure moves chronologically, beginning with early childhood and progressing towards the present. At each developmental period, the clinician asks the patient to identify what happened and what conclusion they drew about themselves, before inviting them to consider the situation again through the lens of what they now understand about the adults who were present. 'You told me your mother never held you when you cried. You concluded from that that you were not worth comforting. I want to ask you now: what do you know about your mother's own history? What do you understand now, as an adult, about why she could not respond to you? Is her inability to comfort you actually evidence about your worth, or is it evidence about her capacity?' This reattribution process is not about exonerating the adults who caused harm; it is about separating the child's legitimate need for comfort and connection — a need that was entirely valid — from the conclusion the child drew about their own worth in the absence of that comfort. The Review works systematically through each period of the patient's history, constructing a revised account of the evidence that does not require the core belief to be true. At the conclusion, the patient and clinician together review the evidence that remains and agree a formulation of the belief that is historically informed and emotionally honest without being totalising.

Therapist Script — Historical Review: 'We have been working with the belief "I am worthless" for several weeks now, and I think it is time to go back to where that belief began and look at the evidence again — not to deny what happened to you, but to examine what it actually proves. I want to go back to the earliest memories you have of feeling worthless. Can you tell me about a time before you were five that connects to this belief?' [...after the patient describes a memory...] 'So your father called you stupid when you spilled the milk. You were four years old. At four, you made sense of that the only way a four-year-old can: by concluding that there is something wrong with you. But you are not four now. When you look at that scene as the adult you are today, what do you understand about your father that the four-year-old could not?'

The Positive Data Log

The Positive Data Log is a CBT-PD between-session tool that directly addresses one of the most consistent cognitive features of personality disorder: the schema-driven selective attention that systematically filters out experience that would disconfirm the core belief. The mechanism is one that every experienced clinician will recognise in their patients: the person who receives ten compliments and one criticism and remembers only the criticism; the person who successfully manages a difficult situation but attributes the success to luck or accident rather than to their own competence. The Positive Data Log provides a structured counter to this filtering by instructing the patient to record, on a daily basis, any experience — however small — that could be interpreted as evidence against the core belief. The log is explicitly framed not as a positive thinking exercise but as an attention-training exercise: the patient is not being asked to pretend that everything is good, but to practise attending to a class of information that their schema-driven cognition has been trained to overlook.

The clinician introduces the Positive Data Log by first establishing, through Socratic questioning, that the patient has been selectively attending to schema-confirming information. 'When you look back at last week, are you more able to recall the moment when your colleague criticised your report, or the moment when your friend told you she values your friendship? Which one do you dwell on?' Having established the pattern of selective attention, the clinician frames the Log as a retraining exercise: 'Your attention has been trained over many years to notice evidence that the belief is true and to skip over evidence that it might not be. The Log is not a thought record; it is more like a camera that you are deliberately pointing in a direction your attention usually avoids. Each day, I would like you to write down one piece of evidence — no matter how small — that does not fit with the belief that you are worthless. Your job is not to decide whether it is convincing evidence, but simply to notice it and record it.' The Log is reviewed in every session, and the patient's responses to the recorded entries — the dismissals, the qualifications, the schema-driven minimisations — become rich material for Socratic questioning and for the identification of specific cognitive processes through which the schema maintains itself.

Schema-Specific Thought Records

The thought record, the foundational self-monitoring tool of the CBT tradition, requires significant adaptation for personality disorder work because the standard format was designed for discrete, situationally triggered distress rather than for the chronic, pervasive, and schema-embedded cognition of personality disorder. The standard instruction to 'identify the automatic thought that preceded the emotion' can founder when the patient's core belief is so chronic and so automatic that it constitutes a continuous background state rather than a discrete triggered thought. In the IPTF's CBT-PD adaptation, the thought record is redesigned as a schema-specific tool that makes the connection between the situation and the core belief explicit, and that focuses the cognitive restructuring column on the schema rather than on the situational interpretation.

The IPTF Schema Thought Record uses five columns. Column One records the triggering situation in brief, factual terms. Column Two records the automatic thoughts, including the hot cognition — the thought that carries the most emotional charge in the moment. Column Three names the schema that was activated and records the core belief in its absolute form ('Defectiveness — "I am fundamentally flawed and unlovable."'). Column Four records the emotional response and its intensity on a zero-to-ten scale. Column Five is the Healthy Adult Response: the patient's attempt, from the Healthy Adult mode, to construct a compassionate, balanced, and evidenced response to the activated schema — explicitly drawing on the Historical Review evidence, the Positive Data Log entries, and the imagery rescripting experience. The Fifth Column response is not merely a rationalisation; it is the patient's practised attempt to inhabit the alternative perspective that the schema work has been constructing, to speak from the voice that is building rather than the voice that condemns. Reviewing the thought records in session allows the clinician to identify the specific points at which the Healthy Adult response breaks down and to use those breakdown points as targets for further experiential or cognitive work.

Conditional Assumption Work and Behavioural Pattern Breaking

At the intermediate level of the CBT-PD hierarchy, the conditional assumptions — the if-then rules through which the patient manages the core belief — require their own targeted intervention, because they are the direct generators of the compensatory strategies that maintain schema avoidance and schema perpetuation. Unlike core beliefs, which are typically experienced as facts, conditional assumptions are more accessible to cognitive examination because they have a recognisable logical structure that the patient can usually identify when it is reflected back to them. The clinician identifies the key conditional assumption through the Socratic process and then invites the patient to examine its costs and benefits: 'You have a rule that says "If I never ask for help, people cannot see my weakness." I would like us to look at what that rule has cost you — and at what you have gained from it. Then I want to ask: is there a version of the rule that would still protect you but cost you less?'

Behavioural pattern breaking at the compensatory strategy level is the CBT-PD analogue of the SFT work on coping mode surrender and overcompensation, and the two conceptualisations can be used simultaneously to provide a richer account of the same behaviour. A patient who habitually overworks to the point of exhaustion in the service of the Unrelenting Standards schema, for example, is both activating the Overcontroller mode (in SFT terms) and enacting the conditional assumption 'If I am perfect, people will have no reason to criticise me' (in CBT-PD terms). The clinician can draw on both formulations in the same session, using whichever language resonates most for the individual patient at that moment. The CBT-PD approach to pattern breaking uses graded task assignment: the patient agrees to test the conditional assumption by temporarily relaxing the compensatory behaviour — leaving work at a set time despite the task being unfinished, for example — and monitoring what actually happens against the catastrophic prediction that the assumption generates.

Behavioural Experiments

Behavioural experiments provide the empirical testing ground for schema modification, and within the CBT-PD tradition they represent the most powerful tool available for bridging the gap between cognitive understanding and lived experience. Where imagery rescripting produces a corrective emotional experience within the consulting room, and where Socratic questioning challenges the belief at the level of logic and evidence, behavioural experiments generate new evidence through direct action in the patient's real-world relational and social environment. They are the mechanism through which the alternative beliefs constructed in therapy are tested against the reality of the patient's actual life, and through which schema-driven avoidance is systematically dismantled through graded exposure to the very situations the schema has been organised to avoid.

The IPTF protocol for behavioural experiments follows a five-stage structured sequence that the clinician and patient work through collaboratively. The first stage is belief identification: identifying the specific core belief or conditional assumption that the experiment will test, stated as a testable prediction ('If I share something personal with my friend, she will think less of me and withdraw'). The second stage is experiment design: designing the specific action that will test the prediction, attending to the three design principles of specificity (the action is clearly defined), manageability (the level of risk is calibrated to the patient's current capacity), and measurability (the outcome can be clearly assessed). The third stage is safety behaviour identification: listing any safety behaviours — the subtle avoidances and compensations that the patient would naturally deploy to reduce anxiety during the experiment, but that simultaneously prevent the experiment from fully testing the prediction. Safety behaviours in personality disorder commonly include emotional suppression during the vulnerable action (sharing something personal but in a flat, minimising tone that prevents genuine contact), premature withdrawal (leaving the situation before the other person can respond), and overpreparation (rehearsing and controlling the interaction to such a degree that it no longer constitutes a genuine test of the prediction). The fourth stage is the experiment itself, conducted between sessions. The fifth stage is the processing review in the following session: what happened, how the patient felt, whether safety behaviours were deployed, what the actual outcome was relative to the prediction, and what this implies for the core belief.

The selection and sequencing of experiments across Phase Three follows a hierarchical structure that begins with lower-stakes experiments in domains where the schema's hold is less intense, and progresses towards higher-stakes experiments in the domains where the schema is most entrenched and the avoidance most profound. A patient with an Abandonment schema, for example, might begin with an experiment involving a low-stakes social encounter (attending a community event and observing whether people respond with interest or indifference), progress to an intermediate experiment (asking a colleague for a small favour and observing the response), and ultimately to a high-stakes experiment (sharing a genuine personal vulnerability with an intimate and observing whether the feared abandonment ensues). Each experiment builds on the evidence generated by the previous one, and the accumulated evidence from a sequence of experiments — processed and integrated within the mentalising frame — progressively erodes the schema's hold on the patient's perception of the social world.

Therapist Script — Designing a Behavioural Experiment: 'We have been working on the belief "If I let anyone see my real self, they will leave." I think it is time to test that. I want to suggest an experiment. This week, I want you to share one thing with your friend Jenna — something real, something you would normally keep to yourself. Not your deepest secret, but something that feels genuinely personal. Before you do it, I want you to write down your prediction: what exactly do you think Jenna will do? Then you do it, and next week you tell me what happened. There are two rules: you are not allowed to share it in a throwaway tone that lets you dismiss the conversation afterwards, and you are not allowed to leave before she has had a chance to respond. The safety behaviours are out. Can we agree on what you will share?'

◆ CLINICAL PEARL

The most effective behavioural experiments are those that are specific, predictable, and personally meaningful. A vague experiment like 'be more open with people' is unlikely to produce useful data. A specific experiment like 'tell Sarah about my anxiety about the party and observe whether she responds with rejection or understanding, predicting that she will reject me' generates a clear, testable prediction with an unambiguous outcome. Help the patient to make their predictions as specific as possible, because the more specific the prediction, the more powerful the disconfirmation. When an experiment produces the feared outcome — when the friend does respond with rejection or distance — this is not a failure of the experiment but extraordinarily valuable data: it invites a mentalising exploration of what happened in that specific relationship, whether the fear was accurate in this case, and what that means about the universality of the core belief. One disconfirming relationship does not refute a core belief formed across an entire developmental history; but it does introduce a crack in the absolutism of the belief, and cracks can be widened.

MBT in Phase Three: A Detailed Clinical Protocol

Mentalisation-Based Treatment, as developed by Peter Fonagy and Anthony Bateman (Bateman and Fonagy, 2004, 2016), contributes to Phase Three in a fundamentally different register from either SFT or CBT-PD. Where SFT and CBT-PD work on the content of schemas and beliefs — what the patient thinks and feels about themselves and others — MBT attends to the process by which the patient thinks and feels: the quality and flexibility of their mentalising, the degree to which they are able to hold the complexity of mental states, and the conditions under which their capacity for reflective function breaks down. In Phase Three, this distinction is clinically consequential because the schema modification work of SFT and CBT-PD requires a level of reflective capacity that can only be sustained when mentalising is intact. When the schema is activated and emotional arousal rises, mentalising degrades — the patient shifts from the flexible, curious, other-aware cognition of the Healthy Adult mode into the rigid, automatic, single-perspective processing of the pre-mentalising modes — and in those moments the SFT and CBT-PD tools are temporarily inaccessible. MBT's distinctive contribution to Phase Three is precisely the restoration and stabilisation of mentalising capacity in these high-arousal moments, enabling the content-focused work of SFT and CBT-PD to resume.

Recognising and Working with Pre-Mentalising Modes in Phase Three

Fonagy and Bateman identified three pre-mentalising modes that characterise the quality of psychological processing when the capacity for genuine mentalising has broken down under the pressure of emotional arousal or relational threat. The IPTF clinician working in Phase Three will recognise these modes regularly, because the schema-activation that Phase Three deliberately induces is precisely the kind of arousal that generates their emergence. Recognising them swiftly and responding with the appropriate MBT intervention is one of the most important clinical skills in Phase Three, because an unrecognised pre-mentalising episode can derail an imagery rescripting session, render Socratic questioning counterproductive, or damage the therapeutic alliance.

Psychic Equivalence is the mode in which the patient's internal reality is experienced as identical to external reality: what they think and feel is what is true and real, without qualification, perspective, or the epistemic humility that genuine mentalising maintains. In Phase Three, psychic equivalence manifests most commonly when the schema is fully activated: the patient who believes 'I am worthless' does not, in this moment, hold the belief tentatively as a hypothesis to be examined; they know it as an unmediated fact, as directly and certainly as they know the chair they are sitting on. When this occurs, Socratic questioning becomes impossible, because the patient is not in a position to entertain alternative perspectives — they are experiencing their cognition as perception rather than as interpretation. The MBT response to psychic equivalence is not to challenge the content of the belief but to gently challenge the mode of processing: 'I notice that right now this feels absolutely certain to you — like a fact rather than a thought. Can we slow down for a moment and notice that quality of certainty, because that itself is something interesting? In my experience, when something feels that certain and that absolute, it is usually a sign that we have hit a very old, very painful piece of experience. Would you be willing to hold it as a possibility for now, rather than a certainty, just so we can look at it together?'

Teleological Mode is the mode in which the patient can only accept mental states — their own feelings of being cared for, valued, or safe — as real if they are demonstrated through concrete physical actions. In Phase Three, teleological mode emerges most frequently in the therapeutic relationship itself: the patient who cannot trust that the clinician's concern is genuine unless it is demonstrated through extended session time, physical touch, or other concrete actions that lie outside the therapeutic boundary; the patient who regards the clinician's verbal validation as hollow unless it is backed by some tangible gesture. The MBT approach is to acknowledge the underlying longing explicitly — 'I understand that words can feel very insubstantial right now — that what you want is something you can hold onto, something that cannot just disappear like a statement in a room' — whilst maintaining the therapeutic frame and exploring, with genuine curiosity, what the concrete action represents: 'What would it mean to you if I extended our session today? What would that prove?' The teleological mode is particularly common in patients with prominent Abandonment and Emotional Deprivation schemas, and recognising it early in Phase Three allows the clinician to address it explicitly in the mentalising stance before it generates acting out, boundary challenges, or premature therapy dropout.

Pretend Mode is the mode in which the patient appears to be mentalising fluently — speaking thoughtfully about their mental states, reflecting on their history, engaging intellectually with the therapeutic material — but in which the cognitive processing is entirely disconnected from any affective experience. In pretend mode, the patient's verbal engagement with therapy is a performance of understanding rather than genuine reflective work: the words are accurate, the insights are articulate, but nothing is felt and nothing changes. Phase Three presents a particular risk of sustained pretend mode engagement, because the intellectual content of CBT-PD work — the belief hierarchies, the evidence worksheets, the thought records — can easily be hijacked by the patient's existing intellectual coping mode and enacted without any genuine emotional engagement. The clinician who fills sessions with productive-sounding cognitive analysis without ever touching the emotional core of the schema is working in the patient's pretend mode. The MBT response is to notice the disconnection and name it compassionately: 'I notice that we have been talking about this very fluently for twenty minutes, but I am finding it hard to locate your feelings in what you are saying. What is happening to your body right now, as we talk about this? Where is the emotion in this material?'

Stop, Rewind, and Explore

The Stop, Rewind, and Explore technique is MBT's primary procedural intervention for addressing the breakdown of mentalising in session, and in Phase Three it functions as the clinician's most important tool for managing the moments when schema activation disrupts the reflective capacity upon which SFT and CBT-PD work depends. The technique is used whenever the clinician detects that mentalising has broken down: that the patient has entered a pre-mentalising mode, that emotional arousal has risen above the threshold at which reflective function can operate, or that there has been a rupture in the therapeutic alliance. Its three components are sequential and non-negotiable in their order.

Stop means literally stopping what is happening — halting the imagery rescripting, interrupting the Socratic sequence, pausing the chair work — and bringing the patient back to the present moment and the present relationship. 'I want to pause what we are doing for a moment. I can see that you have become very distressed and I am not sure we are able to think clearly right now. Let's both take a breath and just be here together for a moment.' Rewind means returning to the point immediately before the mentalising broke down and examining what happened there: what was said, what was felt, what the shift was. 'Let's go back to just before things became overwhelming. What was happening? What did I say, or what did you feel, at the moment things shifted?' Explore means approaching that specific moment with the full mentalising curiosity of the therapeutic stance: examining what the patient felt, what they thought was happening, what they imagined the clinician was thinking, and what the breakdown reveals about the schema that is being activated. 'I'm curious about what happened in that moment. When I said [specific thing], I had the sense that something shifted for you. What did you make of that? What did it feel like I was doing?'

The Stop, Rewind, and Explore sequence is not an interruption of the schema work; it is schema work at a different level. The moments when mentalising breaks down are precisely the moments when the schema is most fully activated and most accessible to observation, and the exploration of what happened in those moments frequently produces the richest clinical material of Phase Three. The Explore phase, in particular, often reveals the specific interpersonal schema that the therapeutic relationship is activating — the way the clinician is being experienced as critical, as distant, as abandoning — and this live relational material, examined with curiosity and without defensiveness, becomes the most powerful and most proximate arena for schema modification.

Mentalising the Emotional Chain

Many patients who present for Phase Three have developed a sophisticated intellectual understanding of their schemas and their history, but retain an experienced disconnection between that understanding and the moment-to-moment emotional chain through which schema activation occurs, crisis behaviour emerges, and interpersonal damage accumulates. They can explain, with great articulacy, why they became furiously angry at their partner last Tuesday; but they cannot, in the moment of anger, track the mental pathway from the trigger to the crisis, and it is that in-the-moment failure of mentalising that perpetuates the problematic patterns despite intellectual understanding. Mentalising the Emotional Chain is the MBT technique for building that in-session capacity: the ability to trace, step by step, the mental pathway from a specific triggering situation to the emotional and behavioural response, attending not to the event but to the sequence of mental states that connected them.

The technique is applied to a specific recent incident, typically one in which the patient's schema was activated and their subsequent behaviour caused relational damage or crisis. The clinician guides the patient through the sequence: 'I want us to slow this right down and follow the mental pathway from the beginning. Not what your partner did — we know what they did — but what happened in here [touching own chest] from the moment that happened. What was the very first thing you noticed? A feeling, a body sensation, a thought? And then what? And then?' The chain typically reveals a sequence of rapidly escalating mental states that the patient has never before examined at this level of granularity: a micro-perception (a slight change in the partner's tone), a schema-driven interpretation ('She's disappointed in me'), a core-belief activation ('I am worthless and she will leave'), a mode shift (from Vulnerable Child to Angry Protector), a pre-mentalising collapse, and finally the behaviour. Each link in the chain is examined with curiosity: was the interpretation the only possible one? What else might have been happening in the partner's mental state? Where in the chain would it have been possible to make a different choice? The technique directly parallels the CBT-PD chain analysis but operates at the level of mental states rather than behaviours, and its integration with the SFT mode map enriches both: the patient can see the mode shift as it occurs within the emotional chain, and can identify the precise point at which the Healthy Adult mode might have intervened.

The Therapeutic Relationship as a Live Mentalising Arena

One of MBT's most distinctive and powerful contributions to Phase Three is its systematic use of the therapeutic relationship itself as the primary arena for schema activation and mentalising practice. In MBT's model, the most potent schema-activating relationship available in Phase Three is not the patient's relationship with their partner, their parents, or their colleagues: it is their relationship with the clinician, because it is this relationship that is immediately present, immediately observable, and capable of being examined in real time with a partner who is trained to hold the mentalising stance even under the pressure of the patient's schema activation. The therapeutic relationship in Phase Three is therefore not merely the container for the work; it is the work itself.

The MBT approach to relational schema work in Phase Three centres on what Bateman and Fonagy describe as the mentalising of the transference: the use of the patient's current experience of the clinician — their attributions, their assumptions, their relational responses — as primary material for mentalising practice. This is not transference interpretation in the classical analytic sense; it is much more immediate, more transparent, and more collaborative. When the patient becomes angry with the clinician, or withdraws, or becomes overly accommodating, or tests the boundary, the MBT response is not interpretation but enquiry: 'I noticed just then that something shifted between us. What were you feeling towards me in that moment?' And then, crucially: 'What do you imagine I was thinking about you?' And finally: 'I want to tell you what was actually happening in my mind, and I want to see whether that matches what you imagined.' This last step — the clinician's transparent disclosure of their own mental state — is one of the most powerful tools in MBT's arsenal for Phase Three, because it provides the patient with direct, immediate evidence about the clinician's actual mental state that can be compared against the schema-driven prediction, constituting in the moment a live behavioural experiment that no between-session assignment could replicate.

Therapist Script — Mentalising the Therapeutic Relationship: 'I want to pause on something that just happened between us. A moment ago, when I suggested we look at the belief from a different angle, you went very quiet and seemed to pull back. I noticed it, and I am curious about it. What were you feeling towards me in that moment?' [Patient: 'Nothing. I just thought you were going to tell me I was wrong again.'] 'That is really important. So in that moment you imagined I was building up to criticising you. I want to tell you what was actually happening in my mind: I was genuinely curious — I was thinking "there is something she knows about this situation that I haven't understood yet, and I want to understand it." Not criticism. Curiosity. Does that match what you imagined?' [Patient: 'No. Not at all.'] 'So your Defectiveness schema gave you one reading, and the actual situation was different. That is exactly the gap we are trying to close — the gap between what the schema predicts and what is actually happening.'

Affect Reconnection in Detachment-Dominant Presentations

For patients with a dominant Detachment trait profile — particularly those whose primary coping mode is Emotional Inhibition or Detached Self-Soother — Phase Three presents a distinctive clinical challenge that neither SFT nor CBT-PD is fully equipped to address: the patient who genuinely cannot access the emotional experience that SFT's experiential techniques require and that CBT-PD's evidence examination seeks to disconfirm. This is not resistance, and it is not pretend mode in the pure sense; it is a deeply established neurological and psychological adaptation in which the connection between somatic sensation, emotional experience, and cognitive awareness has been so thoroughly suppressed, over such a long period, that the patient experiences themselves as genuinely affectless in relation to material that would be expected to generate strong emotion. Imagery rescripting with such patients may proceed technically correctly — the memory is accessed, the clinician enters the image — but with little emotional resonance: the patient reports that they understand what happened but feels nothing about it.

The MBT approach to affect reconnection focuses on building the bridge from the body upwards, attending to the somatic indicators of emotional experience that precede conscious awareness and that the detached patient has learned to suppress at the earliest stage. The clinician begins each Phase Three session with detachment-dominant patients by briefly attending to the body: 'Before we begin, I want to spend just a moment with what is happening in your body right now. Are you aware of any physical sensations — tension, heaviness, emptiness, constriction anywhere?' As the session proceeds, the clinician gently and repeatedly draws attention to any physical or tonal shift in the patient's presentation: 'I notice your voice got a little quieter just then. What is happening in your body right now as you talk about this?' The goal is not to force emotional expression — this would be experienced as violating and would deepen the defensive detachment — but to build the patient's capacity to attend to the early physiological signals of emotional activation before the suppression mechanism engages. Over time, this attentional training creates a wider window for emotional experience, within which the experiential techniques of SFT become increasingly accessible. The MBT marked mirroring technique — reflecting the patient's apparent emotional state back to them in a slightly exaggerated, explicitly tentative way — is also important with detachment-dominant patients: 'I have a sense — and please correct me if I am wrong — that there might be some sadness underneath what you are describing. Is that anywhere near right?'

◆ CLINICAL PEARL

The three modalities of Phase Three — SFT, CBT-PD, and MBT — operate at different levels of the patient's functioning, and their integration in any given session should be driven by clinical observation rather than by adherence to a protocol. MBT attends to the process of mentalising and to the quality of the therapeutic relationship; SFT attends to the emotional core of the schema through experiential techniques; CBT-PD attends to the belief architecture that maintains the schema through cognitive techniques. A useful working rule for Phase Three is as follows. When you notice a pre-mentalising mode, use MBT (Stop, Rewind, and Explore). When the schema is hot and emotionally activated, use SFT (imagery rescripting, chair work). When the patient is reflectively available but cognitively stuck, use CBT-PD (downward arrow, historical review, thought records, behavioural experiments). This is not a rigid protocol; it is a clinical decision-making framework. The three modalities are not competing; they are complementary, and the clinician who can move fluently between them in response to the patient's moment-to-moment presentation is practising the IPTF at its most sophisticated.

Integrating the Techniques: SFT, CBT-PD, and MBT in Phase Three

The IPTF clinician does not follow a fixed sequence of techniques within Phase Three. Instead, they select the technique that is most appropriate for the patient's current presentation, the schema being addressed, and the therapeutic moment — drawing from the full integrated repertoire of SFT's experiential tools, CBT-PD's cognitive and belief-level tools, and MBT's process-level and relational tools. A session might begin with the clinician using MBT's marked mirroring and affect-attending to reconnect the patient to the emotional material they are approaching; move into imagery rescripting when the schema is fully activated; shift to chair work to address the Punitive Parent voice that emerged during the rescripting; then, as arousal settles and reflective function returns, transition to Socratic questioning and a Positive Data Log review from CBT-PD; and conclude with the design of a behavioural experiment and a brief Stop-Rewind-Explore processing of an interpersonal moment that arose during the session. No single modality is sufficient on its own. SFT's experiential work without CBT-PD's cognitive consolidation risks leaving the patient with modified affective memories but unchanged beliefs. CBT-PD's cognitive work without SFT's experiential work risks producing intellectual understanding without emotional change. Both SFT and CBT-PD without MBT's process-level monitoring risk failing to notice the moments when mentalising breaks down and the schema becomes inaccessible — or, worse, producing prolonged periods of pretend mode engagement that feel productive but achieve nothing.

A general principle governs the selection across all three modalities. When the patient is in a pre-mentalising mode — when the schema is in psychic equivalence, when teleological demands are being made of the therapeutic relationship, when pretend mode is producing fluent but affectless engagement — use MBT's process tools first, because mentalising capacity is the prerequisite for all other Phase Three work. When the schema is hot and emotionally activated and mentalising is intact, use SFT's experiential techniques, because they work at the affective level where the activation is occurring and can modify the schema's emotional core in ways that cognitive work cannot reach. When the patient is reflectively available and at a distance from acute activation, use CBT-PD's cognitive tools, because they work at the belief level where the patient's rational capacity is available. These three modalities are not competing alternatives but sequential and complementary layers of intervention: MBT creates the reflective conditions for SFT to do its experiential work, SFT modifies the emotional core that CBT-PD then consolidates at the level of belief, and CBT-PD generates the evidence and the alternative beliefs that, over time, make it progressively harder for the schema to maintain its hold on the patient's perception of themselves and their world.

Chapter Summary

This chapter has provided the detailed clinical protocols for the full range of Phase Three techniques drawn from the IPTF's three Stage 2 modalities. From Schema-Focused Therapy: imagery rescripting across its three-phase protocol with therapist scripts and processing guidance, and chair work including the two-chair and three-chair techniques for mode dialogue. From CBT-PD: the downward arrow technique for excavating the belief hierarchy, Socratic questioning and evidence examination in their adapted form for personality disorder, the Historical Review Method for dismantling the developmental evidence base of core beliefs, the Positive Data Log as an attention-retraining tool, schema-specific thought records, and the full five-stage behavioural experiment protocol with safety behaviour analysis. From MBT: the identification and management of the three pre-mentalising modes (psychic equivalence, teleological mode, and pretend mode), the Stop-Rewind-Explore technique for restoring mentalising after breakdown, the mentalising of the emotional chain, the use of the therapeutic relationship as a live mentalising arena with transparent clinician disclosure, and the affect reconnection approach for Detachment-dominant presentations. The integration of all three modalities within a flexible, formulation-driven, clinically responsive framework — with MBT monitoring the process conditions, SFT addressing the emotional core, and CBT-PD consolidating the belief architecture — is the hallmark of Phase Three within the IPTF. The chapter that follows addresses Phase Four: Consolidation and Preparation for Stage 3.

Chapter 14

Phase Four: Consolidation and Preparation for Stage 3

Overview of Phase Four

Phase Four is the closing movement of Stage 2, typically spanning six to eight sessions. Its purpose is threefold: to consolidate the therapeutic gains of Phases One through Three, to prepare the patient for the transition to Stage 3, and to manage the emotional dynamics of the transition, which can include a complex mixture of hope, anxiety, pride, and grief. The consolidation phase is not a winding-down; it is a critical therapeutic phase in its own right, because it is the phase in which the scattered insights, emotional shifts, and behavioural changes of Stage 2 are drawn together into a coherent narrative of change that the patient can carry forward into the life-building work of Stage 3.

Reviewing and Updating the Schema Map

The first task of Phase Four is to return to the Schema Map constructed in Phase Two and to review it in light of the therapeutic work that has been done. The clinician and patient examine each schema, each mode, and each coping strategy on the map and assess the degree of change that has occurred. Some schemas will have been significantly modified: the core belief may have shifted from absolute conviction to acknowledged tendency, the emotional charge may have reduced, and the coping strategies may have been replaced by more adaptive alternatives. Other schemas may remain active, though perhaps less dominant than they were at the start of Stage 2. The clinician and patient update the map accordingly, noting which schemas have changed, which remain, and which may need continued attention in Stage 3. The updated map provides a visual record of therapeutic progress that is immensely validating for the patient, because it makes the change visible.

The Stage 2 Relapse Prevention Plan

The second task is the construction of a Stage 2-specific relapse prevention plan that addresses the risk of schema reactivation. The plan identifies the situations, triggers, and emotional states that are most likely to reactivate the patient's core schemas; the early warning signs of schema reactivation, including specific thoughts, feelings, body sensations, and behavioural patterns; the specific coping strategies to be deployed at each level of reactivation, drawing upon both the Stage 1 skills and the Stage 2 insights; and the process for seeking support if the reactivation becomes overwhelming, including the availability of booster sessions and the re-access pathway. The plan is expressed in the patient's own language, is kept by the patient in a readily accessible format, and is reviewed with the clinician at regular intervals during Stage 3.

Preparing for Stage 3: The Shift from Understanding to Building

The transition from Stage 2 to Stage 3 represents a fundamental shift in the therapeutic conversation: from the question 'Why am I the way I am?' to the question 'Who do I want to become?' This shift can evoke a complex emotional response. Many patients experience genuine excitement about the prospect of building a meaningful life beyond therapy. But many also experience anxiety about their capacity to sustain the gains outside the therapeutic relationship, grief about the reduction in therapeutic intensity that Stage 3 entails, and a disorienting sense of identity loss: 'If I am not the person in crisis, who am I?' The clinician's task is to normalise these emotions, to hold them within the mentalising stance, and to frame the transition as a collaborative decision rather than an institutional process.

The clinician prepares the patient for Stage 3 by explaining its aims and content: the focus on vocational recovery, social development, identity consolidation, and the building of a life that is aligned with the patient's values. The clinician reviews the patient's recovery goals from Section Three ('The Future') of the IPTF Formulation Worksheet, which was initially completed during the assessment, and updates them in light of the insights gained during Stage 2. The patient may find that their goals have shifted: a patient who initially wanted 'to stop self-harming and get a job' may now articulate goals that reflect a deeper understanding of what they want from life: 'to build relationships in which I can be authentic,' 'to find work that gives me a sense of purpose,' 'to become the kind of parent I never had.'

The Stage 2 Completion Assessment

The transition from Stage 2 to Stage 3 is assessed using a structured completion review that parallels the Stage 1 transition assessment described in Chapter 9. The clinician and patient review the following areas: schema modification, assessing the degree to which the core schemas have been modified and whether the residual schema activity is manageable; mode flexibility, assessing the patient's capacity to recognise their modes, to shift between them with increasing flexibility, and to access the Healthy Adult mode in response to schema activation; mentalising capacity, assessing the patient's ability to reflect on their own mental states and those of others with curiosity, complexity, and tolerance of uncertainty; and readiness for life-building, assessing the patient's motivation, confidence, and practical readiness to engage in the vocational, social, and identity work of Stage 3.

Domain	Assessment Question	Evidence
Schema Modification	Have the core schemas been significantly modified? Has the emotional charge reduced? Have alternative beliefs been developed?	
Mode Flexibility	Can the patient recognise and name their modes? Can they access the Healthy Adult in response to schema activation?	
Mentalising Capacity	Can the patient reflect on mental states with curiosity and complexity? Can they hold multiple perspectives?	
Relapse Prevention	Has a schema reactivation plan been completed? Does the patient feel confident in their ability to manage setbacks?	
Readiness for Life-Building	Has the patient articulated recovery goals? Are they motivated and practically ready for Stage 3?	
DECISION	Transition to Stage 3 / Extended Phase Three / Modified Pathway	

Chapter Summary

This chapter has described the four tasks of Phase Four: reviewing and updating the Schema Map, constructing the Stage 2 relapse prevention plan, preparing the patient for the transition to Stage 3, and conducting the Stage 2 completion assessment. Part III of this manual is now complete. Part IV provides the detailed clinician's guide to Stage 3: Functional Recovery and Identity Consolidation.

PART IV

Stage 3: Functional Recovery and Identity Consolidation

The Clinician's Guide

Chapter 15

Stage 3 Overview: Aims, Delivery Structures, and the Interface with Community Services

> *The third stage asks the hardest question of all: not 'How do I stop hurting?' and not 'Why do I keep hurting?' but 'Now that I have stopped, who do I want to be?'*
>
> — Jayden Josh James, 2026

The Purpose of Stage 3

Stage 3 of the Integrated Personality Treatment Framework addresses the dimension of personality disorder recovery that is most frequently neglected in clinical practice: the translation of psychological change into a meaningful, functional, and sustainable lived reality. Many patients achieve significant reductions in self-harm and emotional crisis through Stages 1 and 2, and many develop genuine insight into the schemas and relational patterns that have maintained their difficulties. Yet these achievements, however real, do not automatically produce a life worth living. The patient who no longer self-harms but who remains unemployed, socially isolated, and without a coherent sense of who they are and what they want from life has been treated but not recovered. Stage 3 exists to bridge this gap.

The primary aim of Stage 3 is to support the patient in translating the psychological changes achieved in the preceding stages into sustained improvements in four domains of everyday life: vocational engagement, including employment, education, and meaningful occupation; social connection, including the development and maintenance of supportive relationships outside the therapeutic context; identity consolidation, including the construction of a coherent, positive, and flexible sense of self that is no longer defined by crisis, diagnosis, or dysfunction; and daily functioning, including the establishment of routines, self-care habits, and practical life skills that provide the structure within which recovery is sustained.

The Clinical Content of Stage 3

The clinical content of Stage 3 is the most eclectic of the three stages, drawing upon all three therapeutic traditions and upon additional approaches from occupational therapy, social prescribing, vocational rehabilitation, and Acceptance and Commitment Therapy. Behavioural experiments from CBT-PD support the patient in testing their capacity to engage in new activities, relationships, and roles. Interpersonal effectiveness skills from DBT support the patient in managing the relational challenges of re-entering the social world. Mentalisation practice supports the patient in navigating the complex interpersonal dynamics of the workplace, the classroom, and the community. Schema-focused work continues to address the schemas of Failure, Defectiveness, and Social Isolation that may emerge, sometimes with renewed intensity, as the patient attempts to build a new life beyond the therapy room. Values clarification, drawn from Acceptance and Commitment Therapy (Hayes, Strosahl, and Wilson, 2012), provides the framework for identity work: helping the patient to identify what matters to them and to align their behaviour with their values rather than with their schemas.

Delivery Structures and Reduced Intensity

Stage 3 is typically delivered at a reduced intensity compared to Stages 1 and 2. Weekly individual sessions may reduce to fortnightly and then to monthly as the patient develops the independence and self-efficacy to manage their life with decreasing therapeutic support. Group-based social and vocational activities may supplement individual sessions, providing structured opportunities for the patient to practise their skills in a supported social context. The reduced intensity is not a sign that the therapeutic work is less important; it is a deliberate clinical strategy that enacts the fifth active ingredient, agency and self-efficacy, by progressively transferring the locus of control from the therapy to the patient.

The interface between the IPTF and external services is particularly important at Stage 3. The clinician functions not only as a therapist but as a broker and coordinator, facilitating the patient's engagement with vocational rehabilitation services such as Individual Placement and Support, social prescribing services, community organisations, peer support networks, educational institutions, and housing and welfare services. The clinician's role at this stage is to support the patient in navigating the systems that can provide the practical infrastructure for sustained recovery, and to address, through the therapeutic lens of the IPTF, the schema-related barriers that may emerge as the patient engages with these systems.

The Existential Challenge of Stage 3

One of the most important and most underappreciated challenges of Stage 3 is the existential disorientation that many patients experience when the crisis and chaos that have defined their lives for years or decades begin to recede. For the patient whose identity has been organised around being the person in crisis, the person who self-harms, the person who cannot cope, the absence of crisis creates a vacuum: 'If I am not the person in crisis, who am I?' This is not a trivial question. It is a profound identity challenge that, if not addressed, can lead to a paradoxical return to crisis behaviour, not because the patient lacks skills but because the crisis provided a structure, a purpose, and an identity that the recovered life has not yet replaced.

Stage 3 addresses this challenge directly through the identity consolidation work described in Chapter 17. The therapeutic task is to help the patient construct a new narrative of self that integrates their past, including the suffering and the survival, with their present capacities and their future aspirations. The patient is not asked to forget or to deny their history; they are asked to enlarge the story, to include not only the chapters of trauma and dysfunction but the chapters of resilience, courage, and growth that their engagement with the IPTF represents.

Chapter Summary

This chapter has provided the operational overview of Stage 3, covering its aims across the four recovery domains, its eclectic clinical content, its reduced-intensity delivery structure, its interface with community services, and the existential challenge of post-crisis identity. The chapters that follow provide the detailed clinical guidance for each dimension of Stage 3, beginning with vocational recovery in Chapter 16.

The Four Recovery Domains in Detail

Domain One: Vocational Engagement

Vocational engagement encompasses paid employment, education, volunteering, and any form of meaningful occupation that provides structure, purpose, social contact, financial independence, and a sense of competence. For many patients with personality disorder, the vocational domain has been devastated by years of crisis-driven withdrawal, abrupt departures from jobs and courses, and the accumulation of gaps, failures, and abandoned projects that confirm the Failure schema. Stage 3 addresses this domain through the structured three-phase process described in Chapter 16: assessment of vocational history and schema-related barriers, preparation through Cope Ahead and practical planning, and graduated engagement through behavioural experiments.

Domain Two: Social Connection

Social isolation is one of the most pervasive and most treatment-resistant features of personality disorder. The patient who has achieved emotional stability and schema modification may nevertheless lack the social network, the relational skills, or the confidence to build meaningful connections outside the therapeutic relationship. Stage 3 addresses social isolation through graduated social engagement, supported by the interpersonal effectiveness skills learned in Stage 1 and the mentalising capacity developed in Stage 2. The clinician facilitates referral to social prescribing services, community organisations, peer support networks, and group-based activities that provide structured opportunities for social contact.

Domain Three: Identity Consolidation

Identity disturbance, the chronic sense of emptiness and the markedly unstable self-image, does not resolve automatically when symptoms improve. Stage 3 addresses this through two complementary approaches: narrative identity construction, in which the patient expands their life story beyond the schema-dominated narrative to include chapters of resilience and growth; and values clarification, drawn from Acceptance and Commitment Therapy, in which the patient identifies what matters to them across life domains and aligns their behaviour with their values rather than with their schemas.

Domain Four: Daily Functioning

The practical infrastructure of daily life, including self-care routines, financial management, housing stability, physical health, and the mundane but essential habits that provide structure, is often severely disrupted in chronic personality disorder. Stage 3 addresses daily functioning through the establishment of sustainable routines, supported where necessary by liaison with housing services, welfare advice, and primary care. The clinician should not assume that patients possess the practical life skills that many people take for granted; years of crisis-driven existence may have prevented the development of skills such as budgeting, cooking, managing correspondence, and maintaining a household.

The Clinician's Changing Role in Stage 3

In Stage 1, the clinician functions primarily as a skills teacher and crisis manager. In Stage 2, the clinician functions primarily as a therapeutic explorer and formulator. In Stage 3, the clinician's role shifts again: they become a facilitator, coordinator, and coach, supporting the patient in navigating the systems and relationships that constitute their recovering life. This shift requires a different clinical posture. The Stage 3 clinician asks fewer questions and offers more encouragement. They celebrate incremental achievements that might seem modest from the outside but represent enormous steps for a patient who has spent years in crisis. They resist the temptation to do things for the patient and instead support the patient in doing things for themselves, because agency and self-efficacy, the fifth active ingredient, is the mechanism through which the therapeutic gains are sustained after treatment ends.

Chapter 16

Vocational Recovery and Graduated Engagement

> ▶ **PATIENT PERSPECTIVE:** *'I had not worked in six years. The thought of going to an interview made me physically sick. My therapist said, "Let us not start with an interview. Let us start with a walk past the building." That was the first step. The next step was a cup of tea in the reception. Then a volunteer shift. Then a supported placement. Now I am six months into a paid job, and last week my manager said she was glad I was on the team. I cried in the car park. Not because I was sad, but because for the first time*

in my life someone at work thought I was good enough.' — Composite patient testimony

The Vocational Dimension of Recovery

Vocational engagement, encompassing paid employment, education, volunteering, and other forms of meaningful occupation, is one of the most powerful predictors of sustained recovery from personality disorder. Employment and education provide structure, purpose, social contact, financial independence, and a sense of competence and contribution that no amount of therapeutic work can replicate. Yet the vocational dimension is routinely neglected in personality disorder treatment, in part because clinicians may assume that vocational goals are premature for patients with complex needs, and in part because the interface between psychological therapy and vocational rehabilitation services is poorly developed in many NHS settings.

The IPTF challenges this neglect by positioning vocational recovery as an integral component of the treatment rather than an afterthought. Stage 3 addresses the vocational dimension through a structured three-phase process: assessment, preparation, and graduated engagement.

Phase One: Vocational Assessment

The vocational assessment explores the patient's vocational history, current aspirations, practical barriers, and schema-related obstacles. The clinician explores previous employment and educational experiences, attending to the pattern of engagement and disengagement: for many patients with personality disorder, vocational history shows a characteristic pattern of promising starts followed by relational conflicts, crises, or abrupt departures that reflect the interpersonal and emotional difficulties addressed in Stages 1 and 2. The clinician helps the patient to understand this pattern through their schema profile. The patient with an Abandonment schema may have left multiple jobs in anticipation of being fired, interpreting routine feedback as evidence of imminent rejection. The patient with a Defectiveness schema may have experienced chronic imposter syndrome, undermining their performance with the conviction that they would inevitably be exposed as incompetent. The patient with a Subjugation schema may have tolerated exploitative working conditions without complaint, building resentment until they left explosively. Understanding the schema-vocational connection enables the patient to anticipate and prepare for the specific challenges they are likely to encounter as they re-enter the vocational world.

The assessment also identifies the patient's strengths, skills, interests, and values. Many patients with personality disorder have significant skills and talents that have been obscured by their difficulties: the patient who survived a chaotic childhood has resilience; the patient who navigated the mental health system has perseverance; the patient who managed complex relational dynamics, however dysfunctionally, has interpersonal intelligence. The vocational assessment makes these strengths visible and positions them as assets for the vocational plan.

Phase Two: Vocational Preparation

Vocational preparation involves addressing the practical and psychological barriers to vocational engagement before the patient enters the vocational environment. Practical barriers may include gaps in the curriculum vitae, lack of recent references, outdated qualifications, or unfamiliarity with job search processes. The clinician works with the patient to address these barriers, drawing upon vocational rehabilitation services, educational institutions, and employment support organisations where available.

Psychological preparation involves using the Cope Ahead skill from Stage 1 and the schema awareness from Stage 2 to anticipate and plan for the specific psychological challenges that vocational engagement is likely to provoke. The clinician and patient identify the situations that are most likely to activate the patient's schemas in the vocational context, for example receiving critical feedback, working in a team, dealing with authority figures, managing performance anxiety, and for each situation they develop a specific plan: which schema is likely to be activated, what the schema-driven response would be, and what the Healthy Adult alternative response looks like.

Phase Three: Graduated Engagement

Graduated engagement builds vocational confidence incrementally through a series of steps, each of which is framed as a behavioural experiment testing a schema-generated prediction. The graduation typically follows a progression: voluntary work or taster sessions provide a low-stakes entry point; structured day programmes or supported employment placements provide more sustained engagement with professional support; part-time work or education provides independent engagement at a manageable intensity; and full-time engagement represents the end goal for patients who seek it. Each step is preceded by a Cope Ahead plan, accompanied by between-session processing with the clinician, and followed by a debrief that examines what happened, what schema was activated, what the patient did in response, and what was learned.

The interface with Individual Placement and Support (IPS) services is particularly valuable at this stage. IPS is an evidence-based model of supported employment that places the patient in competitive employment as quickly as possible and then provides ongoing support to maintain the placement, rather than requiring the patient to achieve 'work readiness' before entering employment. The IPS model aligns well with the IPTF's philosophy of learning through experience rather than waiting for readiness, and IPTF clinicians are encouraged to develop working relationships with local IPS services.

◆ CLINICAL PEARL

The most common clinical error in vocational recovery work is moving too slowly. Clinicians who work with personality disorder patients often develop a protective instinct that leads them to delay vocational engagement until the patient is 'ready,' a state of readiness that may never arrive because the schemas that generate vocational anxiety can only be disconfirmed through vocational experience. The IPTF encourages a 'bold but supported' approach: encourage the patient to take the next vocational step as soon as it is achievable, not as soon as it is comfortable, and provide the therapeutic support needed to process the schema activations that the step will generate.

Chapter Summary

This chapter has described the three-phase vocational recovery process: assessment of vocational history, strengths, and schema-related barriers; preparation addressing practical and psychological obstacles; and graduated engagement through a series of behavioural experiments. The chapter that follows addresses the social and identity dimensions of Stage 3 recovery.

Chapter 17

Social Recovery, Relational Development, and Identity Consolidation

Social Recovery and Relational Development

Social isolation is one of the most pervasive and most enduring features of chronic personality disorder. The patient who has achieved emotional stability and schema modification may nevertheless lack the social network, the relational skills, or the confidence to build meaningful connections outside the therapeutic relationship. For many patients, the therapist is the only person in their life who understands them, and the prospect of finding that understanding elsewhere can feel both desperately desired and impossibly daunting.

Stage 3 addresses social recovery through a structured process that parallels the vocational recovery described in Chapter 16. The clinician begins with a social network assessment, using the Relationship Map exercise introduced in Block Four of Stage 1 and updated at the start of Stage 3. The map identifies the patient's current relationships, including their quality, frequency, and the role each relationship plays; the relationships the patient wishes to develop; the relationships the patient wishes to limit or end; and the gaps in the patient's social network that leave them vulnerable to isolation. From this assessment, the clinician and patient develop a social recovery plan that specifies relational goals, anticipated schema obstacles, and the specific interpersonal skills that will be needed.

The social recovery plan is implemented through graduated social engagement, mirroring the graduated vocational engagement of Chapter 16. Social prescribing and community activities provide structured opportunities that bridge the therapeutic and social worlds: community groups, classes, volunteering, peer support networks, and interest-based organisations offer contexts in which the patient can practise their interpersonal skills with the support of the therapeutic relationship as a processing space. Each social engagement is framed as a behavioural experiment: the patient identifies the schema-generated prediction, engages in the social activity, and processes the outcome with the clinician. The Mistrust/Abuse schema that predicts exploitation can be tested against the experience of a community group that proves welcoming. The Social Isolation schema that predicts exclusion can be tested against the experience of a fellow group member who invites the patient for coffee.

◆ CLINICAL PEARL

One of the most important aspects of social recovery work is helping the patient to develop a tolerance for the ambiguity and uncertainty of new relationships. Established relationships have known parameters; new relationships do not. The patient with personality disorder may interpret the normal uncertainties of developing friendships, such as unreturned messages, cancelled plans, and awkward silences, through the lens of their schemas, generating catastrophic conclusions about rejection or hostility that are not warranted by the evidence. The Check the Facts skill from Stage 1 and the mentalising capacity developed in Stage 2 are deployed continuously throughout the social recovery process.

Identity Consolidation and the Narrative Self

Identity disturbance, the chronic sense of emptiness and the markedly unstable self-image that are among personality disorder's most distinctive features, does not resolve automatically when schemas are modified and social connections are rebuilt. Identity consolidation requires dedicated therapeutic attention, and Stage 3 provides the framework for this work through two complementary approaches: narrative identity construction and values clarification.

Narrative Identity Construction

The narrative approach to identity consolidation holds that our sense of who we are is fundamentally a story we tell about ourselves, a story that selects from the vast archive of our experiences those events and qualities that we consider most defining and weaves them into a coherent narrative that connects past, present, and future. For patients with personality disorder, this narrative is typically dominated by themes of trauma, dysfunction, and failure, and it is organised by schemas that select for confirming evidence and filter out disconfirming evidence. The patient whose life narrative is 'I am a damaged person who has been hurt by everyone and who will never be able to have a normal life' is not lying; they are telling a true story. But it is not the only true story that could be told about their life.

The therapeutic task is to help the patient expand their narrative: not to deny or minimise the painful chapters, which are real and which deserve to be honoured, but to include the chapters of resilience, survival, courage, and growth that the schema-driven narrative has excluded. The clinician guides the patient through a structured narrative construction exercise: 'If your life were a book, what would the chapters be? What would you call each chapter? Which chapters are you most proud of, even if they were painful? Which chapters are you in the process of writing now? What do you want the next chapter to look like?' This exercise enables the patient to step back from the embedded, schema-driven experience of their life and to see it from the authorial perspective of someone who is constructing a story, a perspective that inherently implies agency, choice, and the possibility of a different future chapter.

Values Clarification

Values clarification, drawn from Acceptance and Commitment Therapy (Hayes, Strosahl, and Wilson, 2012), provides a complementary framework for identity work that focuses on the direction of the patient's life rather than on their past. Values are distinguished from goals: a goal is a specific, achievable endpoint, such as 'get a job' or 'make a friend'; a value is a direction of travel that can be expressed in any moment, such as 'being a person of integrity' or 'treating others with kindness.' The distinction is therapeutically important because goals can be failed, and the Failure schema will ensure that the patient notices every failure; values cannot be failed, because they describe how you want to move through the world rather than what you want to achieve, and they are available to you in every moment regardless of your circumstances.

The clinician guides the patient through a values exploration across the major life domains: relationships (what kind of friend, partner, family member do you want to be?), work and education (what kind of worker or learner do you want to be, and what kind of contribution do you want to make?), leisure and creativity (what brings you alive, and what would you do if you were not afraid?), health and self-care (how do you want to treat your body and your mind?), and community (what kind of community member do you want to be, and how do you want to contribute to the world beyond yourself?). For each domain, the patient identifies their core values and rates their current alignment with those values. The gap between values and current behaviour provides the agenda for the remaining Stage 3 work: not because the gap represents failure, but because it represents the direction of travel.

Chapter Summary

This chapter has described the social recovery process, including the social network assessment, graduated social engagement, and the management of schema activations in social contexts; and the identity consolidation process, including narrative identity construction and values clarification. The chapter that follows addresses the final phase of the IPTF: ending treatment, relapse prevention, and the planned therapeutic discharge.

Chapter 18

Ending Treatment: Relapse Prevention, Booster Sessions, and Planned Discharge

> *The ending of therapy is not the end of the relationship. It is the transformation of the relationship from one in which the therapist is present to one in which the therapist's voice has been internalised as part of the patient's own Healthy Adult. The goal of a good ending is that the patient no longer needs you, not because you have become unimportant, but because what you provided has become part of who they are.*
>
> — Jayden Josh James, 2026

The Therapeutic Significance of Endings

For patients with personality disorder, whose attachment histories are characterised by loss, abandonment, and the unpredictable termination of significant relationships, the ending of therapy is among the most therapeutically consequential events in the entire treatment. The way the ending is managed communicates a powerful relational message: either it replicates the patient's historical experience of endings that are sudden, uncontrolled, and devoid of meaning, or it provides a corrective experience of an ending that is planned, gradual, collaboratively negotiated, and invested with significance. The IPTF is committed to the latter. The ending of IPTF treatment should be the best ending the patient has ever experienced, and it should provide a template for how relationships can change form without being destroyed.

The IPTF recommends that the ending be discussed explicitly from the very beginning of Stage 3. This may seem premature, but it serves two important functions: it normalises the ending as part of the therapeutic process rather than as an unexpected loss, and it gives the patient time to process their feelings about the ending, to raise concerns, and to work with the clinician on the specific schema activations that the prospect of ending may generate. The Abandonment schema in particular is likely to be activated by the prospect of losing the therapeutic relationship, and the therapeutic work of processing this activation, of recognising the schema, checking the facts, and developing a Healthy Adult response to the loss, is itself some of the most important work of Stage 3.

The Graduated Frequency Reduction

The IPTF recommends a graduated reduction in session frequency across Stage 3, from weekly at the start to fortnightly in the middle phase to monthly in the final phase. This graduated reduction serves a dual purpose: it builds the patient's capacity for independent self-management by progressively increasing the intervals between therapeutic contacts, and it provides a controlled, predictable experience of increasing separation that parallels the developmental process by which a securely attached child gradually extends their exploratory radius from the secure base of the caregiver. Each step down in frequency is discussed with the patient in advance, agreed collaboratively, and processed therapeutically. The clinician checks: 'How did it feel going two weeks between sessions? What was the hardest moment? What did you do? What does it tell you about your capacity to manage?' The patient's experience of successfully managing longer intervals between sessions is itself evidence of recovery, and the clinician names it as such.

The Comprehensive Relapse Prevention Plan

The relapse prevention plan is the final clinical document of the IPTF treatment, constructed collaboratively over the closing sessions of Stage 3 and retained by the patient as a permanent personal resource. It is a more comprehensive and more personalised version of the safety plan developed in Stage 1 and the schema reactivation plan developed in Stage 2, integrating material from all three stages into a single, holistic plan for maintaining recovery.

The relapse prevention plan includes the following components. Personal early warning signs: the specific thoughts, feelings, body sensations, and behavioural patterns that indicate the patient's schemas are being reactivated or their emotional regulation is deteriorating. These should be expressed in the patient's own language and should include both obvious signs, such as increased self-harm urges, and subtle signs, such as withdrawing from social contact or neglecting self-care, that may precede the more obvious ones. Vulnerability factors: the specific life circumstances, stressors, and situations that increase the patient's vulnerability to relapse, including sleep disruption, substance use, relationship conflict, bereavement, anniversaries of traumatic events, and periods of transition or uncertainty. Stage-specific coping strategies: a hierarchical list of coping strategies drawn from all three stages of the IPTF, organised by the level of distress at which each is most appropriate. For mild distress, the patient might use mindfulness, values-based action, or social contact; for moderate distress, they might use emotion regulation skills, Check the Facts, or opposite action; for high distress, they might use TIP, the Distress Tolerance Plan, or contact with a support person; for crisis-level distress, they use the crisis plan and contact the crisis team. Support network: named individuals and services that the patient can contact for support at each level of need, including friends, family, community organisations, their general practitioner, and the crisis team. Re-access pathway: the specific process for re-accessing the IPTF service if the patient's difficulties escalate beyond their capacity to self-manage, including the criteria for re-referral and the availability of booster sessions.

Booster Sessions

The IPTF recommends a planned schedule of booster sessions following the end of formal treatment, typically at three-monthly intervals for the first twelve months post-discharge. Booster sessions serve three functions: they provide a scheduled contact point that prevents the patient from feeling abandoned by the service, which is particularly important for patients with Abandonment schemas; they provide an opportunity to review the relapse prevention plan and to address any emerging difficulties before they escalate; and they provide data on the sustainability of the therapeutic gains, which contributes to the evidence base for the IPTF. Booster sessions are brief, typically thirty to forty-five minutes, and are focused on reviewing current functioning, checking the relapse prevention plan, and addressing any specific concerns. They are not a resumption of therapy; they are a maintenance intervention.

The Final Session

The final formal session of the IPTF treatment is a planned and structured event that honours the significance of what the patient has achieved. The session includes a collaborative review of the therapeutic journey, using the IPTF Formulation Worksheet as a guide: revisiting 'The Now' from the original assessment and comparing it with the patient's current presentation; revisiting 'The Why' and reflecting on how the understanding developed in Stage 2 has changed the patient's relationship with their history; and revisiting 'The Future' and affirming the patient's recovery goals and values. The session also includes a mutual exchange of feedback: the clinician shares what they have valued about the therapeutic relationship and what they have learned from working with the patient, and the patient shares what was most and least helpful about the treatment.

> **Therapist Script:** *'I want to take a moment to acknowledge what you have done over the past [duration]. When you first came to see me, you were [brief reference to presenting difficulties from The Now]. Today, you are [brief reference to current functioning]. That change did not happen because of anything I did. It happened because you had the courage to stay, to do the work, to face the things that were hardest to face, and to keep going even when it felt impossible. The skills you have learned, the understanding you have gained, and the life you are building are yours. They do not belong to this therapy; they belong to you, and you will take them with you. I want you to know that if things get difficult in the future, and they probably will because life is difficult, you are not on your own. You have your plan, you have your support network, and you have the booster sessions. But most importantly, you have yourself, a self that is stronger, wiser, and more compassionate than the self that walked through my door [duration] ago.'*

The session concludes with the clinician presenting the patient with a copy of their completed IPTF Formulation Worksheet, encompassing all three sections, and with the relapse prevention plan. For some patients, a certificate of completion may be appropriate, particularly if the patient's history includes experiences of educational failure or exclusion that make formal recognition of achievement therapeutically meaningful.

> **◆ CLINICAL PEARL**
>
> Do not underestimate the emotional impact of the final session on yourself as the clinician. Working with a patient through the full IPTF pathway, from crisis and chaos through understanding and modification to recovery and life-building, is one of the most rewarding experiences in clinical practice, and the ending can evoke grief in the therapist as well as in the patient. Process your own feelings

about the ending in supervision or in your consultation team. You have been a significant figure in this patient's life, and their departure is a loss for you too, even as it is a celebration of their growth.

Chapter Summary

This chapter has described the final phase of the IPTF treatment: the therapeutic significance of endings, the graduated frequency reduction, the comprehensive relapse prevention plan, the booster session schedule, and the structure and content of the final session. Part IV of this manual is now complete.

PART V

Specialist Adaptations

Chapter 19

The IPTF in Forensic Settings: Adapting the Framework for the OPD Pathway

The Forensic Context

The Offender Personality Disorder (OPD) Pathway, jointly commissioned by NHS England and His Majesty's Prison and Probation Service, represents the United Kingdom's primary framework for addressing personality disorder within the criminal justice system. As described in Chapter 13 of the parent textbook, the OPD Pathway provides a continuum of personality-disorder-informed services across prisons, approved premises, and the community, ranging from awareness training for frontline staff through to specialist treatment programmes delivered within Psychologically Informed Planned Environments (PIPEs). The IPTF is designed to be compatible with the OPD Pathway, and this chapter provides the specific adaptations required to deliver the framework within forensic settings.

Key Adaptations for Forensic Delivery

Adapting Stage 1 for the Prison Environment

The delivery of Stage 1 within a prison setting requires adaptations to account for the constraints of the custodial environment and the specific presentations prevalent in forensic populations. The skills group may need to be delivered in shorter sessions to accommodate prison regime timetables, and the between-session practice assignments must be adapted for the limitations of the cellular environment. Telephone coaching is not feasible in most prison settings and should be replaced with written coaching cards that the patient can consult independently, or with brief between-session contact with a trained wing officer who can prompt skill use during acute distress. The treatment hierarchy requires adaptation to include offence-related behaviours alongside self-harm and suicidality: violent behaviour towards others, institutional rule-breaking that jeopardises the patient's progression, and offence-paralleling behaviours that replicate the relational dynamics of the index offence are all treatment targets within the forensic IPTF.

Adapting Stage 2 for Dissocial and Antisocial Presentations

Forensic personality disorder presentations frequently include prominent Dissociality trait domain elevations, encompassing callousness, manipulativeness, deceitfulness, and hostility, alongside or instead of the Negative Affectivity and Disinhibition that predominate in community presentations. The Stage 2 schema work must be adapted to address the schemas characteristic of dissocial presentations, which may include Entitlement, Mistrust/Abuse, and Insufficient Self-Control rather than the Abandonment and Defectiveness schemas more common in Borderline presentations. Imagery rescripting with forensic patients requires particular attention to the risk of retraumatisation, particularly where the patient has both experienced and perpetrated violence, and the clinician must be prepared to work with the complex moral and emotional terrain of a patient who is simultaneously a survivor and a perpetrator.

Multi-Agency Working and Risk Management

The IPTF in forensic settings operates within a multi-agency framework that includes the prison establishment, the probation service, the OPD Pathway team, and, where applicable, Multi-Agency Public Protection Arrangements (MAPPA). The IPTF clinician must integrate the therapeutic aims of the framework with the risk management requirements of the criminal justice system, maintaining transparency with the patient about the limits of confidentiality and the circumstances under which information will be shared with other agencies. The formulation-based approach to risk assessment that the IPTF employs, using the Schema Map to understand the cognitive and relational patterns that underpin offending behaviour, is compatible with the structured professional judgement approach to risk assessment required by MAPPA.

Adapting the Treatment Agreement for Custodial Settings

The IPTF Treatment Agreement requires significant adaptation for delivery within prison establishments. The standard agreement assumes that the patient has freedom of movement, access to telephone contact, and the ability to practise skills in an environment of their choosing. None of these assumptions holds in a custodial setting. The adapted agreement should specify the arrangements for session scheduling within the prison regime timetable, including contingency plans for regime lockdowns that prevent the patient from attending; the alternative to telephone coaching, which may include written coaching cards, brief wing-based check-ins with a trained prison officer, or a designated 'listener' on the wing; the confidentiality arrangements, including explicit statements about what information will and will not be shared with the prison establishment, the probation service, and MAPPA; and the management of institutional transfers, which can disrupt treatment unexpectedly and for which a transfer protocol should be in place.

Working with Antisocial and Dissocial Presentations

The schema profile of the forensic personality disorder patient frequently differs from the community presentation. Where community patients typically present with prominent Abandonment, Defectiveness, and Emotional Deprivation schemas, forensic patients may present with prominent Mistrust/Abuse, Entitlement, and Insufficient Self-Control schemas, reflecting developmental histories characterised by exploitation, violence, and the absence of consistent external boundaries. The Stage 2 schema work with these patients requires the clinician to maintain the mentalising stance whilst addressing the specific cognitive and relational patterns that underpin offending behaviour: the Mistrust/Abuse schema that interprets benign interactions as threatening and generates pre-emptive aggression; the Entitlement schema that overrides the rights and feelings of others; and the Insufficient Self-Control schema that produces impulsive, consequence-blind behaviour.

Imagery rescripting with forensic patients presents particular challenges. The patient may have both experienced and perpetrated violence, creating a complex moral and emotional landscape in which the clinician must hold the dual reality that the patient is both a survivor of trauma and a perpetrator of harm. The rescripting protocol should not be modified to avoid the patient's offending behaviour; rather, it should be used to explore the developmental origins of the schemas that drive the offending, whilst the clinician maintains clear moral boundaries about the unacceptability of the behaviour itself. The schema explains the behaviour; it does not excuse it. Both things must be held simultaneously.

> **◆ CLINICAL PEARL**
>
> Working with forensic patients requires explicit attention to your own countertransference. The patient who has committed acts of serious violence

may activate your own threat schemas, disgust responses, or moral condemnation. These responses are natural and do not make you a bad therapist; they make you a human being. The consultation team is the essential support structure for processing these reactions. A therapist who is unable to acknowledge their countertransference to a forensic patient will either unconsciously withdraw from the therapeutic relationship or overcompensate with excessive warmth that the patient will immediately detect as inauthentic.

Risk Management Within the IPTF

The IPTF in forensic settings operates within a multi-agency risk management framework. The clinician must integrate the therapeutic aims of the framework with the risk management requirements of the criminal justice system, maintaining transparency with the patient about the limits of confidentiality. The IPTF formulation, particularly the Schema Map, provides a clinically rich contribution to the risk assessment process: it explains not just what the patient did but why, in terms of the schema activations, mode shifts, and coping strategy failures that produced the offending behaviour. This formulation-based approach to risk assessment aligns with the structured professional judgement model and provides a more nuanced and more useful contribution to MAPPA than a checklist-based risk tool alone.

Chapter Summary

This chapter has described the key adaptations required to deliver the IPTF within forensic settings, including modifications to Stage 1 for the prison environment, adaptations to Stage 2 for dissocial and antisocial presentations, and the multi-agency working framework within which the forensic IPTF operates.

Chapter 20

The IPTF and Neurodiversity: Detailed Adaptations for Autistic Individuals and Those with ADHD

The Neurodiversity-Personality Disorder Overlap

As described in Chapter 14 of the parent textbook, the overlap between neurodevelopmental conditions, specifically Autism Spectrum Condition (ASC) and Attention Deficit Hyperactivity Disorder (ADHD), and personality disorder is one of the most significant diagnostic and therapeutic challenges in contemporary mental health practice. The clinical features shared between these conditions, including emotional dysregulation, interpersonal difficulties, identity disturbance, and impulsive behaviour, can result in diagnostic overshadowing, with one condition being misidentified as the other, or in the co-occurrence of both conditions being missed entirely. The IPTF clinician must be alert to the possibility of neurodevelopmental co-occurrence and must adapt the framework accordingly when it is present.

Stage-by-Stage Adaptations for Autistic Patients

Stage 1 Adaptations

The Stage 1 skills group requires several adaptations for Autistic patients. The sensory environment of the group room should be assessed and modified: fluorescent lighting should be replaced with softer lighting where possible, background noise should be minimised, strong scents should be avoided, and the patient should be permitted to use sensory regulation tools such as fidget items, weighted blankets, or noise-reducing headphones. The session structure should be communicated in advance, in writing, with explicit notice of any changes, because unexpected alterations to routine can be profoundly destabilising for Autistic individuals. The language used in skills teaching should be concrete and specific rather than metaphorical and abstract: the mindfulness instruction 'let your thoughts float away like clouds' may be confusing for an Autistic patient who processes language literally, whilst the instruction 'notice each thought, label it as a thought, and return your attention to your breathing' achieves the same purpose with greater clarity. The interoception difficulties common in autism, specifically the difficulty in identifying and interpreting internal body signals, require modified approaches to emotion identification: beginning with external sensory observations and building gradually towards internal awareness, rather than assuming that the patient can readily identify bodily correlates of emotional states.

Stage 2 Adaptations

The imagery rescripting and chair work techniques of Stage 2 may require adaptation for Autistic patients. Some Autistic individuals find imaginative visualisation difficult and may benefit from concrete visual aids, such as photographs, drawings, or written descriptions, to support the imagery process. Chair work may need to be adapted to address the specific mode presentations characteristic of autistic personality disorder: the Detached Protector mode in Autistic patients may represent autistic shutdown rather than schema-driven emotional withdrawal, and the clinician must distinguish between these presentations to ensure that the intervention addresses the correct mechanism. The mentalising stance of Stage 2 must account for the Autistic patient's cognitive empathy profile: Autistic individuals may have difficulty in spontaneously reading others' mental states but may develop sophisticated mentalising capacity through explicit cognitive routes when these are taught systematically.

Stage 3 Adaptations

The vocational and social recovery work of Stage 3 requires particular attention to the interface between personality-related difficulties and neurodevelopmental needs. The Autistic patient's vocational plan should account for sensory sensitivities in the workplace, the need for clear and explicit communication from managers, the potential for masking fatigue in social work environments, and the possibility that conventional employment structures may need to be adapted. Social recovery work should distinguish between the social isolation that arises from schema-driven avoidance and the social preference that may reflect an Autistic individual's genuine need for solitude, ensuring that the treatment supports the patient's authentic social needs rather than imposing a neurotypical model of social engagement.

Adaptations for ADHD

Patients with co-occurring ADHD require adaptations that address the executive function difficulties, attentional variability, and emotional impulsivity characteristic of the condition. Session duration may need to be reduced, with more frequent breaks. Between-session practice assignments should be simplified, made concrete, and supported with written reminders. The diary card should be adapted to a format that minimises the executive function demands of daily completion: a simplified digital version or a brief daily text-message check-in may be more achievable than the standard paper diary card. The timing of therapy sessions should, where possible, be coordinated with the patient's stimulant medication schedule to ensure that sessions occur during periods of optimal attentional capacity. In Stage 2, the chain analysis and schema identification processes may need additional scaffolding, because the ADHD patient's attentional variability can make sustained reflective engagement more difficult.

Chapter Summary

This chapter has provided stage-by-stage adaptations of the IPTF for Autistic patients and patients with ADHD, covering sensory, communicative, cognitive, and structural modifications across all three stages.

Chapter 21

The IPTF in Primary Care and Stepped Care: Working with Personality Difficulty

Personality Difficulty: The Sub-Threshold Presentation

The ICD-11 category of Personality Difficulty describes individuals who display some features of personality dysfunction that cause problems in daily living but that do not meet the threshold for a formal personality disorder diagnosis. These individuals are commonly encountered in primary care psychological therapy services, where they may present with anxiety, depression, or relationship difficulties that are underpinned by personality-related patterns but that do not warrant referral to specialist personality disorder services. The IPTF's modular design permits a scaled-down intervention for this population, delivered within the resource constraints of primary care settings.

The IPTF Brief Intervention for Personality Difficulty

The brief intervention is a structured, twelve-to-sixteen-session programme that draws upon Stage 1 skills and selected elements of Stage 2 formulation. It includes a brief assessment using the SAPAS and a simplified IPTF formulation focusing on the patient's predominant patterns and their impact on current functioning; a skills-focused intervention covering core mindfulness, distress tolerance, and emotion regulation skills, delivered in individual sessions or in a brief group format; a brief formulation exercise in which the clinician and patient identify one or two core patterns connecting early experience to current difficulties, using a simplified version of the Schema Map; and a relapse prevention plan identifying the patient's vulnerability factors and coping strategies. The brief intervention is not intended as a treatment for moderate to severe personality disorder but may serve as a sufficient intervention for personality difficulty, as a preparatory intervention for patients who are waiting for specialist services, or as a maintenance intervention for patients who have completed the full IPTF pathway and require periodic support.

Chapter Summary

This chapter has described the scaled-down IPTF intervention for personality difficulty in primary care settings, including the brief assessment, the skills-focused intervention, the simplified formulation, and the relapse prevention plan.

Chapter 22

The IPTF with Adolescents and Young Adults: Developmental Adaptations

The Case for Early Intervention

As discussed in Chapter 12 of the parent textbook, the diagnosis and treatment of personality disorder in adolescents is one of the most ethically complex areas in contemporary mental health practice. The tension between the imperative for early intervention, supported by evidence that personality pathology is identifiable in adolescence and that earlier treatment produces better outcomes, and the risk of premature labelling, which may stigmatise a young person with a diagnosis that was historically considered permanent and untreatable, is real and must be navigated with care. The IPTF's position is that the ICD-11 dimensional model, with its severity continuum and its emphasis on patterns rather than labels, provides a framework within which personality-related difficulties in adolescents can be identified and treated without the categorical labelling that carries the greatest risk of harm.

Developmental Adaptations Across the Three Stages

Stage 1: Skills for Young People

The Stage 1 skills curriculum requires adaptation for the sixteen-to-twenty-five age group. Session length should be reduced to sixty to ninety minutes, with more frequent breaks and more active, participatory exercises. The language of the skills teaching should be adapted to use age-appropriate vocabulary and culturally relevant examples, drawing upon the young person's own interests, social media use, and peer culture. The skills group format may be adapted to include mixed-modality delivery, combining face-to-face sessions with digital resources, app-based practice reminders, and brief video demonstrations of skills. Family involvement should be considered: the IPTF recommends a parallel family psychoeducation programme that helps parents and carers to understand the young person's difficulties, to support skill use at home, and to modify their own relational patterns where these contribute to the maintenance of the young person's difficulties.

Stage 2: Age-Appropriate Schema Work

Stage 2 with adolescents requires particular sensitivity to the developmental reality that identity formation is a normative adolescent task, not a pathological one. The clinician must distinguish between the identity disturbance that is a feature of personality disorder and the identity exploration that is a healthy feature of adolescent development. Schema work with young people should be briefer and more action-oriented than with adults, using creative media such as art, music, and digital storytelling alongside the standard cognitive and experiential techniques. Imagery rescripting should be used with caution in this age group, with careful attention to the young person's developmental readiness for the emotional activation that the technique generates.

Stage 3: Building a Life in Transition

Stage 3 with young people addresses the developmental tasks that are specific to the transition from adolescence to adulthood: completing education, entering employment, establishing independent living, developing adult relationships, and consolidating a post-adolescent identity. The interface with educational institutions, careers services, and youth transition services is particularly important at this stage. The clinician functions as an advocate and coordinator as well as a therapist, supporting the young person in navigating the systems that will shape their adult life.

Chapter Summary

This chapter has described the developmental adaptations required to deliver the IPTF with adolescents and young adults, including age-appropriate modifications to the skills curriculum, schema work, and functional recovery process, and the involvement of families and educational institutions.

PART VI

The Client Workbook

Materials for Individuals Receiving IPTF Treatment

The following chapters are written at an accessible reading level and are designed to be photocopied for clinical use.

Chapter 23

Understanding Your Personality Difficulties: A Guide for You

This chapter is for you. It is written to help you understand what personality difficulties are, why you might have developed them, and what your treatment is designed to do. You do not need any special knowledge to read it. If anything is unclear, please ask your therapist to explain it.

✍ My Reflection Space

Use these pages as your own private space. There are no right or wrong answers. Write whatever feels true for you.

My thoughts as I start reading this chapter

....

....

....

....

....

....

Something that resonated most with me in this chapter

....

....

....

Something I want to discuss with my therapist

....

....

. . . .

My Weekly Emotional Stability Rating

Rate how emotionally stable you have felt this week on a scale of 1 (very unstable) to 10 (very stable). There is no right answer — this is just for you to notice patterns over time.

Scale: 1 — 2 — 3 — 4 — 5 — 6 — 7 — 8 — 9 — 10

Week 1 — Date: ______________ My rating: _______ One word that sums up my week: ______________________

Week 2 — Date: ______________ My rating: _______ One word that sums up my week: ______________________

Week 3 — Date: ______________ My rating: _______ One word that sums up my week: ______________________

Week 4 — Date: ______________ My rating: _______ One word that sums up my week: ______________________

Week 5 — Date: ______________ My rating: _______ One word that sums up my week: ______________________

Week 6 — Date: ______________ My rating: _______ One word that sums up my week: ______________________

Looking at these ratings over time, what do you notice? Are there patterns? Are things changing?

. . . .

. . . .

. . . .

What Are Personality Difficulties?

Everyone has a personality. Your personality is the way you think about yourself, the way you relate to other people, and the way you manage your feelings. It is shaped by your experiences, especially your early experiences with the people who looked after you when you were young.

When someone has personality difficulties, it means that some of the patterns they developed early in life — ways of thinking, feeling, and relating — are now causing them significant problems. These patterns often made sense at the time they were formed. If you grew up in an environment where people were unpredictable or unkind, learning to be on guard, to expect the worst, or to push people away before they could hurt you was a reasonable way to protect yourself. The problem is that these patterns, which were helpful then, can become unhelpful now, because they keep running even when the situation has changed.

> **An Important Message**
> Having personality difficulties does not mean there is something wrong with who you are as a person. It means that the experiences you went through shaped the way you see yourself and the world in ways that are causing you pain. These patterns were learned through experience, and they can be changed through new experience. That is what your treatment is for.

Why Did This Happen to Me?

Personality difficulties usually develop because of a combination of things. Your biology plays a part: some people are naturally more sensitive to emotions than others, which means they feel things more intensely. Your early experiences play a big part: if the people who were supposed to care for you were absent, inconsistent, frightening, or hurtful, your developing brain adapted to that environment in ways that affect how you respond to the world now. Your wider circumstances also play a part: poverty, instability, bullying, and other difficult life experiences all contribute to how your personality patterns formed.

None of this was your fault. You did not choose your biology, you did not choose your early experiences, and you did not choose the circumstances you grew up in. The patterns you developed were survival strategies, not character defects. Understanding this is the first step towards change.

What Will Treatment Involve?

Your treatment is organised into three stages, each designed to help you with a different aspect of your difficulties.

Stage 1 is about safety and skills. You will learn practical skills for managing intense emotions, surviving crises without harming yourself, and communicating more effectively with the people in your life. This stage is about getting stable — giving you the tools to manage the day-to-day challenges so that you feel safer and more in control.

Stage 2 is about understanding. Once you are more stable, you and your therapist will explore why you developed the patterns you have. You will look at your early life, identify the beliefs about yourself and others that were formed by your experiences, and work to change those beliefs. This stage can be challenging because it involves looking at painful things, but the skills you learned in Stage 1 will help you manage the emotions that come up.

Stage 3 is about building your life. The final stage is about taking everything you have learned and using it to build the kind of life you want: getting back into work or education, building relationships, discovering who you are beyond your difficulties, and making plans for the future.

You Are in Control

Your therapist will work with you, not on you. You will make decisions together about your treatment. If anything feels too much, you can say so. If you disagree with something, you can say so. Your voice matters in this process, and your experience is valued.

Chapter 24

Stage 1 Skills: Your Skills Workbook

Your Mindfulness Skills

Wise Mind

You have three states of mind. Emotion Mind is when your feelings are completely in charge — you act on impulse without thinking. Reasonable Mind is when logic is completely in charge — you analyse everything without feeling. Wise Mind is the balance between the two — you notice your feelings, consider the facts, and make a choice that fits your values. Wise Mind is always there, even when it is hard to find. It is like the stillness at the bottom of a lake, even when the surface is stormy.

The Five Senses Grounding Exercise

When you feel overwhelmed, use this exercise to bring yourself back to the present moment. Name: 5 things you can SEE. 4 things you can HEAR. 3 things you can TOUCH. 2 things you can SMELL. 1 thing you can TASTE. This works because it anchors your attention in the here-and-now through your senses, pulling you out of the spiral of distressing thoughts.

Your Distress Tolerance Skills

TIP: Temperature

When your distress is very high (8, 9, or 10 out of 10), use the Temperature skill to bring it down quickly. Fill a bowl with cold water, hold your breath, and put your face in the water for 15 to 30 seconds. This activates a natural reflex in your body (the dive reflex) that slows your heart rate and calms your nervous system. If you do not have a bowl, splash cold water on your face, hold ice cubes in your hands, or put a cold flannel across your forehead. It is not pleasant — but it works.

Paced Breathing

Breathe in through your nose for 4 counts. Hold for 1 count. Breathe out through your mouth for 6 to 8 counts. The key is making the out-breath longer than the in-breath. This activates the calming part of your nervous system. Practise this every day, even when you are not distressed, so that it becomes automatic when you need it.

Radical Acceptance

Pain is part of life. Suffering is what happens when we fight against pain that we cannot change. Radical Acceptance means accepting that something has happened, without fighting it, without judging it, and without insisting that it should be different. Acceptance does NOT mean approval. You can accept that something terrible happened AND believe it was wrong. Acceptance means stopping the war with reality so that you can use your energy to move forward.

Your Emotion Regulation Skills

Check the Facts

When you are feeling a strong emotion, check whether it fits the facts of the situation. Ask yourself: What happened? (Just the facts, not my interpretation.) What am I assuming? Am I confusing my thoughts about the situation with the actual facts? Does my emotion fit the facts, or is it responding to my assumptions? If your emotion fits the facts, honour it. If it is responding to assumptions, consider whether a different interpretation might be possible.

Opposite Action

Every emotion comes with an urge to do something. Fear urges you to avoid. Sadness urges you to withdraw. Shame urges you to hide. When the emotion does not fit the facts, or when acting on the urge will make things worse, try doing the opposite. If shame says hide — share something with someone you trust. If fear says avoid — approach what you are afraid of, gently and in small steps. If sadness says withdraw — reach out to someone or engage in an activity.

Your Interpersonal Effectiveness Skills

DEAR MAN: Asking for What You Need

Describe the situation factually. Express how you feel using 'I' statements. Assert what you want, clearly and specifically. Reinforce the benefit to the other person of giving you what you want. Stay Mindful — do not get sidetracked. Appear Confident — even if you do not feel it. Negotiate if necessary — be willing to give to get.

Chapter 25

Understanding Your Patterns: A Guide to Schema Work

What Is a Schema?

A schema is a deep belief about yourself, other people, or the world that was formed by your early experiences. Schemas are like invisible lenses that colour the way you see everything. If you grew up being told you were worthless, you may carry a schema that says 'I am defective.' This schema will make you interpret neutral situations, like a friend not replying to a text, as evidence that confirms the belief: 'See, she does not care about me. Nobody does. Because I am not worth caring about.'

Schemas feel absolutely true because they have been part of you for so long. But feeling true and being true are not the same thing. In Stage 2, you and your therapist will identify your schemas, understand where they came from, and work to change them.

What Are Schema Modes?

Modes are the emotional states you go into when your schemas are activated. Think of them as different parts of yourself. The Vulnerable Child is the part of you that feels the pain of your unmet needs: the fear, the sadness, the loneliness. The Angry Child is the part of you that protests: the rage, the indignation. The Detached Protector is the part of you that shuts down: the numbness, the withdrawal, the 'I do not care.' The Punitive Parent is the part of you that attacks yourself: the inner critic that says you are worthless, stupid, or deserve to suffer. The Healthy Adult is the part of you that can step back, see what is happening, and respond with compassion and wisdom. Your treatment aims to strengthen the Healthy Adult so that it can look after the Vulnerable Child and stand up to the Punitive Parent.

Your Schema Map

During Stage 2, you and your therapist will create a Schema Map together. This is a visual picture that shows: your core schemas (the deep beliefs), where they came from (your early experiences), what triggers them now, and how you cope with the pain they cause. Seeing this map can be a powerful moment — it is often the first time the chaos starts to make sense.

Chapter 26

Building Your Future: The Recovery Workbook

Values: What Matters to You?

Values are different from goals. A goal is something you achieve: 'get a job.' A value is a direction you travel in: 'being someone who contributes.' You can express a value in any moment, regardless of your circumstances. Even on the hardest day, you can choose to act in line with your values.

Think about what matters to you in each of these areas of life: Relationships — what kind of friend, partner, or family member do you want to be? Work and Learning — what kind of contribution do you want to make? Leisure — what brings you alive? Health — how do you want to treat yourself? Community — how do you want to relate to the wider world? Write your answers in your own words. There are no right or wrong answers.

Your Recovery Goals

Working with your therapist, write down your goals in each area: What kind of relationships do you want? What work or study would be meaningful to you? What does a good day look like? Who do you want to become?

Stage 3 is about building your future. You have learned skills to manage your emotions (Stage 1) and you have understood the patterns from your past (Stage 2). Now it is time to ask the most important question of all: what do you want your life to look like?

Exercise: Your Values Compass

Think about what matters most to you — not what other people think should matter, but what genuinely matters to you. Values are not goals. A goal is something you achieve ('get a job'). A value is a direction you travel in ('being someone who contributes'). You can express a value right now, today, regardless of your circumstances. For each area, write down what matters to you: Relationships: What kind of friend, partner, or family member do I want to be? Work and Learning: What kind of contribution do I want to make to the world? Leisure: What brings me alive? What would I do if I were not afraid? Health: How do I want to treat my body and my mind? Community: How do I want to relate to the wider world around me?

Exercise: My Recovery Goals

Working with your therapist, set specific goals in each area. Make them realistic but stretching — not so easy that they do not challenge you, and not so hard that your schemas tell you not to bother trying. Relationship goal: ____ Work/education goal: ____ Daily life goal: ____ Identity goal (who do I want to become?): ____

Exercise: My Strengths Inventory

You have survived some terrible things. That required strengths — even if you do not see them as strengths. What qualities helped you survive? What strengths have you discovered during treatment? What do other people say they value about you? My strengths: ____

____

____

Chapter 27: Your Safety Plan

Your Safety Plan

Your safety plan is a step-by-step guide for what to do when you are in distress. Fill it in with your therapist and keep it somewhere you can always find it — in your bag, on your fridge, saved as a photo on your phone.

Step 1: Warning Signs

What are the first signs that things are getting worse for me? (Specific thoughts, feelings, body sensations, or behaviours that tell me my distress is rising.)

Step 2: Things I Can Do On My Own

Skills I can use without needing anyone else: (List your best skills from Stage 1 — paced breathing, TIP, mindfulness, ACCEPTS, etc.)

Step 3: People I Can Contact

People who can help when I need support: (Names and phone numbers of friends, family, or fellow group members.)

Step 4: Professional Contacts

My therapist: ________________ My care coordinator: ________________

Crisis team: ________________

Step 5: Emergency Plan

If I am in immediate danger, I will go to my nearest A&E: ________________

Or I will call 999.

Chapter 28: Your Formulation: Understanding Your Story

Your Formulation: Understanding Your Story

Your formulation is a shared document that you and your therapist create together. It has three parts:

The Now
What is happening for me right now? My current difficulties, my current risk, and the skills I am learning to manage them. This is completed during your assessment.

The Why
Why did I develop these patterns? My early experiences, the beliefs they created, and the coping strategies I use. This is completed during Stage 2.

The Future
What do I want my life to look like? My goals, my values, and my plan for building the life I want. This is completed during Stage 3.

This formulation belongs to you as much as it belongs to your therapist. You will have your own copy to keep.

Chapter 29: Your Relapse Prevention Plan

Your Relapse Prevention Plan

As you approach the end of treatment, you and your therapist will create a relapse prevention plan. This is a document that helps you stay well after treatment ends. It includes:

My Early Warning Signs

What are the first signs that I might be slipping back into old patterns? (List specific thoughts, feelings, and behaviours.)

My Vulnerability Factors

What makes me more likely to struggle? (Poor sleep, stress, relationship conflict, anniversaries, etc.)

My Coping Plan

What will I do at each level of difficulty? Mild distress: _________ Moderate distress: _________ High distress: _________ Crisis: _________

How to Get Help Again

If I need more support, I can contact: _________ I am entitled to booster sessions at: _________

Chapter 30: Resources and Further Reading

Resources and Further Reading

Crisis Support

Samaritans: 116 123 (free, 24 hours, 7 days). SHOUT: Text 'SHOUT' to 85258 (free, 24/7 text support). NHS 111: Dial 111 for non-emergency medical advice. Your local crisis team: ask your therapist for the number and keep it in your phone.

For Further Understanding

If you wish to understand the science and theory behind your treatment in greater depth, the parent textbook to this manual is: James, J.J. (2026) The Definitive British Textbook of Personality Disorders: Science, System, and Synthesis. Liverpool: Talking Therapies UK.

PART VII

Implementation, Training, and Quality Assurance

Chapter 31

Setting Up an IPTF Service: An Implementation Guide

Service Specification

The implementation of an IPTF service requires a clear service specification that defines the target population, the referral criteria, the staffing model, the delivery configuration, and the expected throughput and outcomes. The target population for a full IPTF service is adults aged eighteen and above, or sixteen and above where adolescent adaptations are employed, who meet ICD-11 criteria for personality disorder at any severity level. Referral criteria should specify the minimum severity threshold for acceptance into the programme, typically Mild Personality Disorder or above, with sub-threshold Personality Difficulty directed to the primary care brief intervention described in Chapter 21.

Staffing and Skill-Mix

The minimum staffing for a full IPTF service delivering all three stages in the full intensive configuration includes two Stage 1 skills group facilitators, trained in DBT skills delivery and IPTF principles; at least one Stage 2 therapist, trained in schema-focused or CBT-PD approaches to personality disorder, with competence in imagery rescripting and chair work; a clinical lead with advanced training in personality disorder treatment and experience in service management; and access to a psychiatrist for diagnostic consultation, medication review, and risk management support. In the skills-focused configuration, the Stage 1 skills group facilitators may be drawn from the existing community mental health team workforce, with IPTF training provided through a structured programme, and the Stage 2 therapist may be a shared resource across multiple teams.

◆ SERVICE READINESS CHECKLIST

To be completed by the clinical lead prior to IPTF service commencement. Each item should be marked complete (✓), in progress (→), or not yet initiated (○).

SECTION A: Staffing and Workforce	
○	A minimum of two qualified Stage 1 skills group facilitators with documented DBT skills training have been identified and are available.
○	At least one Stage 2 therapist with schema therapy or CBT-PD competence, including imagery rescripting and chair work, has been confirmed. Evidence of formal training or supervised practice is documented.

○	A clinical lead with advanced personality disorder training and documented experience in service management has been appointed. Their IPTF supervisory responsibilities are clearly defined.
○	Psychiatric consultation arrangements for diagnostic review, medication management, and acute risk episodes are confirmed and documented.
SECTION B: Training and Supervision	
○	All clinical staff have completed the IPTF Foundation Training Programme (minimum 16 hours). Training records are held centrally and are current.
○	A regular, structured clinical supervision arrangement is in place for all IPTF clinicians, with minimum frequency of fortnightly for Stage 2 therapists and monthly for Stage 1 facilitators. Supervision provision is documented.
○	A peer consultation group or multi-disciplinary team meeting specifically focused on IPTF caseload is scheduled. Frequency and format are agreed.
SECTION C: Environment and Physical Resources	
○	A dedicated group room is available for Stage 1 skills group delivery, with sufficient seating for up to twelve participants, a whiteboard or flipchart, and adequate ventilation and privacy. The room is consistently bookable for weekly sessions.
○	Individual therapy rooms for Stage 2 sessions are available and are adequately private, soundproofed, and equipped with two chairs for chair work exercises. Rooms are accessible to patients with physical disabilities.
○	Client Workbook materials are printed, collated, and available for distribution at the first session. Arrangements for photocopying, storage, and replenishment of materials are in place.
SECTION D: Governance and Patient Pathway	
○	A clear referral pathway from all relevant referral sources (primary care, CMHT, crisis services, inpatient, forensic) is documented, agreed with referrers, and communicated to all parties. A named referral coordinator is in post.
○	The IPTF Treatment Agreement template has been reviewed and approved by the service's legal, information governance, and clinical governance leads. Signed agreements are stored in patient records.
○	A risk management protocol specific to IPTF patients has been developed and communicated to all clinical staff. Out-of-hours crisis contact procedures are clearly documented and accessible to patients.
○	Outcome measures (HoNOS, CORE-OM, or equivalent) are integrated into the patient pathway at baseline, mid-treatment, and discharge. Data collection processes and responsible staff are identified. Data will feed into the service's outcome reporting framework.
○	Stage 1 to Stage 2 transition criteria have been communicated to all clinical staff and are embedded in the patient's clinical record. A formal transition meeting process is scheduled and documented for each patient who completes Stage 1.
Clinical Lead sign-off: ______________________ Date: ________________ This checklist should be reviewed annually and following any significant service change. A copy should be retained in the service governance file.	

Referral Pathways and Waiting List Management

The IPTF service should establish clear referral pathways from primary care, community mental health teams, crisis services, inpatient services, and forensic services. Waiting list management should include an assessment-at-point-of-referral process using the SAPAS to prioritise referrals by severity and risk, and a waiting list intervention that offers brief psychoeducation and skills-based support to patients awaiting full assessment. The rolling entry design of the Stage 1 skills group, in which patients can join at the start of any block rather than waiting for the start of a new cycle, minimises waiting times and maximises group utilisation.

The Business Case for Commissioners

The economic case for personality disorder treatment is well established. The costs associated with untreated personality disorder, including repeated accident and emergency presentations, inpatient admissions, crisis team contacts, criminal justice involvement, and welfare dependency, substantially exceed the costs of structured psychological treatment. The IPTF's modular design and its three delivery configurations provide commissioners with a flexible, scalable investment that can be adapted to the available budget whilst delivering the evidence-based components that produce the greatest return on investment.

Workforce Planning and Skill-Mix

The workforce requirements for an IPTF service depend on the delivery configuration chosen. The following table provides the recommended minimum staffing for each configuration, based on a caseload of twenty to thirty patients at any one time.

Role	Full Intensive	Skills-Focused	Community-Adapted
Clinical Lead (Band 8a+)	1.0 WTE	0.5 WTE	0.2 WTE
Stage 1 Group Facilitators	2.0 WTE	1.0 WTE	0.5 WTE
Stage 2 Therapists	2.0 WTE	1.0 WTE	N/A
Stage 3 Practitioner	1.0 WTE	0.5 WTE	N/A
Care Coordinators	2.0 WTE	Via CMHT	Via PCN
Peer Support Worker	0.5 WTE	0.5 WTE	Optional
Admin Support	0.5 WTE	0.3 WTE	0.1 WTE

The Commissioner's Business Case

The economic argument for investing in structured personality disorder treatment is compelling. Research consistently demonstrates that untreated personality disorder generates costs across the health and social care system that substantially exceed the cost of effective treatment. A single patient with untreated borderline personality disorder typically generates annual costs of fifteen thousand to thirty thousand pounds through repeated A&E presentations, crisis team contacts, inpatient admissions, GP consultations, prescription costs, and involvement with social services and the criminal justice system (van Asselt, Dirksen, Arntz, and Severens, 2007). By contrast, the cost of delivering a full IPTF programme, including all three stages across two to three years, is estimated at eight thousand to twelve thousand pounds per patient, depending on the delivery configuration. The return on investment is realised through reductions in emergency presentations, inpatient bed-days, and crisis contacts that typically become apparent within the first twelve months of treatment.

Chapter 32

Training and Supervision: Developing IPTF Competence

Training Pathway

The IPTF training pathway is designed to build competence incrementally, beginning with foundation-level awareness training and progressing through to advanced practitioner certification. The foundation level, a two-day workshop, provides an introduction to the IPTF model, the ICD-11 dimensional framework, the five active ingredients, and the three-stage structure, and is suitable for all mental health professionals who may encounter personality disorder in their practice. The practitioner level, a five-day intensive training programme supplemented by six months of supervised practice, provides the competence to deliver Stage 1 skills groups and to contribute to Stage 2 and Stage 3 delivery under supervision. The advanced practitioner level, requiring completion of the practitioner training plus a further year of supervised practice with demonstrated competence in imagery rescripting, chair work, and the mentalising stance, provides the competence to deliver all three stages independently and to supervise others. The training curriculum should include didactic teaching, experiential skills practice, video demonstration, role-play, and, at the advanced level, supervised clinical work with real patients.

Supervision Structure

The IPTF supervision structure mirrors the DBT consultation team model described in Chapter 5, adapted for the integrated nature of the framework. Individual supervision is provided fortnightly for all IPTF practitioners, covering case discussion, technique review, and therapist wellbeing. Group supervision or consultation team meetings are provided weekly or fortnightly, following the agreements described in Chapter 5. External supervision from a clinician with advanced expertise in personality disorder treatment is recommended for new services during the first two years of implementation.

The Three-Level Training Pathway

Level One: Foundation (Two-Day Workshop)

The Foundation level provides an introduction to the IPTF model suitable for all mental health professionals. Content covers the ICD-11 dimensional model, the IPTF's three-stage structure and five active ingredients, an introduction to the formulation worksheet, an overview of the evidence base, and practical guidance on personality-informed communication. This level is appropriate for general mental health nurses, social workers, occupational therapists, support workers, and other professionals who encounter personality disorder in their practice but who do not deliver the IPTF directly. The Foundation training equips these professionals to recognise personality-related presentations, to communicate with patients in a validating and schema-aware manner, and to refer appropriately to IPTF services.

Level Two: Practitioner (Five-Day Intensive plus Six Months Supervised Practice)

The Practitioner level equips clinicians to deliver Stage 1 of the IPTF, including the skills group curriculum, diary card review, and basic chain analysis, and to contribute to Stages 2 and 3 under supervision. The five-day intensive training covers the Stage 1 session-by-session curriculum with role-play practice, the diary card and chain analysis protocols, crisis management and safety planning, the formulation worksheet, and the mentalising therapeutic stance. Following the intensive training, the clinician completes six months of supervised practice during which they co-facilitate a Stage 1 skills group and carry a minimum of two individual Stage 1 cases under fortnightly supervision.

Level Three: Advanced Practitioner (Practitioner Level plus Twelve Months Further Supervised Practice)

The Advanced Practitioner level equips clinicians to deliver all three stages of the IPTF independently and to supervise others. The training requires completion of the Practitioner level plus a further twelve months of supervised practice during which the clinician delivers Stage 2 (including imagery rescripting and chair work) and Stage 3 under weekly supervision from an experienced personality disorder therapist. Assessment for Advanced Practitioner certification includes submission of recorded sessions demonstrating competence in each therapeutic modality and evidence of the IPTF's fidelity criteria being met.

Chapter 33

Fidelity and Outcome Measurement

The IPTF Fidelity Checklist

Treatment fidelity, the degree to which the IPTF is delivered as intended, is essential for both clinical effectiveness and research evaluation. The IPTF Fidelity Checklist provides a structured tool for assessing adherence to the model across its core components. The checklist assesses whether the three-stage structure is maintained; whether the treatment hierarchy is applied in every session; whether the 7/10 Arousal Rule is consistently implemented; whether the five active ingredients are present across all sessions; whether the IPTF Formulation Worksheet is completed collaboratively and updated at stage transitions; whether the stage transition criteria are applied; and whether the consultation team is functioning. The checklist is designed to be completed through a combination of session observation, audio recording review, and clinician self-report, and should be used in supervision to identify areas of fidelity drift and to guide corrective action.

Recommended Outcome Measurement Battery

Instrument	What It Measures	When Administered
CORE-OM	Global psychological distress, risk, functioning	Assessment, every 3 months, discharge, follow-up
PHQ-9	Depression severity	Assessment, every 3 months, discharge, follow-up
GAD-7	Anxiety severity	Assessment, every 3 months, discharge, follow-up
BSL-23	Borderline-specific symptomatology	Assessment, Stage 1 completion, Stage 2 completion, discharge
YSQ-S3	Early Maladaptive Schemas	Assessment, Stage 2 midpoint, Stage 2 completion

IIP-32	Interpersonal problems	Assessment, Stage 2 completion, discharge
LPFS-BF 2.0	Personality functioning severity	Assessment, each stage completion, discharge, follow-up
Session Rating Scale	Therapeutic alliance	Every session
IPTF Stage Completion Measures	Stage-specific readiness criteria	Each stage transition

Routine outcome monitoring should be embedded into the IPTF service from the outset, with outcome data collected at the specified time points and reviewed in supervision to inform clinical decision-making. Aggregated outcome data should be reported to commissioners at least annually and used to demonstrate the effectiveness of the service and to identify areas for quality improvement.

The IPTF Fidelity Checklist: Detailed Domains

Treatment fidelity is assessed across eight domains, each rated on a three-point scale: Fully Adherent (the component is consistently delivered as specified), Partially Adherent (the component is present but inconsistently delivered or modified beyond the framework's tolerance), and Non-Adherent (the component is absent or delivered in a manner that contradicts the framework's specifications). The eight domains are as follows.

Domain 1: Three-Stage Structure. Is the treatment organised into the three sequential stages? Are stage transitions determined by clinical criteria rather than by session count? Is the non-linear movement between stages (the 7/10 Rule) consistently applied?

Domain 2: Treatment Hierarchy. Is the target hierarchy (life-threatening, therapy-interfering, quality-of-life) applied in every individual session? Does the diary card review follow the hierarchy sequence?

Domain 3: Five Active Ingredients. Are structure/consistency, validation/empathy, therapeutic alliance, affect regulation, and agency/self-efficacy identifiable across all sessions?

Domain 4: Collaborative Formulation. Is the IPTF Formulation Worksheet completed collaboratively? Is it updated at stage transitions? Is the relational stance (side-by-side) maintained?

Domain 5: Stage 1 Skills Delivery. Are the four DBT skills modules delivered? Is the session structure maintained? Are experiential exercises included?

Domain 6: Stage 2 Technique Integration. Are imagery rescripting, chair work, cognitive restructuring, and behavioural experiments deployed flexibly based on formulation? Is the mentalising stance maintained?

Domain 7: Stage 3 Recovery Focus. Are vocational, social, identity, and daily functioning domains addressed? Is the graduated frequency reduction implemented?

Domain 8: Consultation Team. Is the consultation team meeting regularly? Are the consultation team agreements followed?

Chapter 34

The Research Agenda: Evaluating the IPTF

The Current Evidence Base

As acknowledged in Chapter 1, the IPTF is a new framework that has not yet been subjected to a randomised controlled trial. Its evidence base is theoretical and derivative, drawing upon the established evidence bases of the constituent modalities. Building an independent evidence base for the IPTF is a priority, and this chapter outlines the research programme needed to achieve it.

Recommended Research Programme

Phase One: Feasibility Study. A single-site feasibility study with fifteen to twenty patients, using a pre-post design with the outcome measurement battery described in Chapter 33, to establish whether the IPTF can be delivered as specified, whether patients can be recruited and retained, and whether the outcome measures are sensitive to change. Duration: eighteen to twenty-four months.

Phase Two: Pilot Randomised Controlled Trial. A multi-site pilot RCT comparing the IPTF to treatment as usual in two to three NHS personality disorder services, with sixty to ninety participants, to estimate effect sizes, refine the treatment protocol, and establish the parameters for a definitive trial. Duration: thirty-six months.

Phase Three: Pragmatic Definitive Trial. A multi-site pragmatic RCT with sufficient statistical power to detect clinically meaningful differences, comparing the IPTF to an active comparator such as Structured Clinical Management, embedded within routine NHS service delivery. Duration: forty-eight to sixty months.

Parallel Qualitative Programme. A qualitative research programme running alongside the trial programme, using interviews and focus groups with patients, clinicians, and carers to understand the experience of receiving and delivering the IPTF, to identify the mechanisms of change as perceived by participants, and to inform ongoing refinement of the framework.

An Invitation to Researchers and Clinicians

The IPTF is offered as an open framework that will evolve in response to evidence. Researchers who wish to evaluate the IPTF, clinicians who wish to implement it and share their outcome data, and experts by experience who wish to contribute their perspectives to its development are all warmly invited to contact the author through Talking Therapies UK. The ultimate measure of any treatment manual is not the elegance of its theory but the quality of the lives it helps to build. The IPTF will be judged by that standard, and the author welcomes the scrutiny.

Consolidated References

A full list of references cited throughout this manual, and in the parent textbook, is available in the Consolidated References section of The Definitive British Textbook of Personality Disorders: Science, System, and Synthesis (James, 2026). Key references that are specific to this manual include:

Ainsworth, M.D.S., Blehar, M.C., Waters, E. and Wall, S. (1978) Patterns of Attachment: A Psychological Study of the Strange Situation. Hillsdale, NJ: Erlbaum.

Arntz, A. and Jacob, G. (2013) Schema Therapy in Practice: An Introductory Guide to the Schema Mode Approach. Chichester: Wiley-Blackwell.

Bateman, A. and Fonagy, P. (2004) Psychotherapy for Borderline Personality Disorder: Mentalisation-Based Treatment. Oxford: Oxford University Press.

Bohus, M. et al. (2009) 'The Short Version of the Borderline Symptom List (BSL-23)', Psychopathology, 42(1), pp. 32–39.

Bowlby, J. (1969) Attachment and Loss, Volume 1: Attachment. London: Hogarth Press.

Davidson, K. (2007) Cognitive Therapy for Personality Disorders: A Guide for Clinicians. 2nd edn. London: Routledge.

Hayes, S.C., Strosahl, K.D. and Wilson, K.G. (2012) Acceptance and Commitment Therapy: The Process and Practice of Mindful Change. 2nd edn. New York: Guilford Press.

James, J.J. (2026) The Definitive British Textbook of Personality Disorders: Science, System, and Synthesis. Liverpool: Talking Therapies UK.

Linehan, M.M. (1993a) Cognitive-Behavioral Treatment of Borderline Personality Disorder. New York: Guilford Press.

Linehan, M.M. (1993b) Skills Training Manual for Treating Borderline Personality Disorder. New York: Guilford Press.

Nader, K., Schafe, G.E. and Le Doux, J.E. (2000) 'Fear Memories Require Protein Synthesis in the Amygdala for Reconsolidation After Retrieval', Nature, 406(6797), pp. 722–726.

Wampold, B.E. (2015) 'How Important Are the Common Factors in Psychotherapy?', World Psychiatry, 14(3), pp. 270–277.

World Health Organisation (2019) International Classification of Diseases, Eleventh Revision (ICD-11). Geneva: WHO.

Young, J.E., Klosko, J.S. and Weishaar, M.E. (2003) Schema Therapy: A Practitioner's Guide. New York: Guilford Press.

THE INTEGRATED PERSONALITY TREATMENT FRAMEWORK

Reproducible Worksheets and Clinical Tools

Companion to the IPTF Clinical Treatment Manual

Jayden Josh James
MSc, PGDip CBT, PGDip DBT, MBT, EMDR
Talking Therapies UK

IPTF | INTEGRATED PERSONALITY TREATMENT FRAMEWORK

IPTF Formulation Worksheet

Section One: 'The Now' — Stage 1: Stabilisation and Safety

Name:		**Date:**	

ICD-11 DIMENSIONAL DIAGNOSIS

Severity Level (circle one): Personality Difficulty | Mild | Moderate | Severe

Borderline Pattern Specifier (circle): Applies | Does Not Apply

Trait Domain Profile (indicate prominence: Prominent / Present / Not Elevated):

Negative Affectivity: __________ Detachment: __________ Dissociality: __________

Disinhibition: __________ Anankastia: __________

Brief Narrative Justification:

CURRENT RISK PROFILE (Treatment Hierarchy)

TARGET ONE: Life-Threatening Behaviours

Type, frequency, method, function, most recent episode:

Current suicidal ideation (passive / active / plan / intent):

TARGET TWO: Therapy-Interfering Behaviours

Patterns of non-attendance, non-engagement, boundary issues:

TARGET THREE: Quality-of-Life-Interfering Behaviours

Substance use, housing, employment, social isolation, other:

CURRENT COPING STRATEGIES

Adaptive strategies (strengths to build on):

Maladaptive strategies (targets for replacement):

STAGE 1 SKILLS TARGETS

Priority modules for this patient (tick and note focus areas):

- ☐ Mindfulness: ____
- ☐ Distress Tolerance: ______________________________________
- ☐ Emotion Regulation: ______________________________________
- ☐ Interpersonal Effectiveness: __________________________________

Completed by (clinician): __________________ Date: __________ Reviewed with patient: ☐ Yes

IPTF | INTEGRATED PERSONALITY TREATMENT FRAMEWORK

IPTF Formulation Worksheet

Section Two: 'The Why' — Stage 2: Cognitive Mapping and Schema Work

Name:		**Date:**	

DEVELOPMENTAL TIMELINE

Record significant events, attachment relationships, and adverse experiences at each stage:

Early Childhood (0–7 years):

Middle Childhood (7–12 years):

Adolescence (13–18 years):

Early Adulthood (18+ years):

ATTACHMENT PATTERN

Predominant pattern (circle): Secure | Anxious-Preoccupied | Dismissing-Avoidant | Disorganised-Fearful

Evidence and clinical rationale:

EARLY MALADAPTIVE SCHEMAS AND CORE BELIEFS

For each identified schema, record in the patient's own words:

Schema 1: ______________ **Core Belief: 'I am...'** ______________ **'Others are...'** ______________

Developmental origin:

Current triggers:

Schema 2: ______________ **Core Belief: 'I am...'** ______________ **'Others are...'** ______________

Developmental origin:

Current triggers:

Schema 3: ______________ **Core Belief: 'I am...'** ______________ **'Others are...'** ______________

Developmental origin:

Current triggers:

PREDOMINANT SCHEMA MODES

Vulnerable Child — triggers and presentation:

Angry Child — triggers and presentation:

Detached Protector — triggers and presentation:

Punitive Parent — key messages and voice:

Healthy Adult — current strength and access:

Completed by: ________________ Date: _________ Reviewed with patient: ☐ Yes

IPTF | INTEGRATED PERSONALITY TREATMENT FRAMEWORK

IPTF Formulation Worksheet

Section Three: 'The Future' — Stage 3: Functional Recovery

Name:		**Date:**	

RECOVERY GOALS (in the patient's own words)

Relationships — What kind of relationships do I want?

Occupation — What kind of work, study, or activity do I want?

Identity — Who do I want to be?

Daily Life — What does a good day look like?

VALUES CLARIFICATION

What matters most to me in relationships:

What matters most to me in work and contribution:

What matters most to me in how I treat myself:

What matters most to me in my community:

SOCIAL CAPITAL AND SUPPORT NETWORK

Named supportive individuals and the role each plays:

Community organisations, groups, or activities I am or could be involved in:

Completed by: ___________________ Date: ___________ Reviewed with patient: ☐ Yes

IPTF | INTEGRATED PERSONALITY TREATMENT FRAMEWORK

IPTF Stage 1 Daily Diary Card

Complete daily. Bring to every session.

Name: ____________________ Week beginning: ____________________

	Mon	Tue	Wed	Thu	Fri	Sat	Sun
Distress (0-10)							
Self-Harm Urges (0-5)							
Self-Harm (Y/N)							
Substances (Y/N)							
Skills Used (list)							
Most Significant Event							

Skills Key: M = Mindfulness | DT = Distress Tolerance (specify: TIP / ACCEPTS / Radical Acceptance) | ER = Emotion Regulation (specify: Opposite Action / Check the Facts / ABC PLEASE) | IE = Interpersonal Effectiveness (specify: DEAR MAN / GIVE / FAST)

IPTF | INTEGRATED PERSONALITY TREATMENT FRAMEWORK

Behavioural Chain Analysis Worksheet

Stage 1 — Individual Therapy Tool

Name:		**Date:**	

1. VULNERABILITY FACTORS

What factors made you more vulnerable before the event? (poor sleep, hunger, illness, substance use, conflict, stress, anniversary)

2. PROMPTING EVENT

What specific event set the chain in motion? (Be precise: what happened, when, where, who was involved?)

3. THE CHAIN: Links from Event to Target Behaviour

Trace each link: Thought → Body Sensation → Emotion → Urge → Action

Link 1 — Thought:

Link 2 — Body sensation:

Link 3 — Emotion:

Link 4 — Urge:

Link 5 — Action taken:

(Continue on reverse if needed — add further links as the chain developed):

4. TARGET BEHAVIOUR

What did you do? (Be specific: method, severity, duration, function)

5. CONSEQUENCES

Immediate consequences (within minutes/hours):

Longer-term consequences (within days/weeks):

6. SOLUTION ANALYSIS

At which links could a different response have changed the outcome?

Link ___: I could have used [skill]: ____________________________

Link ___: I could have used [skill]: ____________________________

Link ___: I could have used [skill]: ____________________________

What will I do differently next time?

IPTF | INTEGRATED PERSONALITY TREATMENT FRAMEWORK

Check the Facts Worksheet

Emotion Regulation Tool — Stage 1

Name:		**Date:**	

THE SITUATION

What happened? (Just the observable facts — what would a camera have recorded?)

MY INTERPRETATION

What did I tell myself about what happened? What did I assume?

CHECKING THE FACTS

What is the evidence that my interpretation is accurate?

What is the evidence that it might not be completely accurate?

Are there other possible explanations I have not considered?

MY EMOTION

What emotion am I feeling?

How intense is it? (circle) 0 1 2 3 4 5 6 7 8 9 10

Does my emotion fit the FACTS, or does it fit my INTERPRETATION?

If my emotion fits my interpretation rather than the facts, what would change if I held the facts more lightly?

IPTF | INTEGRATED PERSONALITY TREATMENT FRAMEWORK

Behavioural Experiment Worksheet

Stage 2 / Stage 3 — Cognitive Restructuring Tool

Name:		**Date:**	

1. THE BELIEF BEING TESTED

What core belief or schema-generated prediction am I testing?

2. THE SPECIFIC PREDICTION

If I do [experiment], I predict that [specific outcome] will happen:

How strongly do I believe this prediction? (circle) 0% 10% 20% 30% 40% 50% 60% 70% 80% 90% 100%

3. THE EXPERIMENT

What exactly will I do? (Be specific: where, when, with whom, what will I say or do?)

What skills will I use to manage my anxiety about the experiment?

4. WHAT ACTUALLY HAPPENED

Describe the actual outcome as precisely as possible:

5. WHAT DOES THIS MEAN?

Was my prediction accurate? What does the result tell me about my core belief?

How strongly do I now believe the original prediction? (circle) 0% 10% 20% 30% 40% 50% 60% 70% 80% 90% 100%

What alternative belief does the evidence support?

IPTF | INTEGRATED PERSONALITY TREATMENT FRAMEWORK

My Safety Plan

Keep this with you at all times

Name: ____________________ Date completed: ____________________

STEP 1: My Warning Signs

How do I know things are getting worse? What are the early signs?

Thoughts I notice:

Feelings I notice:

Body sensations:

Behaviours I notice:

STEP 2: Things I Can Do On My Own

Skills from Stage 1 that help me:

For mild distress (3-4):

For moderate distress (5-6):

For high distress (7-8):

For extreme distress (9-10):

STEP 3: People Who Can Help

Name: ____________________ **Phone:** ____________________ **What they help with:**

Name: ____________________ **Phone:** ____________________ **What they help with:**

Name: ____________________ **Phone:** ____________________ **What they help with:**

STEP 4: Professional Contacts

My therapist: ____________________ **Phone:** ____________________ **Available:**

My care coordinator: ______________ **Phone:** ____________________

Crisis team: ____________________ **Phone:** ____________________

STEP 5: Emergency

If I am in immediate danger, I will:

Go to A&E at: ____________________ **or call 999**

Samaritans: 116 123 (free, 24 hours) | SHOUT: Text 'SHOUT' to 85258

IPTF | INTEGRATED PERSONALITY TREATMENT FRAMEWORK

Pros and Cons of Tolerating Distress

Complete this in advance, when calm. Keep in your crisis toolkit.

The crisis urge I am planning for: ____

ACTING ON THE URGE	TOLERATING THE DISTRESS
PROS (short-term gains):	**PROS (long-term gains):**
CONS (long-term costs):	**CONS (short-term costs):**

IPTF | INTEGRATED PERSONALITY TREATMENT FRAMEWORK

Mode Monitoring Diary

Stage 2 — Track your schema modes through the day

Name: ____________________________ Week beginning: ____________________________

Day / Time	What Happened?	Mode I Was In	Emotion	What I Did

Mode Key: VC = Vulnerable Child | AC = Angry Child | DP = Detached Protector | PP = Punitive Parent | HA = Healthy Adult

IPTF | INTEGRATED PERSONALITY TREATMENT FRAMEWORK

Stage 1 Completion Checklist

Transition Assessment: Stage 1 → Stage 2

Name:		**Date:**	

Criterion	Status	Evidence and Notes
1. Behavioural Safety 8+ weeks reduced life-threatening behaviours with skill deployment evidence	☐ Met ☐ Partial ☐ Not Met	
2. Emotional Regulation Identifies and names emotions; deploys 2+ DT skills in crises; arousal returns to <7/10	☐ Met ☐ Partial ☐ Not Met	
3. Alliance Stability Consistent attendance; honest disclosure; ruptures navigated; collaborative engagement	☐ Met ☐ Partial ☐ Not Met	
4. Cognitive Readiness Distinguishes interpretation from fact; Check the Facts Worksheet completed; reflective capacity emerging	☐ Met ☐ Partial ☐ Not Met	
5. Informed Consent Understands Stage 2 content; has expressed genuine willingness to proceed	☐ Met ☐ Partial ☐ Not Met	
OVERALL DECISION	☐ Transition to Stage 2 ☐ Extended Stage 1 ☐ Modified Pathway	

Clinician signature: ________________________ Patient signature: ________________________ Date: __________

APPENDIX A

Clinical Pitfalls, Recovery Scripts, and Transition Prompts

Teaching Notes for IPTF Clinicians

Teaching Notes: Stage 1 Clinical Pitfalls

The following teaching notes accompany the Stage 1 session-by-session guide in Chapter 6. Each pitfall addresses a common clinical difficulty that arises during skills group delivery, provides a diagnosis of the underlying mechanism, and offers a recovery script that the clinician can adapt to their own voice. These are not theoretical concerns; they are the problems that arise in the room with real patients, and the solutions that experienced clinicians have found to work.

Block One: Mindfulness Pitfalls

⚠ CLINICAL PITFALL: The Patient Who Cannot Close Their Eyes

The Problem: When you ask the group to close their eyes for a mindfulness exercise, one or more patients will refuse or become visibly distressed. This is almost always a trauma response: closing the eyes removes visual monitoring of the environment, which feels intolerable for someone whose survival has depended on hypervigilance. Insisting that the patient close their eyes replicates the experience of having their autonomy overridden.

Recovery Script: *'You absolutely do not have to close your eyes. Many people prefer to keep their eyes open during mindfulness, and that is completely fine. If you would like to try it with your eyes open, just soften your gaze and let it rest on a spot on the floor in front of you. The skill works exactly the same way.'*

⚠ CLINICAL PITFALL: The Patient Who Says Mindfulness Does Not Work

The Problem: The patient has tried a mindfulness exercise and reports that it 'did nothing' or 'made me feel worse.' This typically arises from one of two misunderstandings: the expectation that mindfulness should immediately produce a calm, pleasant state; or the experience that turning attention inward intensifies distress because the patient encounters the emotional material they have been avoiding. Both are clinically significant.

Recovery Script: *'Thank you for being honest about that. Can I ask what you mean by "did not work"? What were you expecting to happen? [Listen.] The purpose of mindfulness is not to make you feel calm. The purpose is to notice* *what you are experiencing without being swept away by it. If you noticed that you were feeling distressed, and you were able to observe that without acting on it, then the skill actually did work — you just did not enjoy it, which is different from it not working. Does that distinction make sense?'*

⚠ CLINICAL PITFALL: The Patient in Angry Child Mode Who Disrupts the Group

The Problem: A patient arrives at the skills group in a state of high agitation and begins challenging the facilitator, criticising the skills as 'pointless,' or expressing frustration loudly in a way that destabilises the group. The temptation is to engage with the content of the complaint or to assert authority. Both are counterproductive: engaging validates the disruption as a strategy, and asserting authority replicates the power dynamics of the patient's schema.

Recovery Script: *'I can hear that you are really frustrated right now, and that is valid. Something is clearly going on for you today. I am not going to ask you to pretend it is not happening. What I would like to do is check in with you briefly after the group to make sure you are okay. For now, I am going to ask if you can stay with us — even if you are frustrated — and see if anything in today's session connects with what you are feeling. Can you do that?'*

Block Two: Distress Tolerance Pitfalls

⚠ CLINICAL PITFALL: The Patient Who Refuses TIP Because 'It Is Stupid'

The Problem: The cold water technique can provoke resistance because it feels undignified, simplistic, or incompatible with the seriousness of the patient's distress. The patient may feel that their suffering deserves more than a bowl of cold water. This resistance is often a manifestation of the Punitive Parent mode, which tells the patient they do not deserve simple, practical help.

Recovery Script: *'I completely understand that putting your face in cold water sounds strange when we are talking about the kind of pain you are in. I am not going to pretend it is elegant. But here is what I can tell you: this technique works on your body directly. It activates a reflex that slows your heart rate and calms your nervous system within thirty seconds. It does not care whether you believe in it. It does not care whether it seems silly. It works on biology, not on belief. Would you be willing to try it once, just as an experiment, and then* *decide?'*

⚠ CLINICAL PITFALL: The Patient Who Uses Radical Acceptance to Justify Staying in an Abusive Situation

The Problem: A patient hears the teaching on Radical Acceptance and concludes that they should accept their abusive partner's behaviour, their exploitative employer, or their intolerable housing situation. This is a dangerous misapplication that must be addressed immediately, because it transforms a distress tolerance skill into a mechanism for perpetuating harm.

Recovery Script: *'I am really glad you raised this, because it gives me a chance to clarify something that is absolutely crucial. Radical Acceptance is about accepting that something has happened — that it is a fact — so that you can decide what to do next. It is never about accepting that something should continue to happen. If someone is hurting you, the radical acceptance is: "This is happening." The next step is not to tolerate it; the next step is to use your Interpersonal Effectiveness skills to change it, to get help, or to leave. Acceptance of reality is the starting point for change, not a reason to stop trying.'*

Block Three: Emotion Regulation Pitfalls

⚠ CLINICAL PITFALL: The Patient Who Cannot Identify Any Emotions

The Problem: When asked to name their emotions, the patient consistently says 'I don't know,' 'fine,' or 'bad.' This is common and may reflect alexithymia (a genuine difficulty in identifying and describing emotional states), the legacy of an invalidating environment in which emotional expression was punished, or the Detached Protector mode cutting off access to emotional awareness. It is not resistance.

Recovery Script: *'That is okay. Lots of people find this really hard, especially if they grew up in a household where feelings were not talked about or were dismissed. Let us try a different route. Can you tell me what is happening in your body right now? Any tension, heaviness, tightness, restlessness? [Patient describes.] Good. That physical sensation is your body's way of having an emotion. We do not need to name it right now. We just need to notice it is there. Over time, the names will come.'*

⚠ **CLINICAL PITFALL: The Patient Who Uses Check the Facts to Intellectualise and Avoid Emotion**

The Problem: A highly intellectualising patient completes the Check the Facts worksheet fluently but in a way that keeps them at a cognitive distance from their emotional experience. They analyse the situation rationally without ever connecting to the feeling. This is Pretend Mode mentalising: talking about emotions without actually experiencing them. The skill has become a defence rather than a tool.

Recovery Script: *'You have done a really thorough analysis of the facts, and I can see that your interpretation may not be completely accurate. But I noticed something: as you were going through the worksheet, your voice was very even and your body was very still. I wonder whether the part of you that is doing the analysis might be keeping a safe distance from the part of you that is actually hurting. What would happen if you put the worksheet down for a moment and just sat with whatever is there, underneath the analysis?'*

Block Four: Interpersonal Effectiveness Pitfalls

⚠ **CLINICAL PITFALL: The Patient Who Delivers DEAR MAN as an Ultimatum**

The Problem: The patient uses the DEAR MAN structure but delivers it with an aggressive tone, rigid body language, and an implicit or explicit threat if the other person does not comply. The assertiveness has become coercion. This typically reflects an overcompensation coping mode: the patient has swung from passive Subjugation to aggressive Entitlement without finding the assertive middle ground.

Recovery Script: *'I noticed that when you practised that just now, your voice was quite forceful and your body was quite tense. Can we slow down and look at what happened? DEAR MAN is about getting what you need, but GIVE is about keeping the relationship. What do you think happened to the GIVE part? [Explore.] I wonder whether, when you start to assert yourself, there is a part of you that is so used to being dismissed that it goes to maximum volume immediately because anything quieter has never been heard. Does that resonate?'*

Teaching Notes: Stage 2 Clinical Pitfalls

⚠ CLINICAL PITFALL: Dissociation During Imagery Rescripting

The Problem: The patient's eyes glaze, their narrative becomes vague or robotic, their body becomes still, or they stop responding. This is a dissociative response to the reactivation of traumatic material and must be addressed immediately. Continuing the rescripting with a dissociated patient is not merely ineffective; it risks retraumatisation because the patient is no longer consciously present to process the new information being introduced.

Recovery Script: *'I want to pause what we are doing for a moment. [Gentle, clear voice.] I need you to open your eyes. Can you look at me? Good. Now tell me five things you can see in this room. [Wait.] What colour is my jumper? Good. Can you feel your feet on the floor? Press them down. Good. You are here with me, in this room, and you are safe. What just happened is that your mind went somewhere far away to protect you from what we were looking at. That is your Detached Protector doing its job. We do not need to go back there today. We are going to spend the rest of this session grounding and making sure you feel settled before you leave.'*

⚠ CLINICAL PITFALL: The Patient Who Cannot Access the Healthy Adult Chair

The Problem: During chair work, the patient moves to the Healthy Adult chair but cannot generate any response to the Punitive Parent's attacks. They sit in silence, become tearful, or revert to the Vulnerable Child. This indicates that the patient's Healthy Adult is not yet strong enough to challenge the Punitive Parent independently, which is common in early Stage 2 and is not a failure.

Recovery Script: *'That is really hard, I know. The voice in that chair [pointing to Punitive Parent chair] has been speaking to you for a very long time, and it has had a lot of practice. The Healthy Adult is newer and quieter. So let me help. If I were sitting in this chair [sits beside patient], what do you think I might say to that voice? [Model the response.] Now, can you try saying something similar in your own words? Even one sentence. You do not have to defeat the voice today. You just have to let it know that someone else is in the room.'*

⚠ CLINICAL PITFALL: Stage Drift: Doing Stage 2 Work with an Unstabilised Patient

The Problem: The clinician begins exploring developmental history or conducting schema work with a patient whose arousal is consistently above 7/10, who is still engaging in regular self-harm, or who has not yet acquired a functional skills repertoire. This is the most common and most dangerous fidelity error in the IPTF: it exposes the patient to emotionally activating material without the regulatory resources to process it, and it can precipitate a crisis that undermines the therapeutic alliance and the patient's confidence in the treatment.

Recovery Script: '*I have been thinking about where we are in the treatment, and I want to be honest with you. I think we may have moved into the exploratory work a bit too quickly. I have noticed that when we start talking about your past, your distress goes up very sharply and we spend most of the session trying to bring it back down. That tells me that we need to spend more time building your skills before we go further. This is not a step backwards — it is making sure the foundations are strong enough to hold the building. Can we agree to focus on skills for the next few weeks and then reassess?*'

IPTF Transition Prompts

The following transition prompts provide scripted language for the most common moments in IPTF delivery when the clinician needs to move between therapeutic modalities within a single session. These moments are the distinctive challenge of an integrative framework: the transition must feel seamless to the patient, not like a jarring gear change. Each prompt is labelled with the direction of the transition and the clinical context in which it is used.

↔ TRANSITION PROMPT: DBT Distress Tolerance → SFT Mode Awareness → You have done really well to bring your distress down using the breathing. Now that it is more manageable, I am curious about what was driving it. Can we take a moment to notice which part of you was activated just then? Was it the Vulnerable Child who was feeling the pain, or the Angry Child who was protesting? What was the Detached Protector trying to protect you from?

↔ TRANSITION PROMPT: SFT Schema Exploration → DBT Skills (Arousal Rising Above 7/10) → I can see that talking about this is bringing up a lot of feeling. Can you tell me where you are on the 0-to-10 scale right now? [Patient: About an 8.] Okay. That tells me we need to pause the exploration for a moment and look after the feeling first. Let us do some paced breathing together — breathe in for four, out for six. [Guide breathing.] We can come back to what we were exploring once you are feeling more settled. The material is not going anywhere.

↔ TRANSITION PROMPT: CBT-PD Cognitive Restructuring → SFT Imagery Rescripting → So we have identified that the core belief is 'I am worthless,' and we have looked at the evidence for and against it. I notice that even though the evidence does not really support the belief, it still feels completely true. That tells me the belief is being held at an emotional level, not just a thinking level. Would you be willing to try something different today? I would like us to go back to where this belief was first formed, to the memory where you first learned that you were worthless, and see if we can change what happened there. We would use the imagery work we talked about. How does that feel?

↔ TRANSITION PROMPT: Stage 1 Skills Group Content → Stage 2 Bridge (Check the Facts as Mentalising Primer) → You have just used Check the Facts to look at whether your interpretation matched the evidence. I want

to add one more layer. You checked your own thoughts — now let us check the other person's thoughts. What do you think your friend might have been thinking when she cancelled? Not what your schema tells you she was thinking, but what a range of possible explanations might be. Can you hold two or three possibilities at once?

↔ TRANSITION PROMPT: Stage 2 Schema Work → Stage 3 Life-Building → We have done some really important work understanding why you developed the belief that you would always fail. Now I want to shift the question. Not 'why do I believe I will fail?' but 'what would I do if I did not believe I would fail?' If that schema was not running the show, what would you want your life to look like? Let us start building towards that.

↔ TRANSITION PROMPT: Any Stage → Crisis Response (Safety Plan Activation) → I can see that things have shifted quite significantly in the last few minutes. I want to check in with you directly: are you safe right now? [Assess.] Okay. Let us set aside what we were working on — it will keep — and focus on what you need right now. Where is your safety plan? Let us look at it together.

IPTF Stage-Gate Decision Flowchart

The following decision flowchart provides a visual guide for the most common clinical decision points in IPTF delivery. It is designed to be printed and displayed in the consulting room as a real-time decision-support tool.

The Session-Level Arousal Decision

SESSION OPENS: Ask patient to rate arousal 0–10

▼

Is arousal ≤ 6?

YES (≤ 6)	NO (7+)
Proceed with planned session content: Stage 1 → Skills teaching Stage 2 → Schema exploration Stage 3 → Life-building work	**PAUSE planned content.** Deploy Stage 1 skills: 1. Paced Breathing (4-in, 6-out) 2. TIP if needed 3. Grounding (5 Senses) *RE-CHECK arousal. If ≤ 6, resume. If still 7+, remain in Stage 1 mode for this session.*

◆ **CLINICAL PEARL**

Print this flowchart and pin it to your consulting room wall. The 7/10 Arousal Rule is the single most important clinical decision in the IPTF. If you remember nothing else from this manual, remember this: when the amygdala is on fire, the prefrontal cortex is offline. Cool the fire first. Everything else can wait.

IPTF | INTEGRATED PERSONALITY TREATMENT FRAMEWORK

IPTF Smart Diary Card

Enhanced Daily Monitoring — Links Skills to Modes and Arousal

Name: ____________________________ Week beginning: ____________________________

	Mon	Tue	Wed	Thu	Fri	Sat	Sun
Peak Distress (0-10)							
Self-Harm Urges (0-5)							
Self-Harm Act (Y/N)							
Substances (Y/N)							
Dominant Mode Today							
☐ Mindfulness used							
☐ TIP / Paced Breathing							
☐ ACCEPTS / Radical Acc.							
☐ Opposite Action							
☐ Check the Facts							
☐ DEAR MAN / GIVE / FAST							
☐ Mode Awareness							
☐ Wise Mind accessed							
Significant Event (brief)							

Mode Key: VC = Vulnerable Child | AC = Angry Child | DP = Detached Protector | PP = Punitive Parent | HA = Healthy Adult

This Smart Diary Card integrates skills tracking, mode monitoring, and arousal recording into a single daily tool. Tick every skill you used, even if it did not seem to 'work.' Using a skill, regardless of outcome, is progress.

IPTF | INTEGRATED PERSONALITY TREATMENT FRAMEWORK

Guide to the IPTF for the Wider Team and Family Members

A One-Page Reference for the Multidisciplinary Team and Support Network

WHAT IS THE IPTF?

The Integrated Personality Treatment Framework is a structured programme that helps people with personality difficulties to manage their emotions, understand the patterns that cause them distress, and build a meaningful life. It works in three stages:

Stage 1 (Safety and Skills): The person learns practical skills for managing intense emotions and crises. During this stage, they may still experience episodes of distress, self-harm, or crisis contact. This is expected and does not mean the treatment is failing.

Stage 2 (Understanding Patterns): The person explores how their early experiences shaped the beliefs and patterns that maintain their difficulties. This stage can be emotionally demanding, and the person may temporarily seem more distressed as they process painful material.

Stage 3 (Building a Life): The person works on practical goals: returning to work or education, building relationships, and developing a positive sense of identity.

HOW YOU CAN HELP

Validate, do not fix. When the person is distressed, the most helpful response is to acknowledge their feelings: 'I can see this is really hard for you.' Avoid trying to solve the problem, minimise the feeling, or tell them to 'think positively.'

Encourage skill use, do not enforce it. You can gently remind the person that they have skills they can use: 'Would any of your skills from the group help right now?' But do not insist or lecture. The decision to use skills must come from them.

Expect setbacks and do not catastrophise. Recovery is not linear. The person will have difficult days, and they may occasionally use old coping strategies. A setback does not erase progress. Respond with compassion rather than alarm.

Respect the treatment boundaries. The person's therapist will not be able to share details of the treatment with you without the person's consent. This confidentiality is essential for the person to feel safe enough to do the work.

Look after yourself. Supporting someone through personality disorder treatment is emotionally demanding. You are allowed to set your own boundaries, to take time for yourself, and to seek support when you need it.

KEY TERMS YOU MIGHT HEAR

The 7/10 Rule: When emotional distress is above 7 out of 10, it is not the right time for deep conversation or problem-solving. Help the person use their skills to bring the distress down first.

Schema: A deep belief formed in early life (e.g., 'I am not good enough') that colours how the person sees themselves and others. These beliefs feel true even when the evidence does not support them.

Mode: An emotional state the person goes into when a schema is triggered. 'Detached Protector' means they have shut down emotionally. 'Punitive Parent' means their inner critic is attacking them. 'Healthy Adult' means they are responding with clarity and compassion.

Radical Acceptance: Accepting that something has happened without fighting it. This does NOT mean approving of it or giving up on changing the situation.

If you are concerned about the person's immediate safety, contact the crisis team on the number provided in their safety plan, or call 999 in an emergency.

SUPPLEMENTARY MATERIAL

Worked Clinical Examples and Visual Tools

Worked Example: A Complete Behavioural Chain Analysis Session

Supplement to Chapter 7: The Stage 1 Individual Therapy Component

The following is a complete, annotated session transcript demonstrating how a behavioural chain analysis is conducted within the IPTF. The transcript follows 'Sarah,' a composite patient aged twenty-eight with moderate personality disorder, Borderline Pattern Specifier, prominent Negative Affectivity and Disinhibition, who is in Week 12 of Stage 1. Sarah self-harmed by cutting her forearm three days ago following an argument with her partner. The session lasts fifty minutes. Clinical annotations are provided throughout to explain the therapist's reasoning.

Part One: The Session Opening and Diary Card Review (Minutes 1–12)

[Sarah enters the room and sits down. She is wearing a long-sleeved top. Her eyes are slightly red. She places her diary card on the table between them. The therapist sits alongside Sarah, not opposite her, as the IPTF relational stance requires.]

Therapist: Hi Sarah. How are you doing today?

Sarah: Not great, to be honest.

Therapist: Okay. Thank you for telling me that straight away. Can you give me a number — where are you on the 0-to-10 scale right now?

Sarah: About a 5, I think. Maybe a 6.

Clinical Annotation: *The arousal check. Sarah is at 5–6, below the 7/10 threshold. The session can proceed with Stage 1 content without needing to begin with skills-based stabilisation. If she had said 7 or above, the therapist would have begun with Paced Breathing or TIP before addressing the diary card.*

Therapist: Alright. Shall we have a look at your diary card together?

[Sarah slides the diary card across. The therapist reviews it, running her finger down the columns.]

Therapist: I can see that your distress was quite high on Tuesday and Wednesday — 8 and 9. And I can see that there is a 'Y' in the self-harm row on Tuesday evening. Can you tell me what happened?

Clinical Annotation: *The therapist has identified a Target One behaviour (self-harm) on the diary card. Under the treatment hierarchy, this takes priority over* *everything else in the session. The therapist's tone is warm and matter-of-fact: neither alarmed nor dismissive.*

Sarah: Yeah. I cut on Tuesday night. [Pause.] It was bad. Worse than it has been for a while.

Therapist: I appreciate you being honest with me about that. I know it takes courage to tell me. Can I also see — on Wednesday, your self-harm urge was still at 4, but you did not act on it. And I can see you ticked 'Paced Breathing' and 'ACCEPTS — Music' in the skills column. That is really important, Sarah. You used your skills on Wednesday when the urge was still there. Can we acknowledge that before we look at Tuesday?

❃ **Clinical Annotation:** *The therapist does two things simultaneously: she validates the difficulty of disclosing the self-harm, and she highlights the skill use on the following day. This is not a gimmick; it communicates that the therapist sees the whole picture, not just the target behaviour. It also reinforces skill use by naming it explicitly.*

Sarah: [Small nod.] Yeah. Wednesday was hard but I managed it. Tuesday... I just couldn't.

Therapist: That is okay. 'Couldn't' is not the same as 'didn't try.' Let us understand what happened on Tuesday, step by step, because the more we understand it, the more choices you will have next time. Is that alright?

Sarah: Yeah.

Part Two: The Chain Analysis (Minutes 12-42)

Step One: Identifying the Target Behaviour

Therapist: So let us start with what actually happened. Can you describe the self-harm to me as specifically as you can — what you did, how you did it, how severe it was, and what time it happened?

Sarah: It was about half ten at night. I used a razor on my left forearm. Three cuts. They were quite deep — deeper than usual. I didn't go to A&E but I probably should have.

Therapist: Thank you for being specific. When you say deeper than usual, can you tell me what you mean — did they need closing, were they still bleeding after a significant time?

Sarah: One of them took about twenty minutes to stop bleeding. I used Steri-Strips from the first aid kit.

Therapist: Okay. We will need to look at the wound care in a moment, but first I want to understand the chain that led you there. Before I ask about the evening, can we look at what was going on earlier in the day? Sometimes the chain starts long before the target behaviour.

⚙ **Clinical Annotation:** *The therapist is now moving to vulnerability factors. Note that she asks about earlier in the day, not just the immediate trigger. The chain often begins hours or even days before the target behaviour, and identifying vulnerability factors is essential for prevention.*

Step Two: Vulnerability Factors

Therapist: Take me through Tuesday. What was your day like before the argument? How did you sleep the night before? Had you eaten? Were there any other stresses?

Sarah: I'd slept badly — maybe four hours. I had a nightmare about my stepdad which I get sometimes. I didn't eat breakfast because I felt sick. I had a coffee and that was it until about 2pm when I had some toast. I'd also had a letter from the Job Centre about my Universal Credit review and that stressed me out.

Therapist: So before anything else happened, you were already operating on four hours of sleep, a nightmare, very little food, and financial stress. That is a lot of vulnerability factors stacked up. On a normal day, your baseline distress might be a 3 or a 4. On Tuesday, before the argument even started, where do you think your baseline was?

Sarah: [Thinks.] Probably about a 6, honestly. I was already wound up.

⚙ **Clinical Annotation:** *The therapist has identified four vulnerability factors: sleep deprivation, nightmare (trauma reminder), inadequate nutrition, and external stressor (benefits letter). By asking Sarah to rate her baseline, the therapist makes visible the concept that the patient arrived at the prompting event already depleted. This is the ABC PLEASE material from Block Three made real: when the body is under-resourced, the emotional system is primed for escalation.*

Step Three: The Prompting Event

Therapist: And then what happened?

Sarah: Dan came home from work at about 7. I asked him if he had remembered to pick up my prescription from the pharmacy, because I had asked him that morning. He said he forgot. And I just — I lost it.

Therapist: Can you tell me exactly what he said and exactly what you said? The exact words, if you can remember them.

Sarah: He said, 'Oh shit, sorry, I forgot.' And I said, 'You always forget. You don't care about me. If you cared about me you would remember the things that matter to me.' And then he said, 'It's just a prescription, Sarah, calm down.' And that's when I really went.

⚙ **Clinical Annotation:** *The prompting event is identified: Dan forgetting the prescription. Note that the therapist asks for the exact words — this specificity is critical because the chain analysis needs to identify the precise thoughts and interpretations that link the event to the emotional escalation. 'He forgot my prescription' is the event; 'he does not care about me' is the interpretation. The interpretation, not the event, is what drives the emotional chain.*

Step Four: Tracing the Chain Link by Link

Therapist: Okay. So the event is that Dan said he forgot. Now I want to slow this right down — like we are watching it in slow motion. The moment he said 'I forgot,' what was the very first thought that went through your mind?

Sarah: [Long pause.] 'He doesn't care.' That was the first thing.

Therapist: And what did that thought feel like in your body?

Sarah: My chest went tight. Like a band across it. And my hands went tingly.

Therapist: And the emotion — what were you feeling right then?

Sarah: Hurt. Really hurt. Like... crushed.

⚙ **Clinical Annotation:** *This is the primary emotion — hurt. The therapist notes it. The primary emotion is often fleeting and quickly covered by a secondary emotion that feels more powerful and more protective.*

Therapist: So the first feeling was hurt. And then — what came next?

Sarah: Then I was furious. Absolutely furious. Like a switch flipped.

Therapist: The anger came on top of the hurt?

Sarah: Yeah. The hurt was there for like half a second and then the anger just took over.

⚙ **Clinical Annotation:** *The secondary emotion (anger) has arrived. In schema terms, the Vulnerable Child felt the hurt, and the Angry Child immediately mobilised to protect against it. This sequence — primary hurt instantly converted to secondary rage — is one of the most characteristic emotional patterns in Borderline presentations, and understanding it is essential for both the patient's self-awareness and the Stage 2 schema work that will follow.*

Therapist: So the chain so far is: Dan says he forgot [event] → 'He doesn't care about me' [thought] → chest tightness, tingly hands [body] → hurt [primary emotion] → anger [secondary emotion]. What happened next? What was the urge?

Sarah: To make him feel as bad as I felt. To hurt him back. So I started shouting.

Therapist: What did you say?

Sarah: I said some horrible things. I told him he was useless, that I wish I had never met him, that no one had ever cared about me and he was just the latest in a long line. He went quiet and walked out of the room. Went upstairs.

Therapist: And when he walked out — what was the thought then?

Sarah: [Voice drops.] 'He's leaving me. Everyone leaves.' And then the shame hit. Like, 'You've done it again. You've ruined it again. You don't deserve him.'

Clinical Annotation: *The chain has now reached the critical juncture. The Angry Child's explosion has been followed by the Punitive Parent mode ('you've ruined it again, you don't deserve him'), which generates shame and self-loathing. This is the point at which the self-harm urge typically intensifies, because the self-harm serves a dual function: it regulates the unbearable shame, and it enacts the punishment that the Punitive Parent demands.*

Therapist: So the shame arrived. Where are you on the 0-to-10 scale at that moment?

Sarah: A 9. Maybe a 10.

Therapist: And what was the urge?

Sarah: To cut. I needed to cut. It was the only thing that would make the noise stop.

Therapist: And then?

Sarah: I went into the bathroom. Got the razor. And I cut.

Step Five: Mapping the Complete Chain

Therapist: Thank you, Sarah. I know that was not easy to talk through. Let me map the whole chain so we can see it clearly.

[The therapist writes the chain on a shared piece of paper between them, building it visually as they go.]

SARAH'S CHAIN	DETAIL
VULNERABILITY	4 hours sleep | nightmare about stepdad | no breakfast | Job Centre letter | baseline distress ~6/10
PROMPTING EVENT	Dan: 'Oh shit, sorry, I forgot [your prescription].'
LINK 1: Thought	'He doesn't care about me.'
LINK 2: Body	Chest tightness, tingly hands, heat rising
LINK 3: Emotion 1°	Hurt — 'crushed' — lasting approximately half a second
LINK 4: Emotion 2°	Anger — 'like a switch flipped' — Angry Child mode activated
LINK 5: Urge	To make Dan feel as bad as she felt — to attack

LINK 6: Action	Shouted at Dan: 'You're useless, I wish I'd never met you'
LINK 7: Dan's response	Went quiet. Walked upstairs.
LINK 8: Thought	'He's leaving. Everyone leaves.' — Abandonment schema activated
LINK 9: Emotion	Shame — Punitive Parent mode: 'You've done it again, you don't deserve him'
LINK 10: Arousal	9-10/10 — amygdala fully activated, prefrontal offline
LINK 11: Urge	To cut — 'the only thing that would make the noise stop'
TARGET BEHAVIOUR	Self-laceration: 3 cuts to left forearm with razor, ~22:30
CONSEQUENCES	Immediate: relief, numbness, shame reduction. Later: deeper shame, wound care, dreading telling therapist

Step Six: The Solution Analysis

Therapist: Now — and this is the most important part — let us look at where you could have done something different. Not to blame you, but to give you more choices next time. Looking at the chain, where do you think the first opportunity was?

Sarah: [Looks at the chain.] The vulnerability factors, I suppose. I shouldn't have gone all day without eating.

Therapist: That is a really good observation. That is ABC PLEASE — looking after the body so the emotional system has fuel. If you had eaten properly and perhaps napped during the day, your baseline might have been a 3 instead of a 6, and the whole chain would have played out differently. What about later in the chain — say at Link 1, when the thought 'he doesn't care' arrived?

Sarah: I could have Checked the Facts. Like, does he really not care? He forgets things all the time. He forgot his mum's birthday last month. It probably wasn't about me.

Therapist: Exactly. Check the Facts would have caught the interpretation before it became the truth. The fact is: he forgot the prescription. The interpretation is: he does not care about me. Those are two very different things. What about at Link 4, when the anger arrived?

Sarah: Opposite Action? The anger wanted me to attack, so the opposite would have been to be gentle. Or at least to not say the horrible things.

Therapist: Yes. And what about at Link 10, when the distress hit 9 out of 10 and the cutting urge was very strong?

Sarah: TIP. Cold water on my face. That's what we've practised.

Therapist: Right. At 9 out of 10, TIP is your first-line skill because it works on your body directly, and at that level of arousal your thinking brain is not available. So the solution analysis gives us four intervention points.

SARAH'S SOLUTION ANALYSIS — FOUR INTERVENTION POINTS

Point 1 — Vulnerability: Eat regular meals, prioritise sleep. Use ABC PLEASE to reduce baseline distress before crises arrive.

Point 2 — Link 1 (Thought): Check the Facts. 'Does the evidence support that Dan does not care? Or does it support that Dan is forgetful?'

Point 3 — Link 4 (Anger): Opposite Action. When the urge is to attack, the opposite is to pause, to be gentle, or to leave the room and come back when calmer.

Point 4 — Link 10 (Arousal 9/10): TIP — cold water to face for 15–30 seconds to activate the dive reflex and bring arousal below 7 before making any decisions.

Key Learning: The earlier in the chain you intervene, the easier it is. At Link 1, a moment's reflection might have prevented the entire escalation. By Link 10, only a physiological intervention (TIP) is realistic because the thinking brain is offline.

Therapist: How does it feel to look at this?

Sarah: [Quiet.] Like... it wasn't inevitable. Like there were moments where it could have gone differently.

Therapist: That is exactly right. And that is the most important thing the chain analysis teaches us: it was not inevitable. There were choice points. You could not see them on Tuesday because your arousal was too high and everything happened very fast. But now you can see them. And next time, you might catch one of them. Even one.

Clinical Annotation: *The session has accomplished its core purpose: the target behaviour has been understood, the chain has been made visible, the choice points have been identified, and the patient has experienced the insight that the behaviour was not inevitable. The therapist now transitions to wound care and safety planning for the remainder of the session.*

◆ CLINICAL PEARL

Notice the rhythm of this chain analysis. The therapist asks specific, concrete questions ('what was the very first thought?', 'what did your body do?', 'what came next?'), building the chain link by link rather than asking the patient to provide a narrative summary. The specificity matters because it slows the experience down, making visible the micro-moments that, in real time, pass in a blur. It also communicates that the therapist is genuinely interested in understanding, not just documenting. If you find yourself writing the chain on the worksheet while the patient talks, you have moved into a data-collection mode. Put the pen down. Listen. Build the chain together, out loud, and only write it up once the full picture is clear.

Worked Example: A Completed Schema Map

Supplement to Chapter 12: Phase Two — Schema Mapping and Mode Identification

The following is a fully completed Schema Map for 'Sarah,' the composite patient introduced in the textbook's case studies, produced collaboratively during Phase Two of her Stage 2 treatment. Sarah's assessment identified Moderate Personality Disorder with prominent Negative Affectivity and Disinhibition, Borderline Pattern Specifier. Her Phase One developmental history revealed emotional neglect and intermittent physical abuse by her mother's partner from the age of four, disrupted education, and a series of volatile adult relationships. Her schema identification process identified three core schemas: Abandonment/Instability, Defectiveness/Shame, and Emotional Deprivation.

The Schema Map is constructed collaboratively on a large sheet of paper, with the core schemas at the centre and connecting lines drawn outward to developmental origins, current triggers, and coping modes. The following representation translates this visual document into a structured table format suitable for reproduction in a clinical manual. In practice, the map is a freehand drawing created together by the clinician and patient, using colours, arrows, and the patient's own handwriting, which gives it a personal quality that a printed form cannot replicate. Clinicians are encouraged to use the template below as a starting framework and to adapt it to the patient's own visual preferences.

SARAH'S SCHEMA MAP — Constructed in Stage 2, Phase Two

CORE SCHEMA 1: ABANDONMENT / INSTABILITY

Core Belief: 'Everyone will leave me eventually. I cannot count on anyone to stay.'

Developmental Origins: Father left the family when Sarah was 4 and made no further contact. Mother was emotionally unavailable due to depression and later substance misuse. Mother's partner was intermittently present, creating a pattern of adults who appeared and disappeared unpredictably. Placed in foster care at age 11 after a period of neglect; moved between three placements in two years.

Current Triggers: Partner not responding to text messages within an hour. Friend cancelling plans. Therapist's annual leave. Arguments with partner (interpreted as precursor to abandonment). Any perceived change in someone's tone or manner.

Coping — Surrender: Clings to partner desperately; tolerates poor treatment to avoid being alone; drops her own plans to be available whenever partner wants her.

Coping — Avoidance: Avoids forming new friendships because 'they will leave anyway'; does not apply for jobs because 'I will just get sacked'; pushes people away before they can leave her.

Coping — Overcompensation: Monitors partner's phone; checks social media obsessively for evidence of rejection; makes excessive demands for reassurance ('Do you still love me? Are you sure? Say it again').

CORE SCHEMA 2: DEFECTIVENESS / SHAME

Core Belief: 'I am fundamentally damaged and worthless. If people really knew me, they would see how disgusting I am.'

Developmental Origins: Mother's partner repeatedly told Sarah she was 'stupid,' 'useless,' and 'a waste of space.' Physical abuse accompanied by the message that she deserved it because she was bad. Bullied at school for having unwashed clothes and for being 'the girl from the children's home.' No adult ever told her she had value.

Current Triggers: Receiving any form of feedback or criticism. Looking in the mirror. Comparing herself to other women on social media. Being asked about her childhood or her family. Filling in forms that ask for employment history or qualifications.

Coping — Surrender: Accepts abusive treatment from partners ('I don't deserve better'). Self-harms as self-punishment ('I deserve the pain'). Does not challenge unfair treatment.

Coping — Avoidance: Avoids social situations where she might be 'exposed.' Refuses to attend job interviews. Wears long sleeves to hide scars. Never allows anyone to see her without make-up.

Coping — Overcompensation: Compulsive cleaning and tidying of her flat (proving she is not the 'dirty girl from the children's home'). Aggressive defensiveness when she perceives criticism ('attack before they attack me').

CORE SCHEMA 3: EMOTIONAL DEPRIVATION

Core Belief: 'My emotional needs will never be met. Nobody will ever truly understand me or care about what I feel.'

Developmental Origins: Mother was physically present but emotionally absent; did not respond to Sarah's distress, did not comfort her after the abuse, and did not protect her. No adult in any of her three foster placements provided sustained emotional attunement. Learned that expressing emotional needs was pointless or resulted in further rejection.

Current Triggers: Partner who is emotionally reserved or who does not ask about her day. Seeing affectionate families in public. Being in a group where others receive attention and she does not. Therapy sessions where the therapist does not 'get it' quickly enough.

Coping — Surrender: Accepts emotional neglect in relationships. Does not ask for what she needs. Silently absorbs her disappointment and then explodes when it becomes unbearable.

Coping — Avoidance: Withdraws into isolation rather than risk asking for care and being disappointed. Uses alcohol to numb the loneliness.

Coping — Overcompensation: Makes excessive emotional demands on partner and therapist. Expects others to intuit her needs without being told. Becomes angry when others fail to meet needs she has not communicated.

SARAH'S MODE PROFILE

Vulnerable Child: Activated when Abandonment or Defectiveness schemas are triggered. Presents as tearfulness, a small or childlike voice, curling up physically, and expressions of hopelessness ('nobody cares,' 'what is the point'). The underlying emotions are fear, sadness, loneliness, and shame.

Angry Child: Activated immediately after the Vulnerable Child, as a protective response. Presents as explosive anger, shouting, throwing things, verbal attacks on partner. Often switches on within seconds of the Vulnerable Child appearing, covering the vulnerability with rage.

Detached Protector: Activated after the Angry Child has exhausted itself or when the shame becomes unbearable. Presents as emotional numbness, flat affect, monosyllabic responses, staring at the wall, and dissociative episodes. Sarah describes this as 'going behind the glass.' Functions to cut off emotional pain when it exceeds tolerance.

Punitive Parent: Active much of the time as a background commentary. Voice of Sarah's mother's partner, internalised and directed at herself. Key messages: 'You are stupid,' 'You are disgusting,' 'You deserve everything you get,' 'Nobody could ever love you.' This mode drives the self-harm: it demands punishment and the self-harm delivers it.

Healthy Adult: Currently weak but present. Sarah can access it when arousal is below 5/10, when she is with her sister, or when she is walking her dog. In therapy, she can sometimes observe her modes with curiosity: 'I think the Punitive Parent just kicked in.' The goal of Stage 2 is to strengthen this mode to the point where it can protect the Vulnerable Child and challenge the Punitive Parent without the therapist's help.

◆ CLINICAL PEARL

When you have completed a Schema Map with a patient, ask them to take a photograph of it on their phone. Many patients report looking at their Schema Map between sessions as a way of making sense of difficult moments: 'I looked at the map and I could see — that was the Abandonment schema being triggered, and I went straight into Angry Child.' This real-time pattern recognition, in which the patient sees their own process as it unfolds rather than only understanding it in retrospect, is one of the most important therapeutic achievements of Phase Two and the foundation upon which Phase Three's modification work is built.

Worked Example: An Imagery Rescripting Session

Supplement to Chapter 13: Phase Three — Experiential Processing

The following is an annotated session extract demonstrating therapist-led imagery rescripting with Sarah, targeting her Defectiveness/Shame schema. Sarah is in Week 8 of Stage 2, Phase Three. Her arousal at the start of the session is 4/10. The memory being rescripted was identified during Phase One: an incident at age seven in which her mother's partner told her she was 'disgusting' and locked her in her bedroom after she spilled a drink on the carpet.

Phase A: Accessing the Memory

Therapist: Sarah, today I would like us to try the imagery work we discussed last week — going back to one of the early memories connected to the belief that you are disgusting and worthless. We talked about the memory of the spilled drink. Are you still willing to work with that memory today?

Sarah: Yeah. I've been thinking about it. I'm nervous but I want to try.

Therapist: That is understandable. Remember that you are in control. If it gets too much at any point, you can open your eyes and we will stop. Your skills are here if you need them. And I am here, right beside you. Okay?

Sarah: [Nods.]

Therapist: I would like you to close your eyes if you feel comfortable, or soften your gaze. Take a few slow breaths. And in your own time, let yourself go back to that kitchen. You are seven years old. It is evening. Tell me what you can see.

[Sarah closes her eyes. Her breathing becomes slightly faster. Her hands grip the arms of the chair.]

Sarah: [Quiet, slightly higher voice.] I can see the kitchen. The lino floor. It's yellow. The table is there, and there's a glass of Ribena on it. I've knocked it over. It's going everywhere. On the floor, on the carpet in the doorway.

Therapist: What can you hear?

Sarah: Him. Shouting. He's coming from the living room. He's saying, 'What the fuck have you done?' And Mum is just sitting there. She doesn't move.

Therapist: What is happening in your body right now, seven-year-old Sarah?

Sarah: [Voice trembling.] I'm shaking. My tummy is really tight. I want to run but there's nowhere to go. He's standing in the doorway.

Therapist: What does he do?

Sarah: He grabs my arm. Hard. He says, 'You're disgusting. You're a filthy, disgusting child. Get to your room.' And he pulls me up the stairs and pushes me into my bedroom and slams the door. And I can hear the lock turn.

Therapist: And what is seven-year-old Sarah feeling right now, alone in that room?

Sarah: [Tears falling.] Scared. And... she thinks it's her fault. She thinks she's bad. She thinks this is what she deserves because she's disgusting.

Clinical Annotation: *The memory is now fully activated. Sarah is experiencing the emotional content in the present tense. Note the shift to 'she' — Sarah has instinctively created slight distance by referring to herself in the third person, which is common and clinically acceptable. The therapist monitors Sarah's arousal through her visible distress and her voice quality. The memory is emotionally alive without being overwhelming. The rescripting can proceed.*

Phase B: The Rescripting Intervention

Therapist: [Voice warm, steady, authoritative.] Sarah, I am going to come into this memory now. I am going to walk into that kitchen. I am there. I can see you. I can see what is happening. And I am going to do what should have happened and did not.

[Pause. The therapist's voice becomes firmer, addressing the abuser.]

Therapist: [Addressing the abuser.] Stop. Take your hand off that child right now. She is seven years old and she spilled a drink. That is what children do. What you are doing — grabbing her, screaming at her, locking her in her room — is abuse. You are the adult here, and you are hurting a child because of a glass of Ribena. There is nothing disgusting about this little girl. The only thing that is disgusting in this room is the way you are treating her.

[The therapist's voice softens, turning towards the child.]

Therapist: [Addressing the child.] Sarah, I want you to listen to me very carefully. This is not your fault. You did nothing wrong. You spilled a drink, and that is okay. Every child spills things. You are not disgusting. You are not bad. You are a little girl who deserves to be treated with kindness, and what just happened to you should not have happened. No child should be treated like that. I am going to take you out of this room and I am going to make sure you are safe. You do not have to be scared any more. I am here.

Sarah: [Sobbing quietly.] She never said that. Nobody ever said that.

Therapist: I know. And she should have. Your mother should have stood up and protected you. She did not, and that was her failure, not yours. You deserved protection, and you did not get it. But I want you to hear it now: you were a child, and you were worthy of love and safety, and none of what happened was because of who you are.

Clinical Annotation: *The rescripting has provided the corrective experience: a protective adult has intervened, confronted the source of harm, and delivered the validation and reassurance that were absent from the original experience. Note that the therapist does not minimise what happened ('it was not that bad') or offer false comfort ('everything is fine now'). The rescripting acknowledges the reality of what happened and provides what was missing: protection, validation, and the explicit message that the child was not to blame.*

Phase C: Processing and Integration

Therapist: Sarah, in your own time, I would like you to let the image fade. Feel your feet on the floor. Feel the chair beneath you. When you are ready, open your eyes and look around the room.

[Sarah opens her eyes. She looks around the room, orienting herself. She takes a deep breath.]

Therapist: How are you feeling right now?

Sarah: [Wiping her eyes.] Shaky. But also... I don't know. Something feels different.

Therapist: Can you describe what feels different?

Sarah: It's like... I've always known that what he did was wrong. In my head. But this was the first time I felt it. That it wasn't about me. That I was just a kid. [Pause.] She was just a kid.

Therapist: She was. And she deserved so much more than she got.

Sarah: [Long pause.] I've spent twenty years thinking I was disgusting because he told me I was disgusting. And he was... he was just a cruel man taking his anger out on a little girl.

Clinical Annotation: *This is the critical therapeutic moment. Sarah is experiencing the shift from schema-level conviction ('I am disgusting because I am defective') to contextual understanding ('I was told I was disgusting by a man who was abusing me'). The core belief has not been eliminated, but it has been recontextualised: it is no longer an unquestionable truth about the self but an internalised message from a specific person in a specific context. This recontextualisation is the mechanism through which imagery rescripting modifies schemas, and it is the foundation upon which subsequent* *cognitive restructuring and behavioural experiments will build.*

Therapist: How does the belief 'I am disgusting' feel right now, on a 0 to 100 scale, where 100 is completely true?

Sarah: [Thinks.] Before we did this, I would have said 90. Right now... maybe 60. It is still there. But it is quieter.

Therapist: Sixty is a significant shift. And it may fluctuate — the schema will push back, because it has been running your life for a long time and it does not give up easily. But something has changed today, and you felt it. We will keep working with this.

◆ CLINICAL PEARL

After an imagery rescripting session, allow at least ten minutes for grounding and processing before the patient leaves. Do not schedule rescripting in the last fifteen minutes of a session. Arrange a brief check-in contact within 48 hours. In supervision, attend to your own emotional response to the work: witnessing a patient's trauma memories activates the therapist's empathy system powerfully, and this exposure requires its own processing. The vicarious trauma literature demonstrates that therapists who do not attend to their own emotional responses to trauma work are at increased risk of burnout, compassion fatigue, and fidelity drift.

APPENDIX A

IPTF Comprehensive Assessment Template

Reproducible Clinical Tool · For use by qualified IPTF clinicians only

This template is completed progressively across all assessment sessions. It constitutes the primary clinical record of the IPTF assessment and provides the data required to produce an ICD-11 dimensional diagnosis, a completed IPTF Formulation Worksheet, and an agreed treatment plan. Use alongside Chapter 3 of this manual.

SECTION 1 Patient and Referral Information	
Patient Name (or reference)	
Date of Birth	
NHS Number (if applicable)	
Preferred Pronouns	
Assessing Clinician	
Role / Grade	
Date Assessment Commenced	
Service / Setting	
Referral Source	
Referral Date	
SAPAS Score at Screening	
Reason for Referral (summarise in the referrer's own language)	
Current diagnoses recorded in referral documentation	
Current medication	
Previous mental health diagnoses (list all)	

Language used in prior records (note terms such as 'manipulative', 'difficult', 'non-compliant' — these indicate prior invalidation)

SECTION 2 Assessment Session One · Presenting Difficulties and Current Functioning	
Session Details	
Date of Session One	
Duration	
Format (in-person / video / telephone)	
2A · Patient's Account of Presenting Difficulties	
Main difficulties in patient's own words (capture key phrases verbatim)	
What the patient wants from treatment (in their own words)	
2B · Current Emotional Difficulties	
Predominant emotions experienced	
Frequency, intensity, and duration of emotional distress (0-10 ratings if useful)	
Primary triggers for emotional distress	
Current coping strategies (adaptive and maladaptive)	
Capacity to identify and name emotions (note alexithymia indicators)	
2C · Current Interpersonal Difficulties	

Current significant relationships (partner, family, friends — note quality and stability)	
Recurrent interpersonal patterns (e.g. idealisation, devaluation, withdrawal, conflict)	
Capacity for trust and intimacy	
Current social support available	
2D · Current Functional Impairment	
Employment / education status	
Housing and finances (note instability if present)	
Self-care capacity	
Current service involvement (MH, substance misuse, social care, CJS)	
2E · Psychometric Battery (completed between Sessions One and Two)	
PiCD — Negative Affectivity	
PiCD — Detachment	
PiCD — Dissociality	
PiCD — Disinhibition	
PiCD — Anankastia	
LPFS-BF 2.0 — Self-Functioning	
LPFS-BF 2.0 — Interpersonal Functioning	
LPFS-BF 2.0 — Total	
YSQ-S3 — Top Five Schemas (list)	

CORE-OM Total / Risk Subscale	
PHQ-9	
GAD-7	
BSL-23	
ASRS-v1.1 Total / Screening Positive? (Yes / No)	
Clinician notes on psychometric results (anomalies, inconsistencies, patient response)	

SECTION 3 Assessment Session Two · Developmental History and Attachment Exploration	
Session Details	
Date of Session Two	
Duration	
3A · Family of Origin and Primary Caregivers	
Family composition and primary caregivers in childhood	
Stability of family structure (separations, bereavements, moves, changes in caregivers)	
Quality of attachment to primary caregiver(s) — emotional availability, responsiveness, consistency, warmth	
Provisional attachment pattern (secure / avoidant / ambivalent / disorganised — note evidence)	
3B · Adverse Childhood Experiences	
Physical abuse (history, perpetrator, duration)	

Emotional abuse (history, perpetrator, duration)	
Sexual abuse (patient discloses as much as they choose at this stage)	
Physical neglect	
Emotional neglect	
Parental mental illness	
Parental substance misuse	
Domestic violence in household	
Parental incarceration	
Parental separation or divorce	
Other adversity (bullying, bereavement, institutional care, poverty)	
Estimated ACE Score (0–10)	

Clinician note on ACE score in relation to severity presentation

3C · Emotional Climate of Family of Origin

How were emotions expressed, tolerated, and responded to in the family?

Were the patient's emotional needs acknowledged, validated, dismissed, or punished? (note the dominant relational message the patient received)

3D · Peer Relationships, Education, and Employment

Quality of childhood peer relationships (isolation, bullying, friendships)

Educational trajectory (disruptions, exclusions, achievements, signs of neurodevelopmental difficulty)	
Occupational and employment history (patterns of difficulty or success)	
3E · Adult Relationship History and Previous Mental Health Treatment	
Pattern of adult intimate relationships (stability, recurrent themes, endings)	
Experience of domestic abuse or coercive control in adult relationships?	
Previous mental health treatment (what was offered, what helped, what did not help, why treatment ended)	
Patient's experience of mental health services to date (validating or invalidating — note specific examples)	

SECTION 4 Assessment Session Three · Risk Assessment Summary	
Session Details	
Date of Session Three	
Duration	
Additional session required for formulation feedback? (Yes / No)	
4A · Risk Summary (complete Appendix B — IPTF Risk Assessment Template in full)	
Current self-harm (Yes / No / Historical only)	
Method(s) and frequency if current	
Most recent episode	

Current suicidal ideation (None / Passive / Active without plan / Active with plan)	
History of suicide attempts (Yes / No) — Number	
Substance misuse (None / Present) — Substance(s) and function	
Risk to others (history of aggression, violence, or offending)	
Vulnerability to exploitation or harm from others	
Overall risk level (Low / Medium / High / Very High)	
Basis for overall risk judgement	

SECTION 5 ICD-11 Dimensional Diagnostic Formulation

5A · Personality Disorder Diagnosis Decision

Does the presentation meet ICD-11 general requirements? (Yes / No / Sub-threshold Personality Difficulty)	
Pervasiveness across situations confirmed? (Yes / No)	
Long duration since adolescence or early adulthood confirmed? (Yes / No)	
Significant distress or impairment confirmed? (Yes / No)	

Not better explained by another mental disorder? (Yes / No)	
5B · Severity Level (rate each domain 0 = none, 1 = mild, 2 = moderate, 3 = severe)	
Self-Functioning — Identity	
Self-Functioning — Self-Worth	
Self-Functioning — Self-Direction	
Self-Functioning — Self-Appraisal	
Interpersonal Functioning — Empathy	
Interpersonal Functioning — Intimacy	
Interpersonal Functioning — Cooperation	
Severity Level (Personality Difficulty / Mild / Moderate / Severe — circle)	
5C · Trait Domain Profile (P = Prominent / Pp = Present not prominent / N = Not elevated)	
Negative Affectivity (P / Pp / N) — Key features observed	
Detachment (P / Pp / N) — Key features observed	
Dissociality (P / Pp / N) — Key features observed	
Disinhibition (P / Pp / N) — Key features observed	
Anankastia (P / Pp / N) — Key features observed	

Borderline Pattern Specifier (Applicable / Not applicable) — Features present	
5D · Differential Diagnostic Summary	
CPTSD indicators (Confirmed / Probable / Possible / Not indicated)	
Re-experiencing symptoms present?	
Avoidance symptoms present?	
Hyperarousal symptoms present?	
ASC indicators (Confirmed / Probable / Possible / Not indicated)	
Referral for specialist neurodevelopmental assessment indicated? (Yes / No)	
ADHD indicators — ASRS-v1.1 screening positive? (Yes / No)	
ADHD referral indicated? (Yes / No)	
Other diagnostic considerations (bipolar affective disorder, psychosis, complex dissociative disorder)	

SECTION 6 Treatment Planning and Patient Agreement	
Recommended IPTF starting stage (Stage 1 / Stage 2 / Stage 3 only — circle)	

Estimated treatment intensity (Full pathway 24–60 months / Reduced 12–24 months / Brief Stage 1 only — circle)	
IPTF adaptations indicated (neurodiversity / forensic / primary care / adolescent — specify)	
Trauma processing as Stage 2 adjunct? (EMDR / TF-CBT / Not indicated — circle)	
Patient's response to formulation feedback (note verbal and non-verbal response, corrections, or additions)	
Informed consent obtained and documented? (Yes / No)	
Date consent documented	
Assessing Clinician Signature	
Date Assessment Completed	
Supervisor Notified? (Yes / No)	

This is a reproducible clinical tool. It may be photocopied for clinical use by qualified IPTF clinicians under the terms described in the copyright notice. It is not a substitute for clinical supervision.

APPENDIX B

IPTF Risk Assessment Template

Structured Professional Judgement Framework · Reproducible Clinical Tool

This template operationalises the IPTF's formulation-based approach to risk assessment. It should be completed at initial assessment, reviewed at each stage transition, and updated whenever there is a significant change in presentation or risk status. It supplements but does not replace service-specific risk documentation.

PART 1 Identifying Information and Assessment Context	
Patient Reference	
Date of Risk Assessment	
Assessing Clinician	
Stage in IPTF Pathway (Initial Assessment / Stage 1 / S1-S2 Transition / Stage 2 / S2-S3 Transition / Stage 3 / Review — circle)	
Context for this assessment (e.g. routine review, crisis presentation, significant life event, clinical concern)	

PART 2 Self-Harm · Functional Analysis	
The IPTF approach prioritises understanding the function of self-harm over cataloguing its form. The functional formulation below directly informs Stage 1 safety planning and the selection of distress tolerance skills.	
Current self-harm (Present / Absent / Historical only — circle)	
Method(s) of self-harm	
Frequency — past month	
Frequency — past three months	
Frequency — past year	

Most recent episode **(date, method, severity, treatment sought)**	
Function of Self-Harm **(tick all that apply and add detail)**	
Emotion regulation	☐ To manage or reduce unbearable emotional states
Self-punishment	☐ To punish the self for perceived wrongdoing or defectiveness
Communication of distress	☐ To signal distress when verbal communication has broken down
Dissociation management	☐ To restore a sense of reality or bodily presence during dissociative states
Sensory seeking (ASC)	☐ To generate regulatory sensory input
Other	☐
Typical antecedents **(triggers immediately preceding episodes)**	
Schema activated in the antecedent period **(if identifiable)**	
Patient's own understanding of why they self-harm	
Trend over past three to six months **(Stable / Increasing / Decreasing / Variable — circle)**	

PART 3 **Suicidality · Detailed Assessment**	
Ask directly, compassionately, and without minimising. Evidence consistently demonstrates that direct enquiry about suicidal ideation does not increase risk and frequently reduces it by communicating that the topic is safe to discuss.	
Current suicidal ideation **(None / Passive — "I wish I were dead" / Active without plan / Active with plan — circle)**	

Frequency of suicidal ideation	
Duration of each episode	
Intensity (0–10)	
Specific plan? (Yes / No)	
If yes — describe plan	
Access to means	
Means restriction actions taken	
History of suicide attempts? (Yes / No) — Number	
Most recent attempt (date, method, medical severity, intent)	
Most serious previous attempt (method, medical severity, intent at time)	
Triggers for elevated suicidal ideation (interpersonal, situational, anniversaries, schema activations)	
Protective factors (reasons for living, responsibilities, relationships, values, future orientation)	
Ambivalence about suicide (is there a part of the patient that wants to live? — note evidence)	
Function of suicidal ideation (escape from intolerable pain / self-punishment / communication / other)	

PART 4 Substance Misuse

Substances used (alcohol, cannabis, prescribed medication misuse, illicit substances)	
Frequency and quantity	
Function of substance use (emotion regulation / social facilitation / dissociation management / other)	
Does intoxication increase risk of self-harm or suicide attempt? (Yes / No / Sometimes — circle)	
Referral to substance misuse service indicated? (Yes / No)	

PART 5 Risk to Others and Vulnerability to Harm from Others	
History of aggression or violence (context, triggers, severity, victim relationship)	
Current risk to identified others	
Safeguarding concerns (children or vulnerable adults in contact with patient)	
Current vulnerability to exploitation, coercive control, or harm from others	

PART 6 Trauma History and CPTSD Risk Considerations	
CPTSD (Confirmed / Probable / Possible / Not indicated — circle)	
Identified trauma triggers relevant to risk (stimuli known to elevate risk through trauma activation)	

Does re-experiencing elevate risk of self-harm or suicide? (Yes / No / Sometimes — circle)	
Grounding techniques the patient has found helpful for managing trauma-related distress	

PART 7 Formulation-Based Risk Summary and Safety Planning	
The formulation-based risk summary moves beyond cataloguing risk factors to provide an integrated account of the conditions under which this particular individual's risk is elevated, and the formulation-derived understanding of why.	
Formulation-based account of this patient's risk (link risk behaviour to schemas, attachment patterns, emotional regulation capacity, and environmental triggers)	
Conditions under which risk is likely to be elevated (specific circumstances, interpersonal events, or schema activations that historically precede crisis)	
Early warning signs (patient-identified indicators that risk is beginning to escalate)	
Agreed Crisis Management Steps	
Step 1	
Step 2	
Step 3	
Crisis Contacts	
Named Clinician	
NHS 111 Option 2 (Mental Health Crisis Line)	
Emergency Services (999)	
Named trusted person (patient-identified)	

Risk Review	
Overall risk formulation rating (Low / Medium / High / Very High — circle)	
Basis for this rating	
Actions agreed and documented	
Supervisor / senior clinician informed? (Yes / No) — Name	
Date supervisor informed	
Date for next risk review	
Assessing Clinician Signature	
Date	

This template is a reproducible clinical tool. It may be photocopied for clinical use by qualified IPTF clinicians under the terms described in the copyright notice. It is not a substitute for clinical supervision. All high-risk presentations must be discussed with a senior clinician or supervisor as a matter of priority.

www.ingramcontent.com/pod-product-compliance
Lightning Source LLC
LaVergne TN
LVHW071200210926
848482LV00014B/699